Essays on Aesthetic Genesis

Edited by
Charlene Elsby and Aaron Massecar

University Press of America,® Inc.
Lanham • Boulder • New York • Toronto • Plymouth, UK

Copyright © 2016 by University Press of America,® Inc.
4501 Forbes Boulevard, Suite 200, Lanham, Maryland 20706
UPA Acquisitions Department (301) 459-3366

Unit A, Whitacre Mews, 26-34 Stannary Street,
London SE11 4AB, United Kingdom

Library of Congress Control Number: 2016935146
ISBN: 978-0-7618-6769-2 (pbk : alk. paper)—ISBN: 978-0-7618-6770-8 (electronic)

Contents

Contents

Foreword

Charlene Elsby and Aaron Massecar

Aesthetic Genesis is the ultimate book in Jeff Mitscherling's trilogy, collectively titled, *The Revision of Hermeneutic Ontology*. It is preceded by *Roman Ingarden's Ontology and Aesthetics* (1997, University of Ottawa) and *The Author's Intention* (co-authored with Aref Nayed and Tanya DiTommaso, 2004, Lexington Books).

Aesthetic Genesis has gained a considerable following amongst scholars in diverse fields of philosophy as well as in related disciplines. It is a contemporary work in a subdiscipline of phenomenology that exists both alongside, and as a point of contrast with, what is commonly called phenomenology. While the broader definition of phenomenology focuses on experience as something essential to its definition, realist phenomenology maintains a stricter definition, emphasizing rigorous analysis of this experience to get outside of the psychological realm in order to provide more generalizable insights. What makes a phenomenology "realist" are two fundamental claims: (1) that there is a real world independent of human consciousness; and (2) that there are intentional entities that subsist in the real world.

One of the main contributions *Aesthetic Genesis* has made to contemporary scholarship is to outline what we now refer to as the New Copernican Hypothesis (NCH): while it has heretofore been assumed that all consciousness is intentional (based on the foundational work of Franz Brentano), the NCH proposes that consciousness arises out of a more basic intentionality subsisting in the real world, thus placing the concept of intentionality squarely amongst the metaphysical (where it would normally be a topic appropriate to the philosophy of mind). *Aesthetic Genesis* now serves as an example of the realist phenomenological method and of the potential contributions to philosophy one can achieve by adhering to the concept of phenomenology as a rigorous science.

Essays on Aesthetic Genesis clarifies, contextualizes, and applies the concepts of *Aesthetic Genesis*, emphasizing how its singular advancements in the field of realist phenomenology might be interpreted within the history of philosophy and how its insights have been integrated within philosophy more broadly. We have divided the book into three main sections: *Major Concepts*, *Historical Considerations*, and *Contemporary Discussion*. The first section, *Major Concepts*, serves to elucidate the major conceptual contributions of *Aesthetic Genesis* to contemporary philosophy: the concept of aesthetic genesis and the New Copernican Revolution regarding the concept of intentionality. The essays which we have deemed *Historical Considerations* are unified in that they examine how Mitscherling's text is influenced by and critiques major figures in the history of philosophy (including Descartes, one of the "principle villains" of Mitscherling's account; Gadamer, who features strongly in *The Author's Intention;* and Ingarden, whose work serves as the foundation to the first part of the trilogy). *Contemporary Discussion* includes a wide range of purposes to which Mitscherling's concepts have been put to work, from the notion of artistic creation to the reconceptualization of man's relation to nature.

It is our intention that this collection be interpreted both as a companion to *Aesthetic Genesis* and as further development in the field of realist phenomenology, building upon and propagating the exemplary work of Jeff Mitscherling.

Major Concepts

Chapter One

On the Concept of Aesthetic Genesis

Charlene Elsby

The purpose of this essay is to introduce the concept of aesthetic genesis, or how human experience entails and arises from our sensitive existence, with reference to its roots in Ancient Greek thinkers, its transmission through phenomenological thinkers (especially Merleau-Ponty), and how it becomes sedimented in Mitscherling's *Aesthetic Genesis*.

Mitscherling cites the opening lines of Aristotle's *Metaphysics*, "All men by nature desire to know. An indication of this is the delight we take in our senses; for even apart from their usefulness they are loved for themselves, and above all others the sense of sight."[1] The senses are the conduit by which we acquire knowledge, and specifically knowledge that seems to stray far beyond what is immediately available to us by the senses. As Aristotle completes his analysis of the proper object of metaphysical studies, begun with these lines above, he concludes that we have moved towards "something which is the opposite of our original inquiries";[2] while sensation is of the particular things immediately available to the senses, we seek the most exact and universal knowledge, that "furthest from the senses."[3]

This reversal does not diminish the importance of the senses in acquiring the knowledge worthy of being sought. While sensation continues to be denigrated throughout the history of philosophy as the doubtable, untrustworthy, misleading source of all of our knowledge, it remains that thing which is valued for its own sake, in which we take delight.

As contemporary phenomenology defines intentionality as the property of directedness towards an object, perception and thought are both intentional. We tend to include both of these faculties under the broader term of "consciousness." What classifies a mental phenomenon as a mental phenomenon is its intentionality, according to which consciousness is that thing directed towards such objects as blueness, a landscape, or justice (despite the radical

3

differences in the nature of these objects). In regarding consciousness in this way, we escape the difficulty of explaining how it is that we have consciousness of a landscape aside from an immediate perception of its colours. Plato and Aristotle's teleological conceptions of sensation attempt to explain why sensation is necessary as a precursor to better, more universal knowledge, but by positing perception and thought as disjunct faculties, their co-existence leads to difficulties in how consciousness of the universal objects of thought arises from their sensible correlates. And it seems necessary that we do make this move beyond bare perceptual knowledge (empiricism be damned), for there is literally no perception to which we might be referring in such common phrases as, "There's a riot on Main Street."[4] There is no perceptual riot, no perceptual street, and no perception of existence. (We may look to the proper objects of each individual sense, what later philosophers refer to as "secondary qualities," and find none of these concepts among them.) Whereas our sensitive existence is all that arms us in our mission to know things of the world, a concept of perception that limits its grasp to proper sensibles seems particularly unsuited to an awareness of the things we want most to know.

I argue that consciousness transcends perception; in a mechanical explanation of how it is that we become aware of some object (as an object), we might argue that a series of inferences takes place whereby we move from perception of proper sensibles (colour blobs) to the awareness that the cat is missing an eye, but this seems wholly contradictory to experience. Rather, what we are more immediately conscious of is the kitten's fate, its imperfection, and our own pity. This does not require that we are ever aware of the colour of the kitten's other eye, the shade of its nose, or the patch on its forehead; these details may well be forgotten, or *they weren't perceived*, in the sense that we were never aware of the sense data; their reception was *not conscious*. The transcendence of consciousness over sense perception is not some supernatural communing with an otherworldly realm, but a process of habituation whereby consciousness likens itself to worldly objects and renders so-called "proper" perception automatic.[5]

The world to which our consciousness becomes habituated is constituted of insensible things: we recognize objects, concepts, meanings, and take for granted that these are the existing things, despite the fact that philosophical explanations thus far have rendered them only inferences, beyond our immediate experience. These explanations suffer on account of a restricted definition of intentionality; with a more expanded account of intentionality comes a much more intuitive account of our encounters with these objects. This intuitive account can be achieved through an application of Mitscherling's New Copernican Hypothesis, that consciousness arises from a more basic intentionality: "Our mind becomes conscious when it operates intentionally, and it does so by engaging with the intentional structures of the world of which it is a part."[6] In this essay, I adopt an interpretation of that claim to specify consciousness' assimilating itself to existing intentional objects; there is a riot on Main St., and I am conscious of that riot. This is a result of consciousness' habituating itself, through the means of perception, to objects seemingly defying perceptual apprehension, at which point the awareness of sense data drops out as an automatic, not conscious process.

The delight we take in our senses reverses this habit; like any habit of which we might become aware and therefore contravene, the delight we take in our senses indicates that our awareness of our use of them is novel, something foreign to our general experience of living in a world of objects, concepts, and meanings (as opposed to colours and sounds). As Aristotle conceived of the soul as becoming identical in form to its object, consciousness arises out of the intentional structure of the things of which it is conscious. These things are already intentional, and the intentionality of consciousness arises from that more basic intentionality.

THE GREEK FOUNDATIONS OF AESTHETIC GENESIS

Sensation, for Plato and Aristotle, is the primary source of information for us, as earth-bound creatures gaining access to the world through physical means. Both Plato and Aristotle hold teleological accounts of sensation, according to which the senses are constructed in such a way that they conform to their intended objects. Sensation is both an end in itself as well as a means by which we access the sorts of objects not immediately available to sense (i.e., anything besides colour, sound, odour, taste, and the multiple objects of touch).

In Plato's creation story presented in the *Timaeus*, he refers to the necessity of perception as a means by which we achieve higher truths:

> As my account has it, our sight has indeed proved to be a source of supreme benefit to us, in that none of our present statements about the universe could ever have been made if we had never seen any stars, sun or heaven. As it is, however, our ability to see the periods of day-and-night, of months and of years, of equinoxes and solstices, has led to the invention of number, and has given us the idea of time and opened the path to inquiry into the nature of the universe. These pursuits have given us philosophy, a gift from the gods to the mortal race whose value neither has been nor ever will be surpassed. I'm quite prepared to declare this to be the supreme good our eyesight offers us. [7]

We must be careful in interpreting this claim about the purpose of our having vision. Plato claims here that among our objects of sight are temporal periods, objects already removed from the proper sensibles. What we strictly see are the sun and stars or, even more strictly, what we see are colour blobs. But the objects of perception which lead us away from sense experience toward higher knowledge are not the proper objects of sense. Strictly speaking, an orbit is imperceptible. And to say that an orbit is only an inference from our sense perceptions would put the existence of an orbit squarely in our own understanding—it would be a mental creation—but it is not. Without leaving the realm of sense perception, Plato claims we observe "the orbits of intelligence in the universe,"[8] and thereby posits the existence of universal orbits to which our own understanding becomes habituated. There is a kinship between the revolutions of astronomical bodies and the revolutions of our understanding, and "we should stabilize the straying revolutions within ourselves by imitating the completely unstraying revolutions of the god."[9] This way of confronting the world leads us to invent number; in effect, our encounter with the visible determines a movement towards its opposite.

In Book VII of the *Republic*, Plato attempts to explain in more detail how it is that perceptions lead to higher knowledge. Socrates claims there are different kinds of sense perceptions, some of which are *summoners* (παρακαλοῦντα). Whenever our sense perceptions would lead us to think that some thing is its opposite, e.g., when the same thing is both light and heavy, our understanding is summoned towards some other knowledge that can account for this contradiction. Plato explains this with reference to fingers. Our perception of a finger is not a summoner, since we perceive that adequately, but our perception of the "bigness and smallness of fingers"[10] does summon the understanding, for in that respect perceptions may contradict each other.

This is one of Plato's sneakiest arguments. While it may seem intuitive that our perception of a finger cannot be contradictory, we need to recall that a finger is not the proper object of any sense. To perceive a finger is already to apply some form of higher knowledge to the proper objects of sense, for that knowledge is necessary to apply object recognition to the proper sensibles, by means of which we perceive a finger. As Plato argues that relative sizes lead us to summon the understanding, he (knowingly, I would argue) contradicts the famous argument from equality in the *Phaedo*, where Socrates argues that we must have a concept of equality before we can recognize that two objects are unequal in size.[11] In the *Phaedo*, Plato argues that knowledge of equality must come first, in order for us to recognize that two objects are unequal. In the *Republic*, Plato parallels the argument, using the same example of unequally sized objects to conclude that some kinds of sense perceptions summon the understanding, leading to our consideration of "what the big is and what the small is."[12] While in the *Phaedo,* our application of the concept of equality to unequal objects provides evidence for our prior knowledge of equality, in the *Republic* our concept of inequality comes from our attempt to resolve the contradiction between disparate perceptions, summoning the understanding: the causal relation is reversed. What gets lost in our consideration of this infelicity of coherence between Plato's texts, the thing from which we are being distracted, is that the first premise of his argument in the *Republic* is that *we see fingers*. We see fingers unproblematically, without any intervention of the understanding in our perception of them. We see fingers like we see orbits. It is not one of our higher faculties that ascribes structure to them; the objects of perception are already formed.

Aristotle also has a teleological account of sense perception as well as thought, such that our sensations and thoughts are the soul's conforming to the world as it is. While Plato would have it that our abstractions from perception are completely divorced from their origins in perception, Aristotle rather concludes that if sense perception is the origin of such knowledge, whatever it is of which we have knowledge must be present in the sensible forms of objects.

For Aristotle, thought and perception are relations to what is thinkable and what is perceivable.[13] Perception is perception of something, and knowledge is knowledge of something. Both what is perceptible and what is knowable exist prior to perception and knowledge: "For the knowable would seem to be prior to knowledge. For as a rule it is of actual things already existing that we acquire knowledge."[14] In *De Anima*, Aristotle explains how these processes work, first by examining sense perception and its objects, and then explaining thought by analogy to sense perception. Thinking is like perceiving, and

> . . . if thinking is like perceiving, it must be either a process in which the soul is acted upon by what is capable of being thought, or a process different from but analogous to that. The thinking part of the soul must therefore be, while impassible, capable of receiving the form of an object . . . Thought must be related to what is thinkable, as sense is to what is sensible.[15]

The trouble we run into in interpreting this claim is how to think of the objects of thought and of perception. According to Aristotle, the proper objects of sensation as well as the common sensibles are perceived by five senses, while the objects we say we perceive (e.g., the son of Cleon) are truly perceived only incidentally. We may think of sensible forms in terms of sensation's proper object, but then our sensible forms become something very restricted, unamenable to Aristotle's later claim that the objects of knowledge are, in some way, already in the sensible forms. And it is hard to believe that an object of knowledge, a universal (while we may perceive only particulars, thought is of universals) is contained in a sensible form, *if* we interpret a sensible form to be equivalent to a proper sensible (e.g., "blue"). There is another analogy at work here: while Aristotle does claim that the sense organ must take on the form of the object (and thus the organ must itself be uncoloured, if it is to have the potential to be coloured), the sense organ and the sense are different (the sense organ is only the material of the sense). The sense organ must have the potential to become coloured, but the sense organ itself is not sufficient for sensation. Actualization by the soul is required for the sense organ to be capable of sense, and actualization (the imposing of forms on matter) would correspondingly apply to the imposition of form on the material of the object as sensed (qualities). On this conception, the sense organ *is* the material for the faculty of sensation, by which we access the *material* of the object of sense, e.g., the visible object is sensed as an object, and the material for that sensation is the sense data provided by the sense organ; the perception of a finger is possible because the colour blobs are already organized as they are sensed.

As I mentioned in the introduction to this essay, thinking universals is knowledge furthest away from our perceptions, though in *De Anima* Aristotle argues for thought's being analogous to perception. The types of object of thought and perception vary with respect to their being (universal versus particular), while the faculties themselves are analogous. In both thought and perception, the soul becomes the object (of thought or perception); the faculties themselves are distinguishable according to the different natures of these objects. "Within the soul the faculties of knowledge and sensation are *potentially* these objects, the one what is knowable, the other what is sensible."[16] More specifically, the faculties become the forms of these objects (the object without the matter). While we may think that we are moving away from the objects of sense perception by instead thinking, the movement away from sensation by thought is only to think of things that exist *as* separate, not to separate them. The ultimate objects of knowledge are not separable from the sensible objects. While Plato's account led us away from sense perception, to the point where we may think that for Plato, our relation to sense perception is done as soon as we start considering what, for example, "equality" is, Aristotle assures us that it is nothing separate from the objects of sense.

> The so-called abstract objects the mind thinks just as, in the case of the snub, one might think of it *qua* snub and not separately, but if anyone actually thought of it *qua* hollow he would think of it without the flesh in which it is embodied: it is thus that the mind when it is thinking the objects of mathematics thinks of them as separate though they are not separate.[17]

This is both a rejection of the orthodox interpretation of Plato's theory of forms as well as a demonstration of how Aristotle emphasizes thought's dependence on sensation, by noting the inseparability of what is thinkable from the objects that precondition both our thought and our perception. There are both sensible and intelligible forms, but sensible forms are accessible by sense directly, while intelligible forms are accessed mediately through sensation. The way to make sense of this, I believe, is to ascribe a general dependence of thought on sensation, as well as a particular dependence. A particular dependence would denote that any particular possible thought is dependent on some particular prior perception, while a general dependence necessitates only that perception of some sort is required before thought is possible. Interpreting thought's dependence on perception as a general dependence has the advantage of coinciding well with Aristotle's conception of the hierarchy of the faculties of the soul; Aristotle claims explicitly that it is impossible for something to think (i.e., have the capacity to think) without also perceiving, while it is possible that something might perceive without thinking. (Animals perceive, but do not think, while we think, but only if we perceive as well.) In the following passage, Aristotle's text seems amenable to either interpretation:

> Since it seems that there is nothing outside and separate in existence from sensible spatial magnitudes, the objects of thought are in the sensible forms, viz. both the abstract objects and all the states and affections of sensible things. Hence no one can learn or understand anything in the absence of sense, and when the mind is actively aware of anything it is necessarily aware of it along with an image; for images are like sensuous contents except in that they contain no matter.[18]

The general dependence of thought on sensation can be reduced to this simple statement: there can be no thought without sensation. This statement applies to the *faculties* of sensation and thought. The particular dependence of thought on sensation is with respect to their *objects;* particular objects of knowledge are in particular sensible forms.

With these concepts of thought and perception in place, we can finally turn to the most relevant contribution of the Greeks to the concept of aesthetic genesis: Through both the faculties of perception and thought, the soul becomes identical to its object. Our contemporary bias towards representational theories of consciousness would lead us to the conclusion that, in thought and perception, a copy is made of the object, in thought or perception, whose form is identical to that of the object. Under that interpretation, the object and the object of thought are related by some form of property identity. But all of Aristotle's claims to the effect that the soul *becomes* the object in perception or thought should lead us to using a stricter notion of identity—numerical identity. The form of the object and the form of the thought *are the same form*, not in the sense that one is an accurate likeness of the other, but in the sense that there is only one form, present in both the object and the soul. As Mitscherling recounts, "The act of cognition is informed, and thereby guided, by the same form as the object of cognition. In other words, one and the same form 'informs' both the activity of cognition and the matter of the individual entity *qua* substance, i.e. as particular instance of being."[19] A problem remaining for the Greek account, or what we have of it, is how it is that intelligible forms are conceived of through sensible forms, when proper sensibles themselves are unstructured qualities (e.g., blue).

AESTHETIC GENESIS IN THE CONTEXT OF REALIST PHENOMENOLOGY

Our account of aesthetic genesis in the context of realist phenomenology must begin with the concept of consciousness. The Greeks used no such concept, referring instead to perception, thinking, understanding, judgment, knowledge, opinion . . . Consciousness, on the other hand, takes on the responsibility of all of these; it is that thing to which we now seem to attribute all mental phenomena, and its defining characteristic is intentionality. Consciousness, in the most common sense, connotes an awareness, distinguished from the things of which we are not aware, which we can differentiate as things of which we are *not* conscious. When we say now that "consciousness is consciousness of," we are referring obliquely to the definition of mental phenomena outlined by Brentano in *Psychology from an Empirical Standpoint*:

> Every mental phenomenon is characterized by what the Scholastics of the Middle Ages called the intentional (or mental) inexistence of an object, and what we might call, though not wholly unambiguously, reference to a content, direction toward an object (which is not to be understood here as meaning a thing), or immanent objectivity. Every mental phenomenon includes something as object within itself, although they do not all do so in the same way. In presentation something is presented, in judgment something is affirmed or denied, in love loved, in hate hated, in desire desired and so on. [20]

Here, Brentano specifies the intentionality of consciousness, its direction towards an object. The objects of consciousness range from bare perceptions of colour to the complex structures constituting whatever it is to which I'm referring when I claim, for instance, that "There's a riot on Main St."

The reduction of our modes of interacting with the world (perception, thought, judgment, etc.) to consciousness is by no means an accidental failure to distinguish among distinguishable concepts, heretofore to be referred to as some ill-defined "consciousness," but a recognition of the fact that the distinguishing of these faculties fails to denote their actual unity; for in experiencing a colour as opposed to experiencing a picture, I am not aware of any difference in the faculty I use in these two supposedly disparate encounters. The idea that perception is limited to colours, sounds, tastes, odours and textures, to the exclusion of all other objects, does not reflect the experience I have of encountering the world as it is. Rather, as Mitscherling explains,

[T]here is already meaning at the most primal stage of cognition—that is, we already 'know' perceptually what the table is as soon as we organize our sensations of it. And again, this 'organization' of sensations consists in the information—that is, the informing—of those sensations.[21]

It is not the case that, as perceivers, we encounter an already distinguished world of colours, from which we infer unities, from which we abstract universals. Rather, what we experience is already distinguished in its being, while consciousness becomes habituated to the forms of the world. The opposition necessary to summon consciousness to attention is not an opposition produced by the deception of sense experience (contra Plato), but a recognition of differences in the objects of the world. As Merleau-Ponty claims in *The Metaphysical in Man*, the first stage of metaphysical consciousness is "surprise at discovering the confrontation of opposites," while the second stage is "recognition of their identity in the simplicity of *doing*."[22] This applies equally well to the so-called objects of sense (the proper sensibles, the secondary qualities) as the so-called higher level objects. Colours, according to Merleau-Ponty, are defined by their opposition to others, a state to which consciousness habituates itself, to perceive a difference in the world it inhabits. Merleau-Ponty states in the *Phenomenology of Perception*: "When a child grows accustomed to distinguishing blue from red, it is observed, that the habit cultivated in relation to these two colours helps with the rest."[23] He goes on to say,

To learn to see colours . . . is to acquire a certain style of seeing, a new use of one's own body: it is to enrich and recast the body image. Whether a system of motor or perceptual powers, our body is not an object for an 'I think,' it is a grouping of lived-through meanings which moves towards its equilibrium.[24]

In Merleau-Ponty's work, we find the resolution to the apparent Greek problem of how it is that our mode of accessing the world is perceptual, while the objects which we encounter extend far beyond the proper sensibles. The higher objects of consciousness are irreducible to sensible forms, conceived of as proper sensibles, while perception is irreducible to a mechanical reception of sense data. This is one of Merleau-Ponty's motivations for the elimination of the subject/object dichotomy. Since we must conceive of "'structure' or 'form' as irreducible elements of being," we must also, "put into question the classical alternative between 'existence as a thing' and 'existence as consciousness.'"[25]

Consciousness arises out of perception because of perception's intentionality—that is to say, the intentionality of the object of perception. What this means is that the object of perception (blue), as well as consciousness, points beyond itself. The tendency of consciousness to move away from bare perception of proper sensibles is its habituation to the intentional structure of the sense object: "The sensation of blue is not the knowledge or positing of a certain identifiable *quale* throughout all the experiences of it which I have . . . It is in all probability intentional, which means that it does not rest in itself as does a thing, but that it is directed and has significance beyond itself."[26] In Mitscherling's words, "sensation itself is already 'meaningful.'"[27] The world is rife with intentional structures that demand that we "rid ourselves of the illusion, encouraged by physics, that the perceived world is made up of colour qualities."[28] The particular object in the world to which we become accustomed has its own intentionality, such that consciousness, becoming "like" it, is also intentional. When we say that consciousness is always consciousness *of*, we mean to say that consciousness is directed. Just as consciousness subsists only as long as it has an object to which it is directed, *blue subsists only as long as it has an object, to which it points.*

Consciousness, the "thing" whereby we become like the world, becomes intentional through its assimilation of intentional forms, by which we become used to treating as objects of consciousness forms of things, relations, and action: "That is, just as the 'form' of 'desk' is said to be the formal cause of the physical desk—it informs the matter of this piece of furniture—so does the form of 'stealing a necklace from a jewellery store' inform the action of the thief."[29] As the form of 'stealing a necklace from a jewellery store' informs the action of the thief, so does it inform our perception of what it is the thief is doing: above altering the spatiality of recognizably valuable objects in relation to himself, he's *stealing* them.

Perception is no longer conceivable as the passive reception of sensibles but a "communication or a communion, the taking up or completion by us of some extraneous intention or, on the other hand, the complete expression outside ourselves of our perceptual powers and a coition, so to speak, of our body with things."[30] The things, we should be clear, are not just spatio-temporal material objects. The potential of consciousness to apprehend objects extends well beyond the spatial magnitudes that are pointed to by our perception of proper sensibles. Abstract concepts, as well, are objects of consciousness, pointed to by those spatial magnitudes, but which are not themselves spatio-temporal. As consciousness becomes habituated to the world, we come to immediately perceive such objects as a riot, without the intervening interpretations of sense data as objects to be recognized that exist within certain relations; it is possible to perceive the riot without ever being aware of any particular individual who is rioting, or the colour blobs out of which that individual is supposed to be constituted.

That is not to say that sense data is inessential to consciousness; in becoming a habitual object of consciousness, the sense data does not fail to be there as a possible object, but it is no longer there as the primary object. As a habit, it becomes automatic, something *not* conscious. As William James noted in the *Principles of Psychology*, "*habit diminishes the conscious atten-*

tion with which our acts are performed."[31] A habit does not simply allow us to take the sense data and interpret it at various levels with greater speed; it renders them not conscious. We cannot say, however, that the habit was always unconscious; rather, a series of actions, performed consciously, through repetition become unconscious. And as with any habit, it is possible to engage in habitual action as if it were non-habitual, by attending to it. Were this not the case, any formed habit would be an irrevocable predictor of behaviour.

Where sense perception is concerned, this is the reason why we take such delight in shifting our consciousness to perceptual qualities—precisely because, as these processes have become automatic, attending to them is novel. The habits of consciousness render it like the objects existing in the world, which are already formed; attending to perceptibles becomes an abstraction. Objects exist as already informed, while certain aesthetic objects lead us to attend to our perceptions, e.g., works of art:

> In settling into a painting I'm discovering and taking on form. That's what the visual aesthetic experience comes down to: the discovery and taking on of form, the aesthetic recognition and assimilation of forms and formal relations, *the aesthetic genesis of information.*[32]

CONCLUSION

Aesthetic genesis, or how human experience arises out of our sensitive existence, consists in consciousness' becoming in relation to already-formed, intentional objects. While the Greeks did not sufficiently explain how it is that higher levels of consciousness arise from our perception of proper sensibles, realist phenomenology redefines the perceptual object to include a concept of intentionality—that thing whereby a perception of blue itself points towards an existent object. The intentionality of consciousness is a result of its becoming like the objects of perception, rather than a quality of consciousness alone. Aesthetic genesis is the expression of an already existent, external intentionality of nature.

NOTES

1. Aristotle, *Metaphysics*, 980a21–24. Greek text from W.D. Ross, *Aristotle's Metaphysics*, 2 vols. Oxford: Clarendon Press, 1924 (repr. 1970 [of 1953 corr. Edn.]): Πάντες ἄνθρωποι τοῦ εἰδέναι ὀρέγονται φύσει. σημεῖον δ' ἡ τῶν αἰσθήσεων ἀγάπησις· καὶ γὰρ χωρὶς τῆς χρείας ἀγαπῶνται δι' αὐτάς, καὶ μάλιστα τῶν ἄλλων ἡ διὰ τῶν ὀμμάτων.
2. Aristotle, *Metaphysics*, 983a12: τοὐναντίον ἡμῖν τῶν ἐξ ἀρχῆς ζητήσεων.
3. Aristotle, *Metaphysics*, 982a25: πορρωτάτω γὰρ τῶν αἰσθήσεών ἐστιν.
4. Roman Ingarden uses the example of a parade on Main Street to emphasize the fact that it is never the case that someone simply *knows*, but it is rather the case that someone always knows *something*. He states, "And one doesn't just *know*; one knows, rather, *of* some event or

state of affairs (say, the parade down Main Street on Thanksgiving Day), or one knows *how* to do something (say, how to repair a broken watch), or one knows *that* something is (or is not, or could be, should be, or possibly will be) the case (say, one knows that inflation will probably persist, despite all measures to halt it)." Roman Ingarden, *The Literary Work of Art* (Evanston: Northwestern University Press, 1973), xvii.

5. Merleau-Ponty uses the example being familiar with a face despite not knowing its eye colour as fodder against the empiricist concept of perception: (referring to the prior discussion of the Müller-Lyer illusion) "In the same way the perceived contains gaps which are not mere 'failures to perceive.' I may, through sight or touch, recognize a crystal as having a 'regular' shape without having, even tacitly, counted its sides. I may be familiar with a face without ever having perceived the colour of the eyes in themselves." Maurice Merleau-Ponty, *Phenomenology of Perception*, tr. C. Smith (New York: Routledge, 1964), 13.

6. Jeff Mitscherling, *Aesthetic Genesis: The Origin of Consciousness in the Intentional Being of Nature* (Lanham: University Press of America, 2010), 47. Hereafter cited as AG.

7. Plato, *Timaeus*, 47a1–b3, tr. Donald J. Zeyl in *Complete Works*, John Cooper ed. (Indianapolis: Hackett, 1997), 1250. Greek text from J. Burnet, *Platonis opera*, vol. 4. Oxford: Clarendon Press, 1902 (repr. 1968): ὄψις δὴ κατὰ τὸν ἐμὸν λόγον αἰτία τῆς μεγίστης ὠφελίας γέγονεν ἡμῖν, ὅτι τῶν νῦν λόγων περὶ τοῦ παντὸς λεγομένων οὐδεὶς ἄν ποτε ἐρρήθη μήτε ἄστρα μήτε ἥλιον μήτε οὐρανὸν ἰδόντων. νῦν δ' ἡμέρα τε καὶ νὺξ ὀφθεῖσαι μῆνές τε καὶ ἐνιαυτῶν περίοδοι καὶ ἰσημερίαι καὶ τροπαὶ μεμηχάνηνται μὲν ἀριθμόν, χρόνου δὲ ἔννοιαν περί τε τῆς τοῦ παντὸς φύσεως ζήτησιν ἔδοσαν· ἐξ ὧν ἐπορισάμεθα φιλοσοφίας γένος, οὗ μεῖζον ἀγαθὸν οὔτ' ἦλθεν οὔτε ἥξει ποτὲ τῷ θνητῷ γένει δωρηθὲν ἐκ θεῶν. λέγω δὴ τοῦτο ὀμμάτων μέγιστον ἀγαθόν.

8. Plato, *Timaeus*, 47b7: ἐν οὐρανῷ τοῦ νοῦ κατιδόντες περιόδους.

9. Plato, *Timaeus*, 47c2–4: μιμούμενοι τὰς τοῦ θεοῦ πάντως ἀπλανεῖς οὔσας, τὰς ἐν ἡμῖν πεπλανημένας καταστησαίμεθα.

10. Plato, *Republic*, 523e3, tr. Grube and Reeve, in *Complete Works*, 1140. Greek text from J. Burnet, *Platonis opera*, vol. 4. Oxford: Clarendon Press, 1902 (repr. 1968): τὸ μέγεθος αὐτῶν καὶ τὴν σμικρότητα.

11. "We must then possess knowledge of the Equal before that time when we first saw the equal objects and realized that all these objects strive to be like the Equal but are deficient in this." Plato, *Phaedo*, 74e9–75a3 tr. Grube, in *Complete Works*, 65. Greek text from J. Burnet, *Platonis opera*, vol. 1. Oxford: Clarendon Press, 1900 (repr. 1967): Ἀναγκαῖον ἄρα ἡμᾶς προειδέναι τὸ ἴσον πρὸ ἐκείνου τοῦ χρόνου ὅτε τὸ πρῶτον ἰδόντες τὰ ἴσα ἐνενοήσαμεν ὅτι ὀρέγεται μὲν πάντα ταῦτα εἶναι οἷον τὸ ἴσον, ἔχει δὲ ἐνδεεστέρως.

12. Plato, *Republic*, 524c11: ἐστὶ τὸ μέγα αὖ καὶ τὸ σμικρόν.

13. See *Categories* 6b1–5.

14. Aristotle, *Categories*, 7b23–5, tr. J.L. Ackrill, in *The Complete Works of Aristotle*, ed. J. Barnes (Princeton: Princeton University Press, 1984). Greek text from L. Minio-Paluello, *Aristotelis categoriae et liber de interpretatione*. Oxford: Clarendon Press, 1949 (repr. 1966): τὸ γὰρ ἐπιστητὸν τῆς ἐπιστήμης πρότερον ἂν δόξειεν εἶναι· ὡς γὰρ ἐπὶ τὸ πολὺ προϋπαρχόντων τῶν πραγμάτων τὰς ἐπιστήμας λαμβάνομεν.

15. Aristotle, *De Anima*, 429a13–18, tr. J.A. Smith in *The Complete Works of Aristotle*, ed. J. Barnes [Princeton: Princeton University Press, 1984]. Greek text from W.D. Ross, *Aristotle. De anima*. Oxford: Clarendon Press, 1961 (repr. 1967): εἰ δή ἐστι τὸ νοεῖν ὥσπερ τὸ αἰσθάνεσθαι, ἢ πάσχειν τι ἂν εἴη ὑπὸ τοῦ νοητοῦ ἤ τι τοιοῦτον ἕτερον. ἀπαθὲς ἄρα δεῖ εἶναι, δεκτικὸν δὲ τοῦ εἴδους καὶ δυνάμει τοιοῦτον ἀλλὰ μὴ τοῦτο, καὶ ὁμοίως ἔχειν, ὥσπερ τὸ αἰσθητικὸν πρὸς τὰ αἰσθητά, οὕτω τὸν νοῦν πρὸς τὰ νοητά.

16. Aristotle, *De Anima*, 431b26–8: τῆς δὲ ψυχῆς τὸ αἰσθητικὸν καὶ τὸ ἐπιστημονικὸν δυνάμει ταὐτά ἐστι, τὸ μὲν <τὸ> ἐπιστητὸν τὸ δὲ <τὸ> αἰσθητόν.

17. Aristotle, *De Anima*, 431b12–17: τὰ δὲ ἐν ἀφαιρέσει λεγόμενα <νοεῖ> ὥσπερ, εἴ <τις> τὸ σιμὸν ᾗ μὲν σιμὸν οὔ, κεχωρισμένως δὲ ᾗ κοῖλον [εἴ τις] ἐνόει [ἐνεργείᾳ], ἄνευ τῆς σαρκὸς ἂν ἐνόει ἐν ᾗ τὸ κοῖλον—οὕτω τὰ μαθηματικά, οὐ κεχωρισμένα <ὄντα>, ὡς κεχωρισμένα νοεῖ, ὅταν νοῇ <ᾗ> ἐκεῖνα.

18. Aristotle, *De Anima*, 432a4–10: ὡς δοκεῖ, τὰ αἰσθητὰ κεχωρισμένον, ἐν τοῖς εἴδεσι τοῖς αἰσθητοῖς τὰ νοητά ἐστι, τά τε ἐν ἀφαιρέσει λεγόμενα καὶ ὅσα τῶν αἰσθητῶν ἕξεις καὶ πάθη.

καὶ διὰ τοῦτο οὔτε μὴ αἰσθανόμενος μηθὲν οὐθὲν ἂν μάθοι οὐδὲ ξυνείη, ὅταν τε θεωρῇ, ἀνάγκη ἅμα φάντασμά τι θεωρεῖν· τὰ γὰρ φαντάσματα ὥσπερ αἰσθήματά ἐστι, πλὴν ἄνευ ὕλης. I should note here the difference between what the English term "image" connotes and the Greek term, "φάντασμά." The Greek term does not necessarily refer to a pictorial image, but denotes a sort of residual sense perception more generally.

19. AG, 100.

20. Brentano, Franz, *Psychology from an Empirical Standpoint*, Linda McAlister ed., Rancurello, Terrell and McAlister trs. (Routledge; New York, 1973), 88.

21. AG, 132.

22. Maurice Merleau-Ponty, "The Metaphysical in Man," tr. H. Dreyfus and P. Dreyfus in *Sense and Non-Sense* (Chicago: Northwestern University Press, 1964), 94.

23. Merleau-Ponty, *Phenomenology of Perception*, tr. C. Smith (New York: Routledge, 1964) 132. Merleau-Ponty's footnote: Koffka, *Growth of the Mind*, 174 and ff.

24. Merleau-Ponty, *Phenomenology of Perception*, 132.

25. Merleau-Ponty, "The Metaphysical in Man," 86.

26. Merleau-Ponty, *Phenomenology of Perception*, 213.

27. AG, 1.

28. Merleau-Ponty, *Phenomenology of Perception*, 305.

29. AG, 123.

30. Merleau-Ponty, *Phenomenology of Perception*, 320. C.f. *The Metaphysical in Man*: "Here we no longer have the positing of an object, but rather we have communication with a way of being," 93.

31. William James, *The Principles of Psychology*, Vol. 1, Chapter 4 (New York: Henry Holt and Company, 1890), 114. Italics his.

32. AG, 2.

Chapter Two

The Copernican Turn
of Intentional Being

Charles Rodger

Kant's Copernican hypothesis was formulated in response to the *aporia* of his time: the seemingly intractable conflict between rationalism and empiricism, both of which, he argued, ultimately led to scepticism. Faced with this *aporia*, Kant suggests that instead of assuming, as had been done up to then, that our cognition must conform to objects, we try the experiment of considering whether it might not be objects which must conform to our cognition, likening this hypothesis to the thought of Copernicus, " . . . who, when he did not make good progress in the explanation of the celestial motions if he assumed that the celestial host revolves around the observer, tried to see if he might not have greater success if he made the observer revolve and left the stars at rest."[1]

Given the importance and revolutionary impact of Kant's Copernican hypothesis, is it any wonder if Mitscherling, in announcing what he calls a new Copernican hypothesis and claiming that it is "no less radical in character . . . "[2] does so with not a little self-deprecating humour, admitting that his proposal is liable, at first, to appear "at the very least presumptuous"?[3] Nonetheless, it appears to me that such a hypothesis is greatly needed in our time, for philosophy, and indeed our entire age, once more seems to face an *aporia*. The aim of the present essay is, first, to lay out the *aporia* of our age and the terms in which a new Copernican hypothesis becomes needful by way of an analysis and critique of scientistic materialism, on the one hand, and the phenomenological tradition on the other. After articulating how these two positions in their conflict constitute an *aporia*, I will then articulate the new Copernican hypothesis and attempt to explain the manner in which this new hypothesis serves to overcome it.

MATERIALISM

Our age is largely characterized by the dominance of materialism, and indeed of scientistic materialism, of which eliminative materialism constitutes the most obvious, but by no means only, example. "Scientism" consists in the identification, whether implicit or explicit, of knowledge and truth *as such* with the method and discoveries of empirical sciences. Materialism is an ontology according to which the only things that are or exist are material beings, i.e., spatio-temporally located and extended objects that interact by means of efficient causality, understood in the sense of one thing bumping into each other. Neither of these doctrines or attitudes necessitates the other, and yet they have become bound together so as to dominate our age and thought. How else can one explain the fact that, despite the most evident failure of both psychologism and logical positivism, the academy is home to and even dominated by individuals who, in the name of philosophy, once more seek to "naturalize" ethics and epistemology and turn to cognitive science on the assumption that this will ultimately provide us with a philosophically and scientifically rigorous and true account of that peculiar thing we call the mind?

To recall, psychologism was the attempt to reduce all logical principles and laws to psychological ones. The sceptical results and absurdities entailed by psychologism in fact constituted one of the major motivating forces behind the development of formal logic that is so essential to logical positivists. According to logical positivism, the only things that count as true and meaningful are analytic *a priori* truths of logic and *a posteriori* knowledge verified by means of the scientific method and empirical observation, while all other claims, assertions and positions beyond these are dismissed as "mere metaphysics" and nonsense.[4] On the one hand, insofar as logical positivism embraced the verification principle, it recognized that the empirical sciences as such could not make ontological assertions without falling into metaphysics, and thus recognized the untenability of scientistic materialism, insofar as the latter roams into the sphere of ontology. On the other hand, logical positivism itself was doomed to failure due to its own scientism, for the claim that all truth is either an analytic truth or a truth susceptible to the verification method of the sciences is itself neither analytically true, nor susceptible to empirical verification.

The failure of positivism is particularly instructive, insofar as it so clearly demonstrates both the untenability of scientism and the fundamental difference between the empirical sciences and philosophy. All regional fields of investigation, including the empirical sciences, begin with the presupposition of a subject-matter and a general method and manner of approach, which delimits both the sorts of questions that can be asked and the kinds of answers that can be given. These presuppositions are meta-disciplinary issues;

issues of the foundation of regional disciplines are not determined or decided from within. By contrast, the peculiarity of philosophy, its peculiar self-reflexivity, requires that at least in principle a philosophical position cannot simply begin from established presuppositions, but must be able to account for them and its own account as well in its own terms.

Given the peculiar self-consciousness that belongs to philosophy, it is little wonder that eliminative materialism has failed to garner universal support. Granted, due to the problems that arise when one attempts to account for the relation between the brain and the mind—that is, between a spatio-temporally located material object that is comprehensible in mechanistic terms and the immaterial mind, which appears to both lack such spatiality and seems to exhibit the peculiar characteristic that we call intentionality (i.e., that consciousness is directed towards and about things)—it might at first appear tempting to attempt to eliminate the problematic element. Yet to simply deny the mind altogether and reject all talk of the self and the first-person perspective as a matter of folk-psychology, i.e., as mere unscientific or prescientific mysticism that, like the belief of primitive peoples in nature-spirits, will eventually appear as a quaint superstition,[5] is to commit oneself to an abstraction that contradicts *one's own experience* at every turn. Insofar as the philosopher is at all self-reflective, eliminative materialism must appear absurd, for if one were to accept it, one must begin to ask, for example, to whom, exactly, will it eventually appear that our previous talk of consciousness, intentionality and the subject was merely a superstition? What does "folk-psychology" even mean, when one denies that there is a *psyche*? Whence, then, am I? Who asserts this, or even asks these questions?

Yet eliminative materialism is by no means the only form that scientistic materialism takes, nor even the most insidious form, for scientistic materialism dominates precisely as a *prejudice*; its presuppositions are manifest as at once inconspicuous and self-evident, and thus as beyond question. How so?

Admittedly, it would be foolish to deny that the empirical sciences teach us *something* about the world. Undoubtedly cognitive scientists, for example, learn and discover *something* when they find that certain acts of consciousness are always correlated with processes in parts of the brain, and that if a part of the brain is removed, certain acts of consciousness are altered or even become impossible. Nonetheless, to identify the brain with consciousness and thus to claim, as do Richard F. Thompson and Stephen A. Madigan for example, that the discovery that "if memory is to occur, hippocampal neurons must be functioning" entails that "memories are hippocampal processes"[6] is to make the basic logical error of conflating a relation of contingency (i.e., the necessity of a condition) with a relation of identity.[7] The problem, however, is that, "[w]hen proceeding on the basis of an uncritically assumed materialist metaphysics, such a conflation appears not only to be legitimate, but in fact to be no conflation at all."[8] Now it may be admitted that, "an uncritical acceptance of this conception of the natural world may be appropriate to those sciences that restrict themselves to the mechanics of the empirically observable workings of the world . . . "[9] The adoption of materialism, in other words, *might* be legitimately presupposed *methodologically*, insofar as every regional science and discipline can, and indeed to some extent must, presuppose a subject-matter and general method or manner of approach which delimits the scope of its research and determines what can serve as a legitimate question and answer within its sphere of investigation. Insofar as materialism is adopted by an empirical science as a foundational presupposition for its investigations, however, that science cannot and does not demonstrate the truth of materialist ontology but *merely* presupposes it. If such a scientist or anyone else then takes this presupposition to be legitimate beyond the restrictions of their particular regional science and thus to have universal scope and ontological significance, such a one conflates a methodological presupposition and prescription, i.e., a heuristic principle, with an ontological and metaphysical claim, and thereby slides into scientism. It is questionable, however, whether the kind of reductive materialism that is implicitly presupposed and adopted by the above cognitive scientists is even *intelligible*, let alone philosophically tenable.

Reductive materialism is, of course, motivated by the attempt to avoid both the patent absurdity of the eliminative position, which denies the most basic evidence of our experience, i.e., the intentionality of consciousness and that the world is not just made up of objects but is also subjective and *for* us. At the same time, and like eliminative materialism, it is motivated by the attempt to avoid the absurdities of naïve Cartesian dualism. The assertions that there are two kinds of stuff, physical or material stuff on the one hand that enjoys spatial extension, motion, etc., and mental or ideal stuff that does not enjoy spatial extension on the other; that human beings (and perhaps they alone) are somehow "composed" of both kinds of stuff; that the mental stuff is somehow "in" the brain—all of this is bound to sound strange, if not outright absurd, if only for the fact that the claim that non-extended stuff could be "in" or "touch" the brain seems outright self-contradictory. We thus find students laughing when they are told that Descartes claimed that the point of contact was the pineal gland, sitting at the centre of the brain and connected to the rest of the body by something like a series of pulleys.[10] What such students fail to recognize, and not they alone, is that despite our more detailed and supposedly more scientifically accurate knowledge of the mechanisms of the brain, Descartes' account of eyesight, for example, differs from the scientifically accurate account we are taught in school by degree alone, and not at all by kind. At the end of a complex story regarding the cornea, electronic signals, and the visual cortex, we make no less of a leap when we add "and this causes us to have the representation of an object." This all too easily slips our notice, however, because scientistic materialism dominates as a *prejudicial structure*, rooted in a double-movement in its relation, on the one hand, to the presuppositions that gave rise to the scientific revolution and, on the other hand, to the success of contemporary empirical science which arose from this revolution.

The path that led to the current success of the empirical sciences was first established in the sixteenth and seventeenth centuries. Of particular note are Galileo and Descartes, who (a) overthrew the Aristotelian and Medieval conception of causality, rejecting formal and final cause as useless or misleading, at least with respect to the investigation of nature; (b) installed the metaphor of nature as a machine; and (c) distinguished what would later come to be known as primary qualities, such as shape, number and motion, all of which were taken to be objective,, from secondary qualities such as color, taste and smell, which were then taken to be subjective and derivative from the latter. Together, these presuppositions allow for (a) the comprehension and formulation of nature as a causally determined system, such that causality is simply equated with efficient cause, in the sense of material beings bumping into each other; (b) the mathematization of nature by means of the reduction of all secondary properties to primary properties, which are susceptible to direct geometrical and mathematical symbolization;[11] and (c) the ideal of an "objective" method and approach to the world which consists in "placing nature on the rack," breaking things into their components and putting them together in the service of technological advancement, that is, in order to learn to construct predictable and controllable results and reliable machines.

Undoubtedly, the empirical sciences, in having adopted these presuppositions at least as ideals, have shown themselves to be remarkably successful, insofar as they have provided and continue to provide human beings with a growing mastery over nature and a wealth of technological tools. Undoubtedly, moreover, the empirical sciences teach us *something*, and quite a good deal at that, about the world. As Aristotle notes, however, causes are ways of asking after and answering the question "why?"[12] Such "whys" determine not only what counts as a legitimate question, but a legitimate answer. The presuppositions adopted by the empirical sciences are, by their very nature, useful in directing empirical investigation to ask questions that will provide answers and results of a certain sort, namely of the sort that are amenable to use in the production of machines that can be produced and assembled by the application of efficient causality on material beings and which operate in a regular, predictable and calculable manner. The *prejudicial structure* of scientistic materialism, however, grows out of the fact that, because the success of the empirical sciences becomes so overwhelming in its conspicuousness, its presuppositions are subsequently taken to be simply and immediately true, and are thereby at once obvious, self-evident, and thus become invisible as habits of understanding. Insofar as causality itself, the scope of every "why," is equated with efficient causality, understood in terms of the spatial and temporal interaction of material beings, the only explanations which are presumed to counts as genuine, fundamental, and rigorous are ones that can be understood as answers to a "why" of this specific kind. Indeed, strictly speaking, to even be counted as a genuine *question*, a question must be conceived to be at least in principle reducible to a "why" of this sort, on pain of being rejected as unintelligible.

Now, to return to Descartes: insofar as he eliminates formal and final causality as causes, in the sense that they were taken to be legitimate questions which could provide genuine answers respecting matters of human enquiry,[13] he thereby excludes the possibility of non-material causality as well as of something non-material having an effect in any meaningful sense on a material being. While the absurdity of Cartesian dualism is often merely understood in terms of the issue of the incompatibility of two kinds of "stuff," the problem is a matter of causality, insofar as the only thing that counts as a causal relation for Descartes is the relation of two material things bumping into each other. Once this is recognized, however, then one must admit that reductive materialism is equally absurd, for it is just the same problem in reverse. Where Descartes had to and yet could not explain how a non-material being could be causally related to a material one, such that it could have a material effect or result, the reductive materialist has to and yet cannot explain how a material thing can effect, and indeed even give rise to or produce, a non-material one. The "hard problem" of consciousness, then, is not just extremely difficult to answer, for it is not just a matter of the extreme complexity of the mechanisms involved. In acknowledging that there *is* an explanatory gap, reductive materialism reveals itself to be nothing but scientism, such that it places *faith* in a particular image of the empirical sciences, including the presupposition of and commitment to the truth of materialism. Indeed, it is not only dogmatic scientism, but sheer absurdity to admit that there is a problem or gap of explanation as to how a material thing like the brain *causes* the intentionality of consciousness and at the same time insist that "everything is matter, and all we have to do to construct a truly 'scientific' account of cognition is to wait for our scientists to build a bigger microscope."[14]

This problem cannot be resolved by cognitive science, the philosophy of mind or epistemology, insofar as they remain committed to materialism, whether they adopt a straight-forward reductive materialism, or attempt to avoid the issue while remaining committed to a materialist ontology by speaking of consciousness as, say, an epiphenomenon, or in terms of property dualism, or as an "emergent" property, or as a function, etc. A property, after all, is something that a thing or substratum *has*, while emergent properties emerge *from* something that is primary. According to materialism, however, what primarily and ultimately *is*, is a collection of spatially and temporally extended beings that are causally related by means of bumping into each other, and everything else is reducible to this. Secondary properties, such as seeing things *as* having a color, etc., are supposed to be merely subjective in the sense of "how things merely appear," and yet if intentionality is inherent to and necessary for consciousness, then not just the appearance, but the very consciousness to which things appear is also a mere appearance, in the sense of an illusion. This, however, is absurd, insofar as the very meaning of "illusion" presupposes that there is a being in the sense of something and that is *as* related and directed towards, i.e., a being-for-whom.

It is again surprisingly easy to be blind to this fact, insofar as the prejudice of materialism dictates that "being as such" just *means* material being. It is thus remarkable how often one can meet a self-confessed reductive materialist who nonetheless happily asserts and presupposes the *a priori* truth and validity of basic logical principles without noticing that they are thereby committed to admitting the being of entities that enjoy neither spatial nor temporal location. These laws of logic, however, are taken to be self-evident, while the question of their ontological status is liable to be dismissed out of hand; the questioner, in calling into question this self-evidence, is liable to dismissed by being accused, on the one hand, of arguing for self-refuting scepticism and, on the other hand, of committing a basic category mistake, since being=existence=material being (for the laws of logic are certainly not material beings!). In this way, the prejudicial structure of scientistic materialism once again rears its head by covering over the fact that, even supposing materialism were able to preserve the intentionality of consciousness so as to avoid the absurdity of eliminative materialism, insofar as it remains committed to materialism, it would have managed thereby merely to resurrect psychologism with all its paradoxes.

PHENOMENOLOGY AND POSTMODERNITY

The scientistic materialism which so dominates our age has, of course, certainly not gone unchallenged. Indeed, if one turns to the works of Husserl, one discovers not only detailed and indeed devastating arguments against psychologism, naturalism and scientism, but a rigorously developed and articulated account and description of intentionality and intentional acts. Furthermore, Husserl's account of intentionality is articulated, side by side with a commitment to careful logical analysis, with the aim of establishing philosophy as a rigorous science.

Given this, one might well expect that the works of Husserl and his successors in the phenomenological movement would be highly regarded by philosophers. Positively, phenomenology would appear to provide, at the very least, an invaluable resource for those faced with the "hard problem" of

consciousness (i.e., its intentionality) by providing an alternative, and perhaps more productive, account of and approach to the concept of intentionality and problem of the relation of consciousness to the material world. At the
very least, negatively speaking, one would expect that the articulation within
this movement of critiques of scientistic materialism would be held to war-
rant careful reading and reply by fellow philosophers. Yet such a rapproche-
ment has not only failed to materialize, but phenomenology "has come to be
regarded as not serious philosophy at all."[15] As Mitscherling argues, however, the dismissive attitude to phenomenology cannot be merely laid at the feet
of the other,[16] nor can the fact that the criticisms by phenomenologists of
scientistic materialism have largely fallen on deaf ears. To the contrary, the
manner in which the phenomenological movement developed after Husserl
has served to reinforce the prejudice of scientistic materialism and its presumption that it is only when questions and answers are formulated in its
own framework that philosophy remains rigorous and avoids the fate of
sinking into poetry or fiction. How did this come about?

At the beginning of the twentieth century, at the same time as, and in part
by means of providing a devastating critique of psychologism, phenomenology appeared to offer a radical and revolutionary new avenue for philosophical investigation. The grounds for this revolution were in part laid in and
through Brentano's recovery of the concept of intentionality, according to
which the distinguishing characteristic of consciousness is that it is always
directed towards an object, i.e., that consciousness is always "consciousness
of." For Brentano, however, intentionality constituted merely the immanent
sphere of experience in distinction from, and in opposition to the real world
and the sphere of the other empirical sciences. Husserl, however, in and
through his critique of psychologism, freed intentionality from its psychologistic interpretation and constraints, demonstrating the untenability of this
position, while arguing in his *Logical Investigations* that, while one must
"accept as obvious the fact that logical concepts have a psychological origin,"[17] one need not, and indeed must not, on pain of absurdity, therefore
take logical facts and ideal meaning unities to be reducible to psychological
states and empirical norms of thought. In working with and through this anti-
psychologistic conception of intentionality, Husserl discovered heretofore
unsuspected and unexplored realms of and for philosophical investigation,
and was thus led to extend the scope of intentionality and intentional analysis. Intentionality became, for Husserl, the field of immanent investigation
that was to serve as the apodictic basis for the sciences, i.e., phenomenology
was to be first philosophy.

With Husserl, a new philosophical movement was born which promised
to overcome not only the "objectivism" of naturalism and positivism, but
subjectivism and the relativistic historicism of *Weltanschauung* philosophy,
and thereby to, at last, place philosophy on the path to establishing itself as a

rigorous science. Insofar as intentionality, conceived as "consciousness of," was always directed towards or about an object, the Cartesian problematic as to how consciousness could get "outside" of itself and grasp the real world appeared to be overcome. Insofar as phenomenology turned to the *Sachen selbst*, i.e., the sense of things as they appear and are given forth in lived experience, phenomenology could claim to undercut psychologism, naturalism, materialism and scientism in general. It did this by pointing out that it was investigating things given and appearing in different attitudes, and that the scientific attitude itself constitutes just one particular attitude and manner of givenness, and indeed a highly abstract and limited attitude which could neither found itself nor claim to be comprehensive and thus philosophically rigorous or adequate. Moreover, insofar as phenomenology did not limit itself to psychological states but pursued eidetic analysis and description, seeking thereby to grasp essences and the essential structures and the layers and levels of what was given in intentional acts in their *a priori*, phenomenology could equally sustain itself against and beyond mere subjectivism and the relativism of *Weltanschauung* philosophy and seek to at last attain for philosophy the status of a rigorous science.[18]

Such, then, was the promise of phenomenology, and yet Husserl's hope of founding philosophy as a rigorous science and making phenomenology into a broad and unified school undertaking investigations was soon shattered. Husserl had sought to secure intentionality as a sphere of immanent investigation by means of a series of reductions and thus to articulate a method which could be followed and carried out by the practitioners of phenomenology. Admittedly, given Husserl's repeated attempts to articulate these reductions, their precise number and order remain a matter of some controversy. Nonetheless, we can isolate four essential moments:

1. The initial *epoché* which leads "us beyond (or beneath) the natural attitude of the investigations pursued by the natural sciences,"[19] putting out of play our natural attitude and theoretical presuppositions, and in particular involving the suspension of judgments regarding any commitment regarding the reality of external objects.
2. The epistemological or psychological or reduction, which "leads us through and beyond the domain of psychology" by bracketing the real being of the psychological empirical subject.
3. The phenomenological reduction proper, where the phenomena and acts are to be conceived not in terms of the relation between a cognizing subject and the cognized object, but instead where the *act* of cognition itself is the object of cognition. Accordingly the intending and intended, what Husserl calls *noema* and *noesis*, are just two poles of the same immanent act.[20] This is the level at which, "by means of

the eidetic reduction, we are enabled to perform the 'essential' analyses appropriate to phenomenology."[21]

4. Finally, the transcendental reduction "entails the further claim that these immanent phenomena are to be analysed *exclusively* as immanent; that is, that they are to be regarded in total isolation from, and *ontologically entirely independent of,* any objectivities 'transcendent' to consciousness . . . "[22] "Consciousness," in this instance, is, of course, not the empirical consciousness from which we began and which was bracketed in the psychological reduction, but the transcendental ego which, as a kind of monad, is now to be developed and unfolded from out of itself in order to encompass the entire realm of inter-subjectivity, science, and everyday experience.

Despite his insistence that this was the only possible path, few of Husserl's students were willing to follow him in adopting the final reduction to the transcendental ego. After all, the notion of intentionality appeared at first to offer a path beyond not just the positivism and materialism of scientism, but beyond subjectivism and idealism as well. Insofar as they took him as placing intentional analysis in the immanent sphere of the transcendental ego and insisting on the heteronomy of real and ideal beings, such that they could only be taken as themselves particular kinds of intentional objects,[23] Husserl's Göttingen and Munich students necessarily rejected Husserl's turn to transcendental idealism as a regression to earlier forms of idealism.[24] Nonetheless, the analyses of Pfänder, Reinach, Stein and Ingarden demonstrate just how rich an ontologically focused realist phenomenology that still embraced the *epoché* and eideteic analysis could be.[25] Unfortunately, the development of phenomenology in this realist direction largely remained unrealized, due to the dispersion and death of Husserl's early students in the World Wars, events which in turn enabled Heidegger to attain pride of place and ultimately usurp the phenomenological movement, overshadowing thereby not only Husserl's early students, but Husserl himself.

In the past, the fact that Heidegger came to be taken as the leading figure and representative of the phenomenological movement understandably provoked confusion, for *Being and Time* not only says nothing of the reductions, but scarcely mentions intentionality at all, and then only in passing.[26] The release of Heidegger's lectures, and particularly the *Prolegomena to the History of the Concept of Time,* however, enables us to recognize the continuity of Heidegger's project with Husserlian phenomenology as well as to comprehend that and how he came to exert such an influence over those who, like Gadamer, were certainly familiar with and took themselves to be faithful still to Husserl and phenomenology. The fact is, Heidegger did not take himself to be giving up on intentionality in asking his "question of Being." On the contrary, he took this question to be identical to the investigation of intentionality in its *a priori*, carried out in a rigorously phenomenological manner. What Heidegger explicitly rejected was not intentionality, but Husserl's reductions, claiming that Husserl's very formulation of the reductions was based upon and presupposed various traditional (uninterrogated and not phenomenologically secured) categories, including *essentia* and *existentia*,[27] *res cogitans* and *res extensa*,[28] and real and ideal being. In order to escape psychologism, on Heidegger's reading, Husserl's initial *epoché* first involved the bracketing of real being. Without investigating and establishing the being of intentionality itself, however, Husserl was led to understand intentionality in terms of and on the model of ideal being. On Heidegger's reading, then, truth in its fullest sense is conceived by Husserl in terms of ideality, which is to say in terms of the universality and repeatability of the proposition. The truth of the proposition is then grounded in the apodicticity of the immanent cognition of the transcendental ego, i.e., of its certainty and self-certainty. Thus, Heidegger claims, *"the question of the being of the intentional is left undiscussed. It is not raised in the field thus secured, pure consciousness; indeed, it is flatly rejected as nonsensical."*[29]

Heidegger's entire project, the outline of which is found in the *Prolegomena*, is the attempt to perform a complete *epoché* and thereby to grasp intentionality more originally than Husserl.[30] Granted, in *Basic Problems of Phenomenology*, Heidegger speaks in such a manner that he appears to limit intentionality to subjectivity and to insist that intentionality is itself founded on something more primordial, which he calls "transcendence." Nonetheless, it is a mistake to think that Heidegger rejects or replaces intentionality with transcendence, for he also insists that "it is precisely intentionality and nothing else in which *transcendence* consists . . . ,"[31] but asserts that "transcendence cannot be explicated by means of the concept of intentionality as it has hitherto been usually conceived."[32] In short, what Heidegger rejects in articulating his "question of Being" is not intentionality *per se*, but what he takes to be the unwarranted and, in particular, the subjectivistic interpretation of intentionality by Husserl in his adoption of transcendental idealism and absolutization of the transcendental ego.

Admittedly, the above account of Heidegger is somewhat unorthodox. Nonetheless, Gadamer at least certainly both interpreted Heidegger in this manner and followed Heidegger along this path. Thus, according to Gadamer, although Husserl's conception of intentionality and phenomenology "transcends in principle the opposition between subject and object and discloses the correlation of act and object as its own great field of study . . . ,"[33] and however much Gadamer claims that, at least in his later writings, Husserl recognizes not merely subjective intentional acts, but an anonymous, horizontal or horizonal intentionality,[34] Gadamer nonetheless insists that the line of analysis, while leading Husserl to the conception of the life-world and to making historicity central to phenomenology, is fundamentally in tension with and threatens to burst asunder[35] Husserl's entire project, due to Husserl's continued commitment to the establishment of philosophy as an apodictic science on the basis of "the purely transcendental sense of reduction to the ego."[36] By contrast, it is Heidegger whom Gadamer claims "burst asunder the whole subjectivism of modern philosophy . . . "[37] Gadamer thus takes himself to be following Heidegger when he claims that what is primordial is horizonal intentionality, while at the same time insisting that the subject is only constituted within this horizon, and indeed within the fusion of horizons that is intersubjective conversation.

Yet, while according to the above account, Heidegger is not guilty of replacing the central place of intentionality with the "question of Being," Spiegelberg was nonetheless justified in bemoaning Heidegger's "fateful and almost fatal"[38] influence on the phenomenological movement. First, Heidegger's critique of Husserl entailed the rejection not only of the reductions but of any notion of eidetic analysis. It is no coincidence that Heidegger's descriptions in *Being and Time*, for example, "speak only to commonality, not to identity of essential structure . . ."[39] for " . . . Heidegger's analyses of *Dasein* deny at the outset the possibility of eidetic analysis . . ."[40] The very *exceptional* character of Heidegger's account of "authentic Dasein" precludes such an eidetic analysis, insofar as Heidegger insists that a universal that is valid for and common to every instance is only an "inessential essence," while "essential essence" is the rare and unique.[41] Accordingly, "the students and followers of Heidegger were not taught to undertake such analyses."[42] Second, critical of the seeming subjectivist bent of Husserl's conception of intentionality, but lacking any possibility of grounding his account in material or ideal being, both of which Heidegger took as derivative from intentionality in a more primordial sense (i.e., as what "gives" Being itself, *Ereignis*), or indeed in any claim to universality and necessity, Heidegger turned language itself into the bearer of intersubjective historical experience. In making this move, Heidegger and his followers thereby identified language as the most basic level and horizon of experience. Worse yet, they were seduced by language such that, lacking any ties or limitation to eidetic analysis, the phenomenological movement largely degenerated into jargon and language mysticism. Its "analyses" became seen as (and not without a lot more justification than those of us who still identify ourselves with continental philosophy would often like to admit) a matter of playing with words and language, or at any rate as no longer deserved of the title of serious philosophy, for:

> [I]n tossing aside the demands of logical analysis and rigour, phenomenology has come to be viewed as something totally unsystematic and unscientific and therefore to be grouped with the more 'artistic' disciplines of the arts, and taught by the same faculty who teach drama, poetry and ballet. The current

dominant movement in academic philosophy toward philosophy of science and materialist-oriented cognitive science may be understood as a rejection of the philosophy of experience wrongly conceived in this manner and as a return to the very sort of scientistic, positivistic thinking that Nietzsche lamented over a hundred years ago. [43]

THE *APORIA* OF OUR TIME:
MATERIALISM AND PHENOMENOLOGY

Materialism can hardly provide satisfaction for philosophy, insofar as it remains attentive to the richness of lived experience. The notion that one can simply *explain*, which is to say explain *away*, consciousness and the wealth of ways in which we relate to the world around us in terms of material beings and efficient causality alone must seem absurd to the one who asks "and yet where am I?"

Such an appeal to first-person experience has long been the trump card of phenomenology. Yet, while legitimate within certain limits, this trick has been overplayed to the point of absurdity. Heidegger and Gadamer, for example, are both willing to admit the importance and efficacy of the empirical sciences *within certain confines* and to grant that the planets would still orbit the sun before there were human beings there to witness them (and likely will continue to do so long after human beings cease to live on this planet). Nonetheless, this admission is only made at the "ontic" level, while such ontic claims themselves are supposed to have their ground in some "disclosure of Being" which, while not reducible to the individual human being or single ego, requires human beings and their understanding or interpretation of Being in order to "Be." Thus, the sciences and their subject-matter, and pre-linguistic experience in general, is given the status of something derivative and "founded" on the inter-humanly, intersubjective "World" which "worlds" as the event wherein Dasein is appropriated to Being. The question of what lies behind or before such an event and the origin of language is thus dismissed out of hand as merely ontic, while language is granted the status of a mystical, quasi-divine gift that arises from nowhere. [44] To this, the materialist can only shake their head in wonder at the anti-scientific pretensions and mysticism of a phenomenology that proclaims its justification to lie in an experience no less alien than the divine intellectual intuition of a Jacobi, a Fichte or a Schelling.

It is tempting to blame Heidegger alone for the degeneration of phenomenology, and no doubt he has a good deal to answer for. Nonetheless, the *aporia* which faces us is not overcome simply by returning to Husserl. Granted,

[t]he sneering charge of eliminative materialism—and indeed of all forms of reductive materialism and material identity theory—against competing non-materialist theories is that the latter all take recourse in some mysterious = mystical = spiritual sort of 'substance' . . . [45]

is indicative of ignorance or dishonesty. Any notion of non-material beings is certainly mysterious, insofar as one remains *dogmatically* committed to materialism, yet intentionality is not in any way mystical in the sense of something supernatural that lies beyond or outside of our everyday experience. There is, however, something mysterious and problematic about the notion of intentionality employed and presupposed by the entire phenomenological tradition. Insofar as intentionality is conceived of or defined exclusively as "consciousness of," intentionality is conceived of as belonging exclusively to beings that have the same kind of consciousness and self-consciousness as human beings. Insofar as intentionality is identified with Being itself, there thus arises once more a paradoxical gap between our experience and the natural world along with the recognition that, as finite beings, we cannot explain this world or even its existence, much less our own, in terms of this intentionality. The appeal to intentionality understood as "consciousness of," far from providing a bridge between subject and object or the subjective and the objective, breaks our world in two no less than did the old dualism, with its opposition between material and ideal being—a dualism that materialism and phenomenology in their own ways sought and claimed to overcome.

THE NEW COPERNICAN HYPOTHESIS

In the face of this *aporia, Aesthetic Genesis* attempts to articulate a new Copernican hypothesis which "turns upside down the way we think not only about thinking itself, but about what we human beings most essentially are, and how we are similar to and distinct from the rest of creation."[46] This hypothesis, simply stated, is as follows:

Hitherto it has been assumed that all consciousness must be intentional. But what if we suppose that not all intentionality is conscious? This suggests the possibility that what we call consciousness arises from intentionality. *Aesthetic Genesis* will adopt as a working hypothesis the claim that what we call 'consciousness' is indeed an emergent feature of organisms comprising complex intentional structures, just as 'sentience' is an emergent feature of organisms comprising less complex intentional structures.[47]

Just as dogmatism and scepticism both presupposed that consciousness had to conform to the object, so scientistic materialism and the phenomenological tradition share the presupposition that intentionality is exclusively the distinguishing mark or property of beings that have the consciousness in the manner enjoyed by human beings, or at most by other sentient higher-level creatures. The above hypothesis reverses this conception of intentionality and along with it the fundamental tenet of phenomenology. Intentionality is not to be conceived of primarily or primordially as "consciousness of" but as *intending*, as *tendere,* tending towards as relational directedness.[48] Intentionality, understood in this manner, suggests not only that consciousness exists already at the level of sense-perception and pre-linguistic experience; it suggests not only that intentionality belongs to the organic realm, but that "sensation itself originates in a still more basic intentionality that is to be found already in what we still misleadingly call the 'non-organic' realm."[49]

In other words, intentionality is something that is discoverable "from the bottom of the Great Chain of Being right up to the top."[50] The new Copernican hypothesis, accordingly

> is *fundamentally* committed to: (i) the independent existence of a real world—that is, a world that exists independently of human consciousness; and (ii) the independent subsistence, within that world, of intentional entities—that is, entities that possess intentional being, such as 'forms.'[51]

Intentionality, then, is conceived as a *kind* of being, i.e., intentional being, which stands alongside material and ideal beings such that *all three* are equally fundamental and thus irreducible to the others.

Is this not, however, all quite fanciful? How does this hypothesis serve to overcome the *aporia* of our time?

RESOLVING THE *APORIA*

At first, the new Copernican hypothesis, with its reconception of intentionality, is liable to sound at the very least idiosyncratic if not purely adventitious. Yet the tendency of philosophy towards the conception of a fundamental, irreducible and primordial kind of being, distinct from materiality and ideality, and conceived of as a tending or relating that precedes the distinctions of self and other and the substantialization of these moments, appears to be manifest in the tradition itself. At the very least, the hypothesis of this kind of primordial intentional being serves to make a good deal of sense of, for example, William James' conception of "pure experience" and Nietzsche's conception of "will to power."[52] Both of these thinkers, in agreement with the new Copernican hypothesis, state that what is fundamental is relationality and directional relating,[53] while the kind of consciousness that is enjoyed by human beings and the subsequent substantialization and distinction between subject and object is a sublimated and more complicated formation of primordial directed relating. Accordingly, they are in agreement with the new Copernican hypothesis; for both of these thinkers, the hypothesis of such a primodial directedness is forced upon us, insofar as we take seriously and examine experience from within.[54]

Admittedly, just like Nietzsche's will to power and James' pure experience, the notion of intentional being is bound at first to be misunderstood in a multitude of directions. It is liable to be seen as ascribing, quite absurdly and without the slightest justification in our experience, the kind of consciousness enjoyed by human beings (who, for example, distinguish self and other, inner and outer, etc.) to plants and paramecium,[55] but this is precisely what the new Copernican hypothesis denies. In a sense, admittedly, and precisely because the new Copernican hypothesis makes us aware of how little we understand what we mean by consciousness and how fundamentally we have falsified our experience, it is legitimate to say that "whenever the intentionality, the directedness of a relation—more precisely of an organic relation—is sustained, we find consciousness."[56] This is to claim, however, that a plant or a paramecium enjoys sentience insofar as such things *are* in being directed and related to their environment so as to constitute themselves as a unity, where the whole is not reducible to but is more than its parts. The problem consists in the fact that we tend to substantialize the organism, to think of it as a unity that is separable from its towards and away-from; but this kind of distinction—that makes the ego into a fixed abstraction—is something that only arises late and is by no means the only kind of experience that human beings enjoy.

In making such claims, the new Copernican hypothesis is undoubtedly liable to provoke the disdain of those who embrace scientistic materialism. Intentionality is, for the materialist, at best something derivative that will be explained away in materialist terms. To claim that simple organisms and even the laws of nature have intentional being is thus liable to be dismissed as anti-scientific. The conception of intentional being does undoubtedly fly in the face of materialism. Negatively speaking, insofar as the new Copernican hypothesis asserts that material being is only one kind of being and that there are even *two* non-material kinds of being, namely ideal and intentional being, that are not reducible to material being, it of necessity stands opposed to and rejects scientistic materialism. The new Copernican hypothesis, however, far from rejecting science, rejects scientistic materialism, because materialism is itself *un-scientific and indeed anti-scientific*.

Admittedly, insofar as scientistic materialism dominates as a prejudice, it has gained sway even with scientists, as was seen in the example of the cognitive scientists who dogmatically embrace and articulate their works in terms of the project of reductive materialism. Materialism insists that the world is, at base, just matter, and that all causality is efficient causality, in the sense of material things bumping into each other. Causality at a distance, accordingly, is dismissed as a mystification, for there cannot be non-material causes, so that such causality, like all non-material being, is to be eliminated as "magic." (And in truth, it would be magic if, as Descartes claimed, human beings and they *alone* enjoyed not only material being but another kind of being and causality!) The reductive materialist, then, while honest enough at least to admit that there is a problem, maybe even a "hard problem" with respect to consciousness, insofar as consciousness seems to possess the peculiar quality called intentionality, promises that this problem will eventually be resolved by means of a better microscope, i.e., by comprehending that which lies at the micro-level. Such a promise, however, is a mere presumption and a dogmatic assertion, for not only can the empirical sciences never prove or demonstrate the truth of materialism, because it is an ontology and a metaphysics, but because it is not itself and has not been strictly bound by these dogmatic presuppositions. Even Newtonian physics, whose proposed billiard-ball universe appears to remain the paradigm and ideal of the materialist, had to admit as its central feature precisely a causality at a distance that the materialist insists is mystical, namely gravity. Current physics, far from eliminating such mystical causality has multiplied it and discovered it at the quantum level with double-slit experiments and quantum entanglement. To follow the sciences, i.e., to follow what scientists themselves actually say, as opposed to what a materialist wants to assume or dogmatically assert they say, requires that we admit the positive existence of causality other than efficient causality as well as the positive existence of indeterminacy, probability and directionally determining relations.

Now, no doubt the materialist will be liable to respond that this is one more instance of "Fashionable Nonsense," where continental philosophy attempts to illegitimately extend discoveries at the micro-level to the macro-level, where the materialist conception of the universe is perfectly viable. Let us recall, however, that it was the materialist who insisted that we gather our microscope, claiming against experience that if one started at the micro-level and worked up, all of our mystical conceptions—of being not reducible to matter, and causality not reducible to efficient causation—would vanish; but this is dogmatism, is metaphysics, is materialistic scientism that is in fact anti-scientific. By contrast, while the new Copernican hypothesis is formulated in response to the prejudice of scientistic materialism which itself dominates as a prejudice in the empirical sciences, it is *not* anti-scientific. Admittedly, a philosopher might, on the basis of this hypothesis, be bold enough to suggest alternate interpretations of the data, and even to suggest other possible avenues of research and experiment, for the prejudice of materialism serves to limit the possibility of scientific research by foreclosing avenues of investigation. Kant was right in claiming that, when it comes to organisms, it is impossible to proceed without a concept of internal teleology, i.e., without the concept of a self-organizing and in-forming directedness, but it was a mere prejudice brought on by his faith that Newtonian physics could explain everything in terms of matter and efficient causality (excepting first-person experience, of course) that allowed him to take internal teleology to be merely a "subjective" heuristic principle.[57]

Intentionality, in the sense proposed by the new Copernican hypothesis, is found all the way up and down "the great chain of being," and thus there is no fundamental ontological difference or gap between us, i.e., between consciousness and its intentionality, and the rest of the world. Nonetheless, and *pace* William James and Nietzsche, the new Copernican hypothesis does not therefore claim that ideal and material being are reducible to intentional being. This would lead ultimately to conceptual confusion, or psychologism, or idealism. While, as Nietzsche and James claim, attending to experience requires that we admit what Mitscherling calls intentional being, it is no less true that the acknowledgement of all three kinds of being is "forced upon us by logic and common sense."[58]

Negatively speaking, the new Copernican hypothesis, insofar as it entails both realism and the fundamental heterogeneity of being, such that there are three kinds of being, of necessity stands opposed not only to the idealism of Husserl, but to the phenomenological movement as it was developed by Heidegger and his followers. It does not, however, entail the rejection of phenomenology as such. To the contrary, this hypothesis is posed with the aim of placing phenomenology back on track and to the end of recovering eidetic analysis and the moments of the reductions essential to the rigour of phenomenological analysis.

That phenomenological analysis can be carried out in a realist vein, and indeed on the basis of the distinction of material, ideal and intentional being, has already been demonstrated by Ingarden, and in particular by his masterful work of ontology that is *The Literary Work of Art*. According to Ingarden, for Husserl not only "real" or material beings, but even ideal beings were ultimately just "intentional formations of a particular kind,"[59] such that "the real world and all its elements [are] purely intentional objectivities which have their ontic and determining basis in the depths of pure consciousness that constitutes them."[60]

Taking the literary work of art—as an object which in Husserl's terms must uncontroversially be considered a purely intentional objectivity and which clearly has its source in the conscious acts of an individual ego (i.e., the artist)—as the starting-point for his analyses, Ingarden demonstrates that (a) the form of such a purely intentional object is fundamentally distinct from that of material and ideal beings; and indeed that (b) while not identifiable with or reducible to beings of these kinds, such a purely intentional being requires and depends for its existence and subsistence on beings such as this; and hence that (c) "even such an intentional object enjoyed a foundation that was not constituted solely by the activity of consciousness."[61]

In no way did adopting this threefold and hence heterogenous ontology exclude Ingarden from employing what is essential in Husserl's reductions (it only excludes the problematic transcendental reduction to the transcendental ego) or from providing careful description and eidetic analyses of the literary work of art. Granted, the possibility of a *complete* reduction is excluded, but this is not a failure but instead a consequence of adopting the position of realist phenomenology.[62] Nonetheless, the very example of the literary work of art serves as rejoinder to those who, like Heidegger, take Husserl's reductions to be something mysterious or artificial. The very act of reading a literary work demonstrates that this assumption is mistaken.

There seem to be numerous ways in which we can relate ourselves to what we call "literary works of art" when we pick up a book. We can merely use the book as the occasion to focus on ourselves, on our moods, history and psychological states ("This reminds me of when I . . . "); we can take the book as an object of psychological analysis and read the work as a symptom of the psychological states of its author ("Clearly *Remembrance of things Past* is the expression of Proust's anxiety regarding his closeted homosexuality!"); we can fetishize the book itself ("This is a first edition!" or "Look at how beautiful the type font is!"); we can read the work as the articulation of some empirical fact ("This fictionalized account of Napoleon is clearly wrong, for at that date, as the historical record shows, his wife was nowhere around!"); we can take it as the expression of some theoretical or ideal truth ("*Pride and Prejudice* is an illustration of Marx's account of class struggle!" or "I refute *Alice in Wonderland*, as it conflates relative and absolute size!") If we really read a literary work, then we recognize that all such ways of relating to a work of fiction are distractions from the *Sache selbst* and bracket all such concerns, or rather, for the most part these matters are put out of abeyance as we attend to the unfolding of the work. In other words, we have already performed the reductions when we read a literary work, and what we have before us is a purely intentional object which, although it requires certain things in order to subsist (e.g., a material basis, certain ideal meaning unities, the peculiarities and particularities of psychological states of the author and the readers) is not identical or reducible to any of them.

Intentional beings, then, are nothing "mysterious" or "mystical," insofar as such beings are manifest in experience all the time as, for example, cultural objects, sentences, symbols and works of art. The new Copernican hypothesis, however, claims something more and goes further than Ingarden at least explicitly ventured, although his admittedly incomplete masterpiece, *Controversy Over the Existence of The World*, tends towards and contains hints in this direction,[63] for Ingarden still appears to have conceived of intentionality as "consciousness of." Granted, on Ingarden's account, a purely intentional object can become separable and independent from the individual conscious acts of an ego which was the source or the author of, for example, the literary work. Indeed, such separation *must* be possible if there are literary works of art that are intersubjectively accessible. Nonetheless, Ingarden still insists that such intentional objects are, on the one hand, still traceable back to such conscious acts[64] and, on the other, that the subsistence of such purely intentional objects is dependent on human consciousness and in particular the continuity of culture and language, without which the work would die.[65] In contrast, the new Copernican hypothesis asserts that a good many intentional beings subsist independently from and even prior to human consciousness, while human consciousness is something derivative insofar as it is simply a higher, more complex formation of intentionality that in different and simpler forms can be found all the way up and down "the Great Chain of Being."[66] Intentional being is thus not only constitutive of animals and plants, but of the most simple material beings insofar as even the laws of nature are *habits*, i.e., a be-having and tending.

Given this conception of intentionality, there is no more difficulty in ascribing intentionality to simple organisms or even inorganic things than there is in ascribing it to other human beings. It is only on the presupposition of some great, and rather implausible, divide between intentionality as tied to consciousness in the sense that we ascribe to human beings, and indeed only to adult human beings, that it is even credible to claim that we have no access and right to ascribe intentionality to anything except human beings. We are not born into a language but acquire it; humans first had to create it, and indeed continue to create new words. Before language, there is a transformation and sublimation of impulses, feelings and even thoughts, and it is only later that these are sublimated into verbal signs.[67] The fact that the form of language and grammar can then itself serve to prejudice, (i.e., direct,) thought, once the habit of a language and the connection of words has be formed, is not a refutation but a consequence of the fact that language has an origin in simpler and more fundamental intentional formations than what we usually call "consciousness," much less "language." It is a mere prejudice, based on the presupposition that intentionality is "consciousness of" and indeed where consciousness is equated with the consciousness of human beings exclusively, to assume and assert that phenomenology has no access to the intentionality that is non-human, much less non-linguistic. There is, in fact, no difficulty in understanding the intentionality of a child who does not yet know the word for something or speaks it wrongly (we find ourselves in this situation all the time!). The mother understands the infant who cries as calling for something that, sometimes frustratingly, is quite specific and different from what she first assumes, and even knows what such an intention is, in the form of the urge not yet verbalized. Similarly, it is not difficult to see—to the contrary, it requires a good deal of self-deceit and blindness to not see—that the paramecium which one views under the microscope, when "it moves in every direction possible, exploring first in this direction and then in that, and it quite vigorously responds to any interference suddenly placed in its path" enjoys intentional being.[68] Admittedly, there is always the possibility of misinterpreting the phenomena, of overestimating the complexity involved in a particular instance. The difficulty here, however, is no more troublesome, and in some ways due to its simplicity far less so than the problem of ascribing particular intentions to another person in a particular instance. Nonetheless, almost miraculously, we find, even with all of the problems and complications that language, with its conventions with all the amorphous diachronic and synchronic displacements would appear to entail, that we more often than not *do* understand each other. This would indeed be a miracle, if there was no "outside-text,"[69] and if all being was intentionality. But intentional being is not the only kind of being, for intentionality also subsists so as to *in-form* material beings, and this kind of being, as well as ideal being, exerts its pressure and limitations on things as well as on our interpretations. Likewise, we are not merely intentional being, but are in-formed matter, i.e., have a body. There is, then, nothing strange in the fact that I can see and understand the intentionality that is exhibited by the chair that, standing on two legs, is quivering and falling, for I am also in that way and, while I recognize that it shall not hurt itself, if I attend carefully to the phenomenon I can identify the form exhibited by the falling chair as a form that I too, have all too often displayed.

How, then, does the new Copernican hypothesis serve to overcome the *aporia* of our time? Because, while it does not deny or reduce ideal or material beings either to each other or to some third thing, it admits a third kind of being which joins these extremes. At the same time, however, the assertion that "intentionality is not 'of consciousness' but is instead a feature of the natural world amounts to a denial of any essential distinction between the mind and the object of cognition."[70] We, accordingly, are not "outside" of the world or essentially different from it, and there is no great gap, either ontological or therefore epistemological, between consciousness and the world, for the world may be regarded "as exhibiting the same three sorts of being that we humans ourselves exhibit."[71] To assert that intentionality belongs to the independent world is not to reduce either the world or consciousness to material being or to idealistically reduce the world to consciousness.

It is, rather, to locate the realm of intentional being at the heart of creation, and to locate the activity of consciousness as in the world, and to identify that activity as that which informs the matter of that world.[72]

NOTES

1. Immanuel Kant, *Critique of Pure Reason,* trans. Paul Guyer, and Allen W. Wood. (New York: Cambridge University Press, 1999), Bxvi.

2. Jeff Mitscherling, *Aesthetic Genesis: the Origin of Consciousness in the Intentional Being of Nature.* (Lanham: University Press of America, 2010), 7. Hereafter cited as AG.

3. See AG, 7.

4. Cf. A.J. Ayer, *Language, Truth and Logic*. (New York: Dover Publications, Inc. 1952), 31-2.

5. See Paul M. Churchland, *Matter and Consciousness*. (Cambridge: Massachusetts Institute of Technology, 1997), 44-5.

6. AG, 102.

7. AG, 102.

8. AG, 102.

9. AG, 39.

10. Descartes's own account is in fact not quite this crude. See René Descartes, *The Philosophical Writings of Descartes, Volume* I, trans. J. Cottingham et al. (Cambridge University Press, 1985), 339–341.

11. See Husserl's analysis account of the mathematization of nature in Edmund Husserl, *The Crisis of the European Science and Transcendental Philosophy*, trans.D. Carr (Evanston: Northwestern University Press, 1970), 21–56.

12. See Aristotle, "Physics," *The Complete Works of Aristotle, Volume I*, ed. J. Barnes (Princeton University Press, 1984), 194b16ff.

13. Descartes, of course, does admit that we can, and indeed must, appeal to formal causality when we turn to the consideration of a first cause, but such formal cause is presented by him as known only by analogy with and through extension of the concept of efficient causality (René Descartes, *The Philosophical Writings of Descartes, Volume II*, trans. J. Cottingham et al. (Cambridge University Press, 1985), 166–7) and as only applicable in a positive sense to God (ibid., 165–6.)

14. AG, 39.

15. AG, 9.

16. See ibid.

17. Edmund Husserl, *Logical Investigations, Volume I*, ed. Dermot Moran (London: Routledge, 2001), 111.

18. See Edmund Husserl, "Philosophy as Rigorous Science" in *Phenomenology and the Crisis of Philosophy*, trans. Q. Lauer (New York: Harper & Row, Publishers, Incorporated, 1965).

19. Jeff Mitscherling, *Roman Ingarden's Ontology and Aesthetics*. (University of Ottawa Press, 1997), 81.

20. Cf. ibid., 56.

21. Ibid., 81.

22. Ibid.

23. Cf. AG, 115–16 and 125.

24. Mitscherling, *Roman Ingarden's Ontology and Aesthetics,* 13.

25. See ibid., 14 and AG, 9.

26. Heidegger only explicitly mentions intentionality at two points in *Being and Time*, first on page 48 and second in a endnote to page H 363, wherein he announces "that the intentionality of consciousness is *grounded* in the ecstatical unity of Dasein, and how this is the case, will be shown in the following Division . . . " Martin Heidegger, *Being and Time*, trans. J. Macquiarrie and E. Robinson (New York: Harper & Row, 1962), 498, i.e., in the unpublished move to Time and Being.

27. Martin Heidegger, *History of the Concept of Time: Prolegomena*, trans. Theodore Kisiel (Bloomington: Indiana University Press, 1992), 110.

28. Ibid., 101

29. Ibid., 13–4.

30. It would take us too far afield to articulate and defend this interpretation here. It may thus merely be indicated that, (A) according to Heidegger's outline of his project in his *Prolegomena*, the penultimate draft of *Being and Time* Heidegger lays out the steps of his project in four steps as the elaboration in these two direction, moving (1) from the *intentio*, (2) from the *intentum*, (3) as the relation between these two, and (4) a refined conception of intentionality that supercedes this threefold division and leads to a more refined conception of the *a priori*. (Heidegger, *Prolegomena*, 148.) (B) in Martin Heidegger, *Basic Problems of Phenomenology*, trans. Albert Hofstadter (Bloomington, Indiana University Press, 1988), Heidegger shifts termi-

nology insofar as he now restricts intentionality to the first moment, while the second moment that begins from the intentum is what Heidegger now calls transcendence (see ibid., 63-4.) (C) As Heidegger indicates in a footnote to *Basic Problems*, this work was intended as "[a] new elaboration of division 3 of part 1 of *Being and Time*."(Ibid., 1 fn.1.) (D) The distinction between intentionality and transcendence, which is according both to the *Prolegomena* and *Basic Problems* constitutes a reversal, coincides with the reversal from *Being and Time* to Time and Being and from *Zeitlichkeit* to *Temporalität*. (E) In *On Time and Being*, Heidegger retrospectively articulates the four steps of his path of thought as leading "from *Being and Time* past what is peculiar to 'Time and Being' to the it that gives, and from this to [Ereignis]."(Martin Heidegger, *On Time and Being*, trans. J Stambaugh (New York: Harper & Row, 1972), 27) (F) Heidegger claims that Ereignis, which he already introduced in 1919 as that originary pre-theoretical lived experience which phenomenology seeks (See Martin Heidegger, *Towards the Definition of Philosophy*, trans. T. Sadler (New York: Continuum, 2002), 63) involves the *epoché* of the various ways in which Being has revealed itself in the various epochs of the philosophical tradition up to the Event itself which "gives" these epochs. With this, according to Heidegger, "one stands before being *as* being, and no longer before one of the forms of its destiny." Martin Heidegger, *Four Seminars*, trans. A. Mitchell and F. Raffoul (Bloomington: Indiana University Press, 2003), 60-61.

31. Heidegger, *Basic Problems*, 63. I cannot agree with Mitscherling's reading of Heidegger on this point. According to Mitscherling, Heidegger's articulation of the concept of intentionality on page 61 entails that Heidegger fundamentally misunderstood and misrepresented Husserl's conception of intentionality as something that is merely subjective and immanent to the ego. Against this reading, Mitscherling insists that, for Husserl, experience consists "in the active engagement of subject with world. Husserl's goal often appears to have been the unification of the subjective and the objective—he repeatedly argued that he *not* be interpreted as dealing exclusively with the subjective. It is well know that he failed to ever give a convincing account of how his phenomenological analyses did not wind up in such a subjectivist position, but he certainly never wanted to restrict experience to the exclusively subjective." (AG, 15) The passage which Mitscherling cites as evidence of Heidegger's misunderstanding, however, belongs to Heidegger's discussion of misunderstandings of the concept of intentionality, at the end of which Heidegger asserts that "intentionality is neither objective, extant like an object, nor subjective in the sense of something that occurs within a so-called subject, where this subject's mode of being remains completely undetermined. Intentionality is neither objective nor subjective in the usual sense . . . " Martin Heidegger, *Basic Problems*, 65.

32. Heidegger, *Basic Problems,*175.

33. Gadamer, *Philosophical Hermeneutics*, trans. D. Linge (Berkeley: University of California Press, 1976), 144–5.

34. Ibid., 118. See also Gadamer, *Truth and Method,* trans. J. Weinsheimer and D. Marshall (New York: Continuum, 1998), 245.

35. See Gadamer, *Truth and Method*, 248. Compare also Gadamer's claim in Gadamer, *Philosophical Hermeneutics*, 196: "the notion of the 'life-world' has a revolutionary power that explodes the framework of Husserl's transcendental thinking."

36. Gadamer, *Philosophical Hermeneutics*, 160.

37. Gadamer, *Truth and Method*, 257.

38. Herbert Spiegelberg, *The Phenomenological Movement: Second Edition, Volume I* (The Hague: Martinus Nijhoff, 1965), 273.

39. AG, 14.

40. Ibid.

41. Cf. Martin Heidegger, *Elucidations of Holderlin's Poetry*, trans. K Hoeller (New York: Humanity Books, 2000), 52.

42. AG, 9.

43. AG, 9.

44. Jeff Mitscherling, Tanya DiTommaso, Aref Nayed, *The Author's Intention* (Lanham: Lexington Books, 2004), 14.

45. AG, 35.

46. AG, 5.

47. Mitscherling, *Author's Intention*, 168, cited in AG, 47.

48. See AG, 51.

49. AG, 7.

50. AG, 5.

51. AG, 19.

52. Regarding Nietzsche's will to power as relational and directed, cf. Friedrich Nietzsche, *Writings from the Later Notebooks*, ed. R Bittner (Cambridge University Press, 2003), 25 (36[21] and 36[22]), and esp. 222 (11[115]).

53. While the notion that relations was fundamental to William James' conception of radical experience from the start (cf. William James, *Essays in Radical Empiricism* (Cambridge: Harvard University Press, 1976), 22–27), the importance of the directedness of pure experience did not dawn on James until 1907 when, after reading Bergson's *Creative Evolution*, he recognized the solution to lie in the non-reciprocality and thus directedness and directionality of relations. It is for this reason that James takes the "flux" of additive relations to resolve both the "pen" problem and the "Fechner problem" at the same time. See William James, *Manuscripts, Essays and Notes* (Cambridge: Harvard University Press, 1976), 108 and 114.

54. Cf. William James, *Essays in Radical Empiricism*, 22-3. Compare Friedrich Nietzsche, *Beyond Good and Evil*, trans. W. Kaufmann (New York: Vintage Books, 1966), §36. It is no coincidence that Mitscherling could turn the Nietzsche's account of language against Heidegger and the Heideggerian inspired conceptions of language operative in Gadamer's *Truth and Method*. (See Mitscherling, *Author's Intention*, 7–19).

55. See AG, 5. Compare also William James, *A Pluralistic Universe* (Cambridge: Harvard University Press, 1977), 77–8.

56. AG, 114

57. Cf. Immanuel Kant, *Critique of the Power of Judgment*, ed. Paul Guyer (Cambridge University Press, 2000), 20:205.

58. AG, 127

59. Roman Ingarden, *The Literary Work of Art*, trans. G. Grabowicz (Evanston: Northwestern University Press, 1973), lxxiv.

60. Ibid., lxxii.

61. Jeff Mitscherling, "The Life of the Literary Work of Art," in *Existence, Culture and Persons: The Ontology of Roman Ingarden*, ed. A. Chrudzimski and W. Huemer (Frankfurt: ontos verlag, 2005), 139.

62. Cf. AG, 15

63. See AG, 18.

64. Cf. Ingarden, *Literary Work*, pp. 117–18, and 126, also Roman Ingarden, *Controversy Over the Existence of the World, Volume.I*, trans. A Szylewicz (Frankfurt: Peter Lang, 2013) 116.

65. Hence, on Ingarden's account, the literary work of art dies when, for example, it is written in a language that has become dead and thus can no longer be concretized.(Ingarden, *Literary Work*, 354. Cf. also ibid., 126.)

66. AG, 5.

67. See Mitscherling, *Author's Intention*, 13.

68. AG, 70.

69. See Jacques Derrida, *Of Grammatology*, trans. G Spivak (Baltimore: The Johns Hopkins University Press, 1998), 158.

70. AG, 26.

71. AG, 69.

72. AG, 13.

Historical Considerations

Chapter Three

Cartesian Soul

Embodiment and Phenomenology
in the Wake of Descartes

Felix Ó Murchadha and Ane Faugstad Aarø

Aesthetic Genesis is a highly original and suggestive work, one which combines a powerful systematic thesis with a provocative overview of the history of philosophy and (to a lesser extent) of theology and science. In approaching this work, we wish to question some aspects of that historical account and in doing so, drawing especially on the emphasis on the corporeal in French thought from Descartes to Merleau-Ponty, sketch an alternative interpretation which, we believe, leads to a more nuanced approach to the "idealism" of Husserl and generally a more inclusive view of phenomenology than is allowed for in Mitscherling's account.

This article consists of four parts. Part one will address some issues regarding the relation of Descartes to Medieval thought (I); part two will trace an account of embodiment from Descartes through to Merleau-Ponty, which indicates another strand in modern thought—which in particular emphasises the place of habit and embodiment (II); part three will turn to Husserl, in order to question the fruitfulness of discussing his account of intentionality under the rubric of realism/idealism (III); and the final part concludes with some brief reflections on recent French phenomenology (IV).

I

It would be fair to say that one of the principle villains in the historical account sketched in *Aesthetic Genesis* is René Descartes. Descartes, Mitscherling tells us, "was simply wrong in maintaining that the ego . . . is the

43

immaterial substantial 'thing' called the 'mind or soul'";[1] Descartes engages in an "unsympathetic and misleading caricature" of intentional species;[2] Descartes provides us with the "first philosophically articulated basis for the modern thinker's view of the soul,"[3] a view which, for Mitscherling, has been disastrous; "Descartes naively conflated the epistemological and the metaphysical; he regarded 'mind' and 'soul' as synonymous terms, concluding that the knowing subject . . . is one and the same as the metaphysical subject."[4] The problem with this account is twofold: it is both a one-dimensional and a decontextualized account of Descartes.

We accept much of the diagnosis Mitscherling offers of the loss of any account of formal causality in Modernity. However, once we see that the roots of this lie not in Descartes, but in the late Middle Ages, and that Descartes is one—albeit highly influential—response to a crisis in the late Medieval world, we can better diagnose our current situation. This is not a mere historical quibble: in effect, Mitscherling's argument is that something important has been lost between the School of Aristotle and today and, if that is the case, then it is important to know why that has been lost. In speaking of final causes, Mitscherling states the following: "when modern science rejected the former sort of final cause [designed for a purpose] as inadmissible to its investigations, it also rejected the latter sort [behaving purposively]."[5] In fact, however, long before science rejected the latter (we may call it) immanent account of final causality, theology has rejected the intelligibility of the former, and that rejection had made immanent teleology impossible. The seeds for this had already been sown in the immediate aftermath of Aquinas' work. In 1277, opposing the influence of so-called "Pagan" philosophy in the theology faculty at Paris, Stephen Tempier, the Archbishop of Paris, issued a condemnation of 219 theses which were associated with the revival of Aristotle.[6] In large part, these condemnations were intended to stress the omnipotence of God, placing him beyond the bounds of reason itself. On this view, the efforts of reason to understand God are ultimately futile, because they assume a limitation on divine power, namely that his will is subordinate to his intellect. The teleological ontology of Aristotelian metaphysics thus becomes ungrounded, as it assumes a *telos* which can be read from created being, while the *telos* can only originate from the will of God, which by hypothesis is unknowable by human reason. The Voluntarism of this position also implies a Nominalism: the universal terms in which human reason speaks have at most heuristic, but not ontological significance; God does not create universals, but rather singular entities, which owe their existence directly to him; universals can have no ontological significance, because to assume they do is to assume that the divine will is limited by the divine intellect apprehending the universals.[7] Universals come to be understood as simply names, words which have a heuristic purpose, but no ontological significance.[8]

The Voluntarist emphasis on the omnipotence of God had the paradoxical effect of dividing the natural from the supernatural: if God's will is hidden from human reason and not subject to divine intellect, then there is no path left from the natural to the supernatural. The problem with the argument from design in such a view then is not that such an appeal to God's plan would hinder scientific research, [9] but rather the presumption of inferring divine design from the natural world around us. It is only when the world—nature— is evacuated by theology of divine reference that an "a-theistic" science is possible. As such, the gap of natural and supernatural, to which Mitscherling points, [10] is premised on a rejection, evident already in the writings of Duns Scotus, of the Thomistic account of analogy. [11] While Aquinas understands nature as intelligible in terms of predicates which are perfectly true of God and imperfectly manifest in nature, for Scotus, being is univocal and as such is predicable of God and nature. But the univocity of being is gained at the cost of making being a most general and empty term. Univocity could be affirmed, so long as being could not be affirmed and denied of the same thing without contradiction. Only if understood as the most general term could being be so employed of God and creatures. [12]

It is not too much to speak here of shock waves going through the intellectual and religious traditions of Europe in these centuries (from the late 13th to the early 17th), which had at their core a certain dualism—of natural and supernatural, of God and world, of grace and nature, of freedom and determinism, of soul and body. Montaigne's sceptical response to these turmoils forms the backdrop to Descartes' encounter with sceptical doubt and sets the tone for the manner in which he grappled with these issues and, along with Galileo, set the parameters for that final response to them which gave us modern science. It is important when we read Descartes' most famous works, *Discourse on Method* and *Meditations of First Philosophy*, that we recognize their strategic purpose. Descartes was about to publish his physics, *Le Monde*, when the condemnation of Galileo (1632) made him hold it back. His work on method and metaphysics were meant to give a first philosophical and methodological basis for his physics: "these six meditations contain all the foundations of my physics . . . I hope that readers will gradually get used to my principles, and recognize their truth, before they notice that they destroy the principles of Aristotle," he says. [13] The *Meditations* begins by making a clear distinction between Philosophy and Theology, but again this distinction was already made by Ockham who, following consistently from the Voluntarist premises, declared that theology was not a science. [14] What this means, in effect, is that philosophy must remain at the level of immanence: reason which follows nothing other than its own laws. This autonomy of reason is appealed to in order to protect philosophy from the sceptical implications of such theology. But the problem is that reason's own laws are obscure to human reason itself. The sceptical challenge for Descartes is a radical one, because theological doubts infect the very foundations of reason itself, namely the analogical relation of human and divine natures, and hence of human and divine reason.

The response to the theological crisis of the late Middle Ages was not for Descartes, as for Montaigne in the "Defence of Raymond Sebond,"[15] one of sceptical fideism, but rather one of strict rationalism. As such, the ego which we find in the cogito argument is one which is in dialogue with itself, seeking to find in that inner dialogue a place which can methodologically suspend the omnipotent, voluntarist God. The whole argument of the *Meditations* aims to disempower that God and, in effect, to instrumentalize him as a guarantee for human reason (a guarantee lost in Voluntarism) and to effectively transform that God into a model of falsity: falsity arises for human beings when they, like the voluntarist God, separate will and intellect.[16] As such, the soul in Descartes is nothing supernatural; it is rather that capacity to think which makes science and human society possible. In this sense, Descartes seeks to relegate the voluntarist God to theological speculation, while reclaiming a God which unites intellect and will for philosophy.[17] This God is one which himself creates the eternal truths,[18] but in creating them creates nature which can be understood in terms of the natural light of reason. Here, Descartes is reflecting in a philosophical key the theological debates on nature and grace—dividing up the "pure nature" of the created world from the supernatural destiny of human beings as believed on the basis of a faith in grace.[19]

The question, for Descartes, then becomes not so much how to reach certainty, as why certainty is so elusive. If we can divide the natural and the supernatural, and if human reason has a natural capacity to reach truth about nature, how can we explain error? Descartes' diagnosis here is that the falsity of his judgments is based in the congruence of two related influences: the twin governance of teachers and appetites, of society and nature.[20] Neither society nor nature is free from the possibility of error, because neither can be thought fundamentally enough. For Descartes, there is no question of a choice between one and the other, neither rejecting nature for the benefits of civilized society, nor rejecting society in the name of nature. Both nature and society are equally complicit, hence the need for a metaphysical meditation, a move away from both nature and society, a movement within.[21] This movement within arises out of the spontaneous skeptical movement, but is for Descartes the precondition of any systematic skeptical reflection. The situation which he describes here, and his means of overcoming it, point to an account of human fallenness,[22] which again reflects the concerns arising from the Voluntarist crisis of late Medieval thought. Indeed, Descartes can be understood as reacting against a radical Augustinian account of grace which places human salvation wholly in the inscrutable will of God.[23] Crucial to understanding this is the place of method in his thought.

For all the rigor of the method which he sets out first in the *Rules*, he denies that it functions prescriptively. Rather, his method is simply describing how the intellect *already* operates: "nothing can be added to the clear light of reason which does not in some way dim it."[24] Hence, the method he is proposing is, in effect, a reflection of the intellect on itself: the intellect by virtue of its own operations attempts to set the limits of these very operations.[25] Yet, if the clear light of reason functioned simply naturally, there would be no need for a method, or that method would be known intuitively by all. Again, he begins the *Discourse* by saying that all people have good sense,[26] yet the very project of the *Discourse* would be meaningless if that good sense were exercised by those who possessed it. Descartes is assuming here a logic of fallenness: the human has both the calling to truth and goodness and yet, for reasons which are constitutive of its present self, fails to reach either. The symptom of this, which shows it to be more than simply a contingent failure, is the classically Augustinian one of disunity and disobedience within the self, between will and desire, a conflict which, for Descartes, is rooted in the relation of body and soul. As the reality and origin of this conflict are not recognized, it is manifest as a conflict of the passions, through which the will can only employ representations to excite opposing passions.[27] This is the fallen state of the human being, one in which no clear distinction of body and soul is achieved and, as such, one in which the human is forever subject to a conflict of the passions. What is lacking here is a purity of judgment,[28] judgment which is purified of bodily influence. The fallen nature of the human being is one in which the soul is clouded by the body. Descartes' response to this situation is, however, radically anti-Augustinian—not the appeal to divine grace, but the employment of method.

Method in Descartes's philosophical project responds to the fallenness of human embodiment, but does so not to escape from that embodiment, but to harmonize the different elements of human nature. We can understand better the complexity of his account when we see the manner in which he is reacting against the embodied understanding of the self in Montaigne. While Descartes shares the latter's conservatism regarding custom (at least in a certain context),[29] he resists Montaigne's account of habituation. The inward movement is one away from the body as external and as subject to the imposition of time. The time of habit is the time of the past in the present, molding the present in terms of the past; the inward movement is a liberation from that time. It is a movement out of the external relations of time, in the causal connections of past and present, towards a domain in which all those forces and connections can be bracketed out and left in abeyance. This temporal indifference, this foreclosing of past and future makes possible the will's indifference, which is operative in systematic doubt. This temporal foreclosure is possible for Descartes only through an inward movement which resists the body, which in thought if not in actuality attempts to undo the fallenness into the body and by that token fallenness as such.[30]

The motif of inward movement is more Stoic than Augustinian. For Augustine, the movement is not away from the world as such, but rather from captivation with it for its own sake. Furthermore and related to this, the movement away from captivation with the world is a precondition for developing a passion for that which is not of the world. For Descartes, on the contrary, understanding of the inner movement of the *Meditations* is (for all its Ignatian influences) rooted in that division of the world into action and passion, which so clearly marks the Stoic writers. We can see this throughout his writings—it is inherent in the basic movement of his method, it guides his provisional moral code and is articulated as follows in the *Passions of the Soul*: "Regarding those things that depend only on us . . . our knowledge of their goodness ensures that we cannot desire them with too much ardour . . . . Regarding the things that do not depend on us in any way, we must never desire them with passion, however good they may be."[31] Reason begins with itself, without any ontological guarantees, as these have been theologically undermined. It is unaffected reason, reason above all not affected by the past. What this means also is that historical authority needs to be questioned. Mitscherling rightly criticizes the misunderstanding of authority in contemporary thought,[32] but again this has its roots in the stoical tenor of the radical Voluntarism of late Medieval thought (Mitscherling acknowledges this in part):[33] for unaffected intellect, the past is simply that which lies prior to its own positing.

The ego which knows itself is, for Descartes, such a being which begins with itself. Already in the fourth century, the incorrigibility of self-knowledge had been asserted, notably by Augustine, who claimed that one cannot doubt that one has mental content, even if one might have doubt about whether this content corresponds to anything external to the mind.[34] Indeed, self-knowledge as a basis can be found in medieval thought amongst those who discussed sceptical arguments. On the lineage from Aquinas, Duns Scotus, William of Ockham and Autrecourt, we find a willingness to accept knowledge of the self as certain truth. Variations of the cogito argument appear here, particularly in Crathorn. Self-knowledge is thus a tradition from medieval thought already, on through Descartes and Malebranche in the early modern era, and although Malebranche resists the idea that any clear knowledge of the soul is possible, he retains the idea that consciousness has certainty in the perceptions of the self.[35]

The knowledge of the self or the soul through rigorous investigation and verification of beliefs and by an *epoché*, a suspension of beliefs, permeates the philosophical tradition from its very beginning in antiquity; indeed the Pyrrhonian sceptics claimed the authority of Socrates for sceptical arguments. The cogito argument in Descartes and his assertion of the existence of the ego is tied to this tradition.

II

Mitscherling presents in *Aesthetic Genesis* his dilemma, the choice of two necessarily opposing views of embodied cognition, the one realist and the other idealist: either that the mind must be embodied for cognition to occur, or that the mind is an "epiphenomenon of cognition, which is essentially and exclusively, bodily."[36] Implicit in this distinction is a dualism of matter and mind, which ignores the modes in which matter and mind are intertwined, particularly with respect to habit. It seems to us that this claim, while to some extent true of contemporary debates, does not account for the rich French tradition of analysis of the corporeality of cognition rooted in Descartes.

As we have seen, Descartes' project of self-knowledge has a long lineage in the Medieval tradition. It is important that neither the novelty of his approach to this question be over-emphasized, nor the claims which Descartes made for the cogito argument be exaggerated. The ego which emerges from the cogito argument is a minimalist ego, a reduced ego which is the only remnant after having performed this profound *epoché*.[37] It is not a soul or a consciousness per se. Contrary to Mitscherling's claims regarding Descartes' naïve merging of epistemological and metaphysical questions, nothing seems to indicate that this ego, purged as it is of all its cogitations, is the true "self" of a person or of any person. It is rather a principle or an idea of a something which must have some sort of ontological status, since it cannot reasonably be doubted.

The place of the body with respect to the ego is simply bracketed in Meditation II, and the result of the considerations of Meditation VI are, as Princess Elizabeth firmly insisted in her correspondence with Descartes, inconclusive.[38] To fully understand the Cartesian inheritance on the question of the body, the *Passions of the Soul* is crucial. This is particularly so with respect to the French tradition, where the importance of this work is recognized more than in the English speaking world. The understanding of the ego and of self-knowledge continued to evolve in the philosophical tradition into a fuller account of the self, a self that is more positively described as a complete human being, as the composite entity of a whole body/soul compound and with a world. In Malebranche and Maine de Biran, we see this view coming markedly to the fore, but already Descartes, in *The Passions of the Soul,* departs from the tradition in the debate of the sceptical arguments.[39] Inspired by the Stoics, however critical of their results, he produced an account of the human passions, the autonomy of the will, and the relationship between the higher and the lower passions, such that ultimately the passions of the soul refer to those noble and most refined emotions of the intellect which allows for a truly human will and longing and love of God, i.e., the metaphysical in man. The body in The *Passions of the Soul* is not a piece of extended matter, which it is all too often termed with reference to the *Meditations*, but rather that which allows for the organic whole to function as a unity of perception, passion, will and intellect. In the *Passions*, we find a delineation of the nature of the soul and its passions in §19, where at the same time he stresses the importance of the passions with regard to self-awareness or self-consciousness:

> . . . For it is certain that we cannot will anything without thereby perceiving that we are willing it. And although willing something is an action with respect to our soul, the perception of such willing may be said to be a passion of the soul. But because this perception is really one and the same thing as volition, and names are always determined by whatever is most noble, we do not normally call it a 'passion,' but solely an 'action.'[40]

The passions of the soul are those perceptions or sentiments that we view as specially pertaining to the soul, i.e., to a sphere of ownness.

Although Descartes begins the *Passions of the Soul* by claiming that he is simply wishing to explain the passions and not deal with them as a moral philosopher, in fact description and prescription intertwine in this work. The strongest souls, he tells us, are those in which the will most easily conquers the passions.[41] In conquering the passions, the will first curbs the bodily consequences of particular passions, e.g., running away in the case of fear, but then further controls the passion itself.[42] This latter task is only possible through firm and determinate judgment concerning truth and goodness, but crucially also requires the cultivation of "higher" passions.[43] Furthermore, while the intellect is an instrument in this task, the will is that which governs: the will, for Descartes, needs both to regulate the passions and to guide the intellect—indeed these are one and the same task. This task is one which cannot, however, be accomplished by mere acts of the will, but rather by the habitual cultivation of higher passions. The will is the middle term in the relation of intellect and body, and indeed a fundamental question for Descartes, already in the *Meditations* but more particularly in the *Passions*, is to understand how it is that thought can "inform" matter, how the soul can move the body. The metaphysical task with respect to the passions is to raise consciousness out of fallenness. This does not mean some kind of angelic delusion of escape from the body, but rather finding within the passions a harmony of mind and body. The body is conceived of as metaphysical in *Passions*; i.e., the meaning and function of the passions, some of which are physical in their origins, is to allow the human will and imagination to exist. Method's place in this context is a way of disciplining the soul.

Mitscherling claims that, while for the Medievals and Ancients the soul permeated the whole body, for Descartes the soul is located in the brain (the pineal gland) and that this leads to the "conventional modern theory" that identifies the soul with the cerebral cortex.[44] But while Descartes does suggest such a view (particularly in Meditation VI), in fact he affirms the opposite. In the *Passions*, §30 he states: "the soul is really joined to the whole body . . . For the body is a unity which is in a sense indivisible because of the arrangement of its organs . . . And so the soul is of such a nature that it has no relation to extension . . . it is related solely to the whole assemblage of the body's organs."[45] Descartes goes on to base this precisely on the non-extended nature of the soul: if the soul is not extended, how, he asks, can it be located in any particular part of the body. The pineal gland is that part of the body where the soul "exercises its functions more particularly than in all the others" or where it "directly exercises its functions."[46] Descartes's arguments for this need not detain us here; more important is the fact that his distinction is not between an inanimate body and a supernatural soul, but rather between the soul as organic unity—or indeed, as form—and how such a soul functions in this forming activity. As already noted, the *Passions* reflects a fundamental ambiguity of "fallen" nature: everyone feels passions within them, yet our understanding of them (reflected in the writings of the Ancients) is obscure.[47] Whatever of the fairness of this judgment (regarding the Ancient Greek and Roman accounts of the passions), what it points to again is the difficulty of error in that which is closest to us. The reason for this, for Descartes, is that we do not understand the relation of body and soul. In understanding this relation correctly, we understand not only how the soul moves the body and the body the soul, but also how we can mould the intertwining of these relations in such a way as to achieve goodness and happiness.[48]

While, as we have seen, Descartes resists Montaigne's account of habit with respect to securing the methodological starting point of philosophical reflection, the peace of mind which such method both requires and should engender depends on the proper relation of mind and body—that is, on the passions. The connection Descartes charts here is a very close one. The passions arise from the manner in which the body affects the soul, which is in terms of a greater force in the blood—beyond what is necessary for survival (§107)—through which an excess of blood enters the heart (and this may even precede birth [§136]). These affections take on a particular form through habit, by which "once we have joined some bodily action with a certain thought, the one does not occur afterwards without the other occurring too."[49] This he sees as a habit which lies at the origin of our being: habitual connection of a bodily action with a thought produces a close alliance of body and soul, which amounts to a unity of the free ego and nature. This unity is such that Descartes, in discussing love, states "this caused the soul . . . to join itself willingly . . . , i.e. to love it."[50] The soul is incited to assent to joining itself willingly to this flow of blood. How can the soul *both* be caused *and* act willingly, or voluntarily? The soul seeks the good of the body, and such flow of blood discloses the vitality of the body to the soul. But an element of volition is necessary, such that the soul can resist that which leads it to give its assent and in fact hate that which at first inspires love. There seems to be an interplay here of habit and volition (§137).

The passions which form here are understood functionally by Descartes, but they fulfil a function, because they dispose the soul towards objects in different ways; the passions inform the soul of the objects as having certain natures. The passions represent objects in certain ways, understand them as having certain natures and as requiring certain dispositions "to wish those things which nature deems useful to us."[51]

The philosophical development of the corporeal in French thought from this starting point in Descartes' *Passions of the Soul* is important for the later development of the concept of corporeality in phenomenology in general. By looking at a few traces in early modern French philosophy, leading up to the concept of "flesh" in Merleau-Ponty, we may discern a line of philosophical thinking about the corporeal, which we think throws light on the various influences in phenomenology. The background is the existing debate in Merleau-Ponty's French tradition before he took up the Husserlian treatments on "*Leib*" (particularly in *Ideas II*).

In the French tradition, analyses of the corporeal go hand in hand with analyses of consciousness. As much as the dualism of mind and matter has been criticized, Descartes has undoubtedly inspired a vast tradition of philosophical analyses of the ego, consciousness and the experiencing subject. That it has profoundly influenced the themes in later French philosophy is evident by the fact that the Cartesian ego continues to figure as one of the most central issues and a point of departure for philosophers such as Malebranche (1638–1715) in the 18th century, Maine de Biran (1766–1824) in the 19th and Bergson (1859–1941), Lavelle (1883–1951) and Merleau-Ponty (1908–1961) in the 20th century. As we have seen, Descartes emphasized the unity of mind and body in his *The Passions of the Soul* as well as in the *Meditations* (as a relationship closer than how "a sailor is present in a ship"), stating, "[. . .]I am very closely joined and, as it were, intermingled with it, so that I and the body form a unit."[52] One might say that the primary goal in the *Meditations* was to attain certainty regarding the ideas and intuitions of the ego and of God.[53] In a response to Descartes' position, Malebranche wrote in the late seventeenth century that the intelligibility of the cogito and of clear and distinct ideas depends on a *sentiment intérieure* and a divine inauguration of touch.[54] Twentieth century phenomenology after Husserl takes up this important aspect of sentiment or affectivity in self-consciousness and perception. Merleau-Ponty treated Malebranche's ideas of the corporeal and affective in self-awareness in a set of lectures (transcribed by Jean DePrun as) under the title *L'Union de l'ame et du corps chez Malebranche, Biran et Bergson.*[55] In Judith Butler's words, Merleau-Ponty's concept of flesh contains "a relation of tactility that precedes and informs intersubjective relations, necessarily disorienting the subject-object account."[56] Butler argues that in the concept of flesh in "The Intertwining" chapter in his later work *The Visible and the Invisible*, something more fundamental is in play than in the account of intentionality in the *Phenomenology of Perception*, a principle of some sort: "[S]omething prior to the subject, but this something is not to be understood on the model of a substance," she writes.[57]

Malebranche's work, partly informed by Augustine, is relevant here, responding to Descartes' *cogito* by way of introducing s*entient being* as a necessary part of the c*ogito,* of knowledge of the self; self-knowledge is acquired over time, with imperfection, and is inaugurated by an initial introduction to tactility by God. (We recall the Cartesian cogito as being more of a sudden insight, and showing minimal characteristics.) In Malebranche, all experience, perceptions and passions follow a principle prior to sensation and objects of sensation, something like an ontological set of relations (to God) that grounds experience and gives rise to the passions.

Writing on the theme of the corporeal and of affectivity, Maine de Biran in *De l'Aperception immédiate* conveys the profound influence of Descartes' *Passions* and throws light on later developments in French philosophy, especially on Merleau-Ponty. Maine de Biran says in this work that the feeling of permanent causality and individuality resides in a sphere of ownness marked by a sense of will and of motility, action and force. All of that which is within the limits of the ownness and the sense of the self's effort is "apperceived as *willed* act or result of an act willed by the identical Self":

> On immediate apperception in relation to the sentiment of co-existence of the own body and the boundaries [*circonspection*] or distinction of its different parts. The meaning of effort, which we may call also the meaning of immediate apperception, in the special exercise of which we attach the feeling [*sentiment*] of permanent causality and individuality, *resides* in all the parts of the motoric system, which is directly influenced by the will, delineates or limits [*circonscrivent*] the domain of ownness where it exercises this force. All that which operates within these limits is immediately apperceived as *willed* act or the result of an act willed by the identical Self; all that which is outside of these limits is not any longer dependent on the same force, nor does it attain the same mode of apperception. [...][58]

It is in the primitive, willed effort to move that the existence of the ego is to be found; "in the apperception of the effort of which it feels itself subject or cause."[59] "The fact of a power of action and of *will,* proper to the thinking being, is certainly as evident to him as the very fact of his own existence; the one does not differ from the other."[60] Maine de Biran wrote, "It is *I* who move or who *will* to move, and it is also *I* who am moved. Here are the two terms of the relation which are required to ground the first simple judgment of personality *I am*."[61] *Volo, ergo sum*; I will, therefore I am.[62]

The spatial and temporal world of tactility, vision, hearing, the aesthesiological body is the domain of the natural attitude in phenomenology, of the empirical world and of psychology. Renauld Barbaras writes that for Merleau-Ponty the reduction poses a problem with regard to natural being: "Merleau-Ponty's phenomenology is really a *phenomenology of life*, which means Merleau-Ponty's thought completes the project of Husserl's phenomenology. Indeed, we can say that Merleau-Ponty's main purpose, from beginning to end, is to give sense to the Husserlian *life-world* as it is described in the *Crisis*."[63] With regard to the discussion of whether there is an idealism at play on Husserl's part, we may bear in mind that whatever is transcendentally there in the *epoché* is fundamentally also first in the life-world.[64] Merleau-Ponty's later theory of the flesh and of reversibility in *The Visible and the Invisible* arose exactly out of the need to address the relationship between subject and object, a duality that jeopardizes the organic unity of the corporeal self in its sentient and intentional experiencing of the situation and its horizons.

That perception is for Merleau-Ponty always a crucial field is evident also in his comments on Maine de Biran and Bergson. As de Biran had stated, perception is in itself already unified and does not, in the course of my sensations, become a compound with my thinking self. The self is in its primordial faith and situatedness always already in a world of perception, and for the latter not to be thought of as a coinciding with the world or a complete transparency of phenomena to a passive spectator, it is a world which, as Pascal said, informs me of myself rather than the other way around. "In one way I understand the world, in another it understands me."[65]

In this context, we can understand what Merleau-Ponty writes regarding Bergson on coincidence:

> The famous Bergsonian coincidence certainly does not mean, then, that the philosopher loses himself or is absorbed into being. We must say rather that he experiences himself as transcended by being. It is not necessary for him to go outside himself in order to reach the things themselves, he is solicited or haunted by them from within. For an ego which is *durée* cannot grasp another being except in the form of another *durée*. By experiencing my own manner of using up time, I grasp it, says Bergson, as a "choice among an infinity of possible *durées*.[66]

Merleau-Ponty goes on to say: "If to do philosophy is to discover the primary sense of being, then one does not philosophize in quitting the human situation; it is necessary rather to plunge into it. The absolute knowledge of the philosopher is perception."[67]

Merleau-Ponty takes up, in *In Praise of Philosophy*, Bergson's understanding of language as furnishing consciousness with an immaterial body in which it can incarnate itself:

> In and through language it is generally the expression with which Bergson is concerned. He saw that philosophy did not consist in realizing freedom and matter, spirit and body apart from one another or in opposing them. In order to be themselves, freedom and spirit must witness themselves in matter or in the body; that is to say, they must express themselves.[68]

Language is thus an immaterial body which bears witness to our incarnate being, expressing both freedom and spirit, as they are idealized as "soul" or "mind" in classical thought.

The themes which interested Merleau-Ponty in Bergson were the expression of being in a continuum of the living word that encompasses the ideal and the material, consciousness and matter, the living word which is always expressed to someone and about something, and carrying out the exchange between the past and the present and between matter and spirit. Freedom must always be realized in matter, through language as act or as that which furnishes consciousness with an immaterial body, incarnates it. "It is as if the spirit which, from the beginning, hovered over the waters had need of constructing for itself the instruments of its manifestation in order to exist completely."[69] In Merleau-Ponty, however, language, or the spoken, living word, does not stand apart from consciousness as such. In speech, being becomes conscious, unfolds its consciousness and lives in its material element. The element is the flesh of the world, where perception and expression take place, and ideation is inaugurated from the hyletic of lived concrete corporeal experience.[70] If we look at *The Visible and the Invisible*, where sight itself comes to the foreground as the archetypical perception, we find this alternative described, not as spiritualism, but as precisely that which allows for an incarnated spirit fully engaged in a historically created generality and a culture, where even pure ideality is not without a material origin, which is shown in particular through language.[71] The radicality of this theory and of the concept of the flesh and of reversibility in offering a middle term between the freedom and necessity, nature and spirit, is that it builds on the life-world of Husserl and historicity, but opens up the opposing characters of these terms and centers all being around the nexus of the flesh of the world.

> When the silent vision falls into speech, and when the speech in turn, opening up a field of the namable and the sayable, inscribes itself in that field, in its place, according to its truth—in short, when it metamorphoses the structures of the visible world and makes itself a gaze of the mind, *intuitis mentis*, —this is

always in virtue of the same fundamental phenomenon of reversibility which sustains both the mute perception and the speech and which manifests itself by an almost carnal existence of the idea, as well as by a sublimation of the flesh. [72]

When Mitscherling proposes intentional being as a middle way between realism and idealism, this may be entirely in line with the various uses made of the concept of intentionality in phenomenology, in particular the way it relates to the subject and the world in a reciprocal manner, most notably in Merleau-Ponty. In the latter's work (both early and late) a certain sense of standing apart seems to be operative in perception, which stretches intentionality beyond its limits in a concrete, natural world and points to that which exceeds our everyday horizon. This gap or openness is twofold transcendence, both of the world and of the seer/perceiver. In the "Cogito" section of *Phenomenology of Perception*, Merleau-Ponty explicitly discusses Descartes' cogito in the *Meditations* and his resistance to the idea of the self as an absolute constituting consciousness, eternal and atemporal, and the meaning he himself ascribes to transcendence in perception. For now, it is sufficient to highlight the following passage:

> Vision is an action, not, that is, an eternal operation (which is a contradiction in terms) but an operation which fulfils more than it promises, which constantly outruns its premises and is inwardly prepared only by my primordial opening upon a field of transcendence, that is, once again, by ek-stase. [73]

Sight is not in possession of itself; it does not coincide with its objects, but instead *escapes* from itself into the thing seen. [74] The cogito finally means that what I discover is not immanence or a constituting consciousness. Nor is it a coinciding with the phenomena. It is rather "the deep-seated momentum of transcendence which is my very being, the simultaneous contact with my own being and with the world's being." [75] The standing apart or ek-stasis in perception bears witness to and safeguards the two-folded nature of perception; the transcendence of the world and of the seer, and the close-knit relationship between the seer and the seen that it entails. The world informs us of ourselves, as we mentioned, through the exceeding of ourselves in perception, and here Merleau-Ponty makes yet another reference to Descartes and the nature of the cogito, but now it is clearly and indubitably a cogito active and creatively perceiving a world: "And since the consciousness of an object necessarily involves *a knowledge of itself*, without which it would escape from itself and fail even to grasp its object, to will and to know that one wills, to love and to know one loves are one and the same act; love is consciousness of loving, will is consciousness of willing." [76]

Perception necessarily carries always with it a sense of unity between the subject of perception and the world. As mentioned earlier, the body is conceived of as bearing a metaphysical meaning in Descartes *Passions.* In that sense, the corporeal in perception, such as also the passions of the soul is that which reaches above and beyond the actual situation, creating an openness as regards possible experiences and horizons. This aspect of Descartes' philosophy may be said to have been brought out also in phenomenology as transcendence and openness in perception and as an intertwining of the world of the sentient, moving, acting self and its metaphysical being.

The tradition of thought leading from Descartes in the 17th century to Bergson and Merleau-Ponty in the 20th century was marked by an emphasis on spirit rather than matter or science, and was primarily a reaction against reductionist and/or naturalist accounts of perception and cognition. In the three hundred years, the theories and counter-arguments proliferated across the continent in various forms, taking as their point of departure Descartes' poignant "cogito, ergo sum." Its influence echoes through the works of Malebranche and Maine de Biran, as well as Bergson and Merleau-Ponty. The aspects of the corporeal, of will and affectivity, sensibility and activity are always made prominent, in elaborating on the sense of self-consciousness as informed by and enacted by a fully corporeal and affective being. Crucial in this movement of thought are not realist or idealist stances, but rather the attempt to explain being, perception and consciousness on an ontological or metaphysical level. At that level, the central topic is one of affectivity, which binds the tradition from Descartes to Merleau-Ponty in articulating the complex co-constitution of perception by ego and world through the mediation of the body.

III

Early in *Aesthetic Genesis*, Mitscherling allies his project with that of the later Merleau-Ponty, in particular the latter's "elusive mentions of 'the flesh of the world.'"[77] However, if as we have shown in the previous section, Merleau-Ponty is strongly embedded in a Cartesian-inspired tradition of corporeal consciousness, and further, if we take seriously Merleau-Ponty's continual claims of indebtedness to Husserl's transcendental phenomenology, it is necessary to complicate Mitscherling's account of Phenomenology, particularly of Husserl's "idealism."[78] We do this not so much to challenge the substance of Mitscherling's conclusions as to demonstrate that the dichotomy of idealist/realist which Mitscherling employs may be misleading.

When speaking of the phenomenological reduction, Mitscherling emphasises the eidetic reduction. He states: "We strip away all the 'non-essential' habits and ways of being . . . the suspension of the non-essential was the original motivation behind Husserl's introduction of the *epoché*."[79] The question of the motivation of the reduction is not a simple one, but if we look at Husserl's earlier account of the reduction in the lecture course *The Idea of Phenomenology*, it seems clear that the context was one of bracketing naturalistic assumptions, both in the natural sciences and in common sense. Furthermore, the reduction here centres around the question of givenness—to lead back reflectively to the original givenness of phenomena. [80] This sceptical (in the Pyrrhonian sense) strategy of suspension is indifferent to the distinction of idealism and realism, because it operates in neither the active nor the passive, but in the middle voice: allowing things to appear as they are to a perceiver. This position is one which is reflective, in the sense that it must purify both science and common sense of both of their unreflective positions and (at least in the case of science) of naturalistic assumptions which reduce reality to a mechanical causal system. The latter is a product of a particular process of idealization [81] which replaces sense experience with mathematical points and lines which cannot be made intuitive to sensibility. The eidetic reduction is subsequent—in motivation at least—to this prior transcendental reduction, which suspends existence not as its initial or final move, but rather as a moment in the reflective process of clearing experience of that which is foreign to it. [82]

The life of consciousness, for Husserl, is characterized not by causal but by motivational laws, which function in a kind of circularity [83] of activity and passivity, anticipation and fulfilment/disappointment, allurement and projection. In his genetic account of phenomenology, Husserl develops an understanding of intentionality much richer than the label "transcendental idealism" would seem to allow. He speaks in particular of "webs of motivation," "built through and through from intentional rays, which with their sense-content and filled content, refer back and forth, and they let themselves be explicated in that the accomplishing subject can enter into these nexuses." [84] This notion of "intentional rays" is especially interesting, because it indicates the manner in which phenomena affect a perceiving subject through what Husserl terms their allure (*Reiz*). [85] This allure in the phenomena, Husserl understands as having "an affective binding force on consciousness." [86]

Crucial to understanding this is to appreciate the temporal structure of consciousness. It is not so much that consciousness is temporal for Husserl, but rather that temporality structures consciousness: there is an I only because there is a temporal flow which constitutes it. [87] Furthermore, this temporal flow is intersubjective: it forms a horizon of possibility, which is one of my subjectivity in co-existence with others. [88] To explore this, let us take a term which we find in Husserl's *Analyses of Passive Synthesis*: "rhythmatization." He is referring to the way in which "a tone as affectively unitary appears for itself, and in such a way that a new tone and then another new one do not merely appear in the same way, but rather forthwith takes hold of what has just past, as bestowing an affective salience on an objective uniform to it or similar to it." [89] Clearly, such rhythmatization is already implicit in

Husserl's account of retention, where precisely the melody maintains a unity not alone through the retention of tones, but also through the rhythmic relation of tones to one another. But such a rhythmic unity is possible only through the embodiment of experience and consciousness. While Husserl may employ dualistic categories—nature/spirit, body/lived body (*Körper/ Leib*)—he does so precisely in line with the tradition we have drawn from Descartes to Merleau-Ponty: within lived experience, the extremes of objective nature and psychic life are mediated. The ego is not a sovereign consciousness but a person living within circumstances which she embodies as habit: "To yield to a drive establishes the drive to yield: habitually. Likewise, to let oneself be determined by a value-motive . . . establishes a tendency . . . to let oneself be determined once again by such a value-motive . . . Here *habit and free motivation intervene.*"[90] Habits do not alone form a unity between past and present, but also situate the ego within a meaningful circumstance, which themselves form the motivation for habitual behaviour.[91]

In his genetic phenomenological analyses, Husserl understands human consciousness as necessarily embodied and in its embodiness, as *Leib*; the conscious ego is both constituted and constituting. Such a being is, for Husserl, necessarily ensouled (*Beseelung*). Without such ensoulment, without that is a living body, we can have no sense of time or space.[92] In other words, it is only through our experience of the life world as a domain which we co-constitute meaningfully that we can speak of entities in that world. This is not to say that the ego alone constitutes the world,[93] but that without the empathetic capacity to be as experiencing beings in the world, there can be no intentional meaning. The picture of Husserl, which emerges from *Aesthetic Genesis*, particularly with respect to intentionality, does not seem to take account of the richness which, for many years now, has been revealed in his Nachlaß. The account of intentionality which he quotes from Heidegger[94] is, as he says, false, but seems to be implicitly accepted (by Mitscherling) as true of Husserl's "idealism." When he quotes Ingarden on the literary work of art,[95] he could just as well have quoted from Husserl's *Phenomenological Psychology*: "A tool or a work of art is a physical thing, but not merely that: in it a rich mental sense is embodied; in it a formation originating from a subjective performance is objectified."[96] It is indeed true that Husserl does speak of that which he nonetheless calls an abstract "pure nature," nature appearing "as a self-enclosed causal nexus of physical things, stretching to eternity,"[97] but in doing so he is not expressing a thesis of transcendental idealism, but rather describing the practice of modern science, while adding the caveat: "we are not saying . . . that a pure physis ever exists or could exist on its own, as if the world were conceivable as pure nature."[98] Ironically, the world *is* conceivable as this, but only in the abstract theoretical approach of science. In other words, the movement of Husserlian phenomenology is pre-

cisely to recognize and account for the "rich mental sense" of the phemome-
na, something which is most evident in the work of art, but is by no means
confined to it. We can see this if we take our point of orientation with respect
to Husserl not from the static phenomenology of *Ideas I*, but from the more
dynamic account of generative phenomenology which so inspired Merleau-
Ponty.

IV

Aesthetic Genesis ends with a plea for "the notion of an incarnated soul, a
natural soul that is an integral part of the organism of the natural world."[99]
Our claim is that there are rich resources within the Cartesian tradition stem-
ming from the *Passions* (rather than the *Meditations*) for working out such a
notion. The advantage of such an approach—apart from the acknowledgement of this tradition of thought—is that it allows for a more inclusive
account of phenomenology (one not riven by an idealist/realist divide, which
we believe to be already overcome in Husserl) and one which facilitates a
rethinking of the historical legacy of Modernity. If, as we have argued, the
core crisis which still haunts philosophy generally and phenomenology more
specifically is that of late Medieveal Nominalist Voluntarism, it may be
beneficial to think Mitscherling's project in conjunction with the latest twist
in the history of the French thought, the "so-called" theological turn in
French Phenomenology, which, in the figures of Marion, Chrétien and La-
coste has its theological roots in the questioning of that legacy by the Nou-
velle Théologie.[100] Motivated by Heidegger's critique of onto-theology, this
turn in phenomenology seeks a way of thinking God not as inscrutable will,
but rather as a trace within the world of phenomena. Such a phenomenology
is necessarily "realist," at least in the sense of seeking that in the phenomena
which is in excess of any capacity of the subject to project or constitute.[101]
Crucial here are not specifically the theological concerns which may moti-
vate these thinkers, but the implications of this move on the questions which
Mitscherling raises. Specifically, from Merleau-Ponty's *The Visible and the
Invisible* and Levinas's *Totality and Infinity* (both published in 1961), the
underlying question can be understood to be that of accounting for the way in
which phenomena overwhelm the constituting action of consciousness. In
thinking through Mitscherling's project in *Aesthetic Genesis*, we propose that
what is required is a phenomenological articulation of the manner in which,
as habituated and embodied, the human capacity to think and know continually encounters that which exceeds its powers of constitution. Taking our
clue from both Merleau-Ponty and Levinas (who, in turn, are both strongly
influenced by Husserl and Heidegger in this respect), we might think this
problem as essentially one of temporal constitution: the constant referral

back to a past which is always already constituted, which is a "past which has never been present," "a past older than ever present."[102]

NOTES

1. Jeff Mitscherling, *Aesthetic Genesis* (Lanham: University Press of America, 2010), 33. Hereafter cited to as AG.

2. AG, 35.

3. AG, 100.

4. AG, 134.

5. AG, 89.

6. See E. Grant: "The Effect of the Condemnation of the Condemnation of 1277" in *The Cambridge History of Later Medieval Philosophy*, ed by N. Kretzmann et al (Cambridge: Cambridge University Press, 1982), 537-39.

7. On this Nominalist and Voluntarist revolution in late Medieval thought see M. Gillespie: *The Theological Origins of Modernity* (Chicago: University of Chicago Press, 2008), 19–43

8. On the late Medieval debates concerning Universals, see M. McCord Adams: "Universals in the Fourteenth Century," in N. Kretzmann et al (1982), 411–439.

9. AG, 89.

10. AG, 101.

11. On the question of analogy in Aquinas and later Medieval thinkers, see J. Ashworth: *Les Theories de L'Analogie Du Xiie Au Xvie Siecle* (Paris: Vrin, 2008).

12. Ockham develops the same thought concluding that "'Being' stands only for the concept in the mind, not for substance or accident." Ockham: *Philosophical Writings* (Cambridge: Hackett, 1990), 113.

13. Descartes: "Letter to Mersenne, 28th January 1641" in Cottingham et al: *The Philosophical Writings of Descartes vol. 3* (Cambridge: Cambridge University Press, 1991), 173; AT III, 298.

14. Ockham *Quodlibet Questions* (New Haven: Yale University Press, 1998), 103–4: "In order to demonstrate the statement of faith that we formulate about God, what we would need for the central concept is a simple cognition of the divine nature in itself—what someone who sees God has. Nevertheless, we cannot have this kind of cognition in our present state."

15. In Montaigne *Complete Works* (Stanford: Stanford University Press, 1971).

16. See Descartes "Meditation IV"in Cottingham et al: *The Philosophical Writings of Descartes vol. 2* (Cambridge: Cambridge University Press, 1984), 40–1; AT VII, 58.

17. "Letter to the Sorbonne," Cottingham et al: (1984), 3: AT VII, 1: "[God and the soul] are prime examples of subjects where demonstrative proofs ought to be given with the aid of philosophy rather than theology."

18. "Letter to Mersenne, November 1631" in Cottingham et al: *The Philosophical Writings of Descartes vol. 3* (Cambridge: Cambridge University Press, 1991), 24–5; AT I, 175

19. On the question of grace and "pure nature" see H. de Lubac, *Augustinianism in Modern Theology* (New York: Crossroads Publishing, 2000); on Descartes and this question see Marion: "What is the Ego Capable of?" in *Cartesian Questions: Method and Metaphysics* (Chicago: University of Chicago Press, 1999), 67–95.

20. "Discourse," in Cottingham et al: *The Philosophical Writings of Descartes vol. 1* (Cambridge: Cambridge University Press, 1993), 117; AT VI, 13: "we are all children before being men and had to be governed for some time by our appetites and our teachers."

21. On the Augustinian parallels in this inward movement cf. Menn: *Descartes and Modernity* (London: Routledge, 1998), 134–178

22. On this issue, see Ó Murchadha: "Sceptical Wisdom: Descartes, Pascal and the Challenge of Pyrrhonism" in R. Edmondson and K-H. Hülser: *Practical Reasoning and Human Engagement: Language, Ethics and Action.* (London: Rowman and Littlefield, 2012), 247-50.

23. In the *Meditations* Descartes alludes to this account of grace when he states "[N]either divine grace nor natural knowledge ever diminishes freedom."

24. Descartes: "Rules," Cottingham et al (1993), 16; AT X, 373, .

25. Cf. Ibid, 30: "– he will indeed discover by means of the rules we have proposed that nothing can be known prior to the intellect, since knowledge of everything else depends on the intellect, and not *vice versa.*" while presumably this discovery is itself an act of knowing.

26. "Discourse" Cottingham et al: (1993), 111: AT VI, 1–2

27. Descartes: "Passions of the Soul," §45, in Cottingham et al (1993), 345. In this Descartes might be responding directly to Montaigne, for whom to dissuade someone from entering a foolish course of action it is more productive to incite in them the opposite appetite than to give them good reasons against their chosen course. C.f. Montaigne (1971), 703. Only God touching the heart of man can give him the courage to listen to his reason, in which case the appetite is not diminished, but reason becomes stronger (ibid., 620). Against Montaigne, Descartes seeks to uncover the human capacity for reason, independent of grace.

28. "Discourse," Descartes in Cottingham et. al. (1993), 117; AT VI, 13

29. See Ó Murchadha (2012), 256–8.

30. As we will see, however, this cannot be dismissed as an angelic view of the human (as Maritan amongst others would have it), but rather is a breaking from the body as fallen in order to retrieve it following its methodological "cleansing."

31. "Passions of the Soul" in Cottingham et al (1993), 379: AT XI, 437.

32. AG, 56.

33. AG, 54.

34. Augustine: On the Trinity, 15.12.21 (New York: New City Press 1991); Bodyard, 2013; http://plato.stanford.edu/entries/skepticism-medieval/

35. See Schmaltz, T. M.: *Malebranche's Theory of the Soul: A Cartesian Interpretation.* (New York: Oxford University Press, 1996).

36. AG, 121.

37. Husserl, terms it a "tag-end of the world;" see his *Cartesian Meditations* (Dordrecht: Kluwer, 1999), 24.

38. *The Princess and the Philosopher: letters of Elisabeth of the Palatine to René Descartes* (London: Rowman and Littlefield, 1999), 11–15.

39. Descartes: *Comments on a Certain Broadsheet,* in, Cottingham et al (1993), 299; AT-VIIIB, 351: "But that which we regard as having at the same time both extension and thought is a composite entity, namely a man – an entity consisting of a soul and a body."

40. *Passions of the Soul,* §19, in Cottingham et al (1993), 335-6, AT 343.

41. Ibid, 347; AT XI, 366–7.

42. Ibid, 345; AT XI, 364.

43. Ibid, 347; AT XI, 367.

44. AG, 100.

45. "Passions of the Soul" in Cottingham et al (1993), 339; AT, 351.

46. Ibid, 340; 352.

47. Ibid, 328; 327.

48. Ibid, 404; 488.

49. Ibid, 365; 407.

50. Ibid, 366; 407

51. Ibid, 349; 372.

52. Descartes: "Meditations on First Philosophy," in Cottingham et al., (1984), 56; AT 81.

53. "Synopsis of the following six Meditations," in Cottingham et al, (1984), 11; AT 15.

54. Malebranche, *The Search After Truth,* (Ohio State Univ. Press: Columbus, 1980). On this topic see Judith Butler, "Merleau-Ponty and the Touch of Malebranche," *Cambridge Companion to Merleau-Ponty,* Taylor Carman and Mark B. N. Hansen eds., (Cambridge: Cambridge University Press, 2005), 182.

55. Maurice Merleau-Ponty, *L'Union de l'ame et du corps chez Malebranche, Biran et Bergson,* Jean DePrun ed., (J. Vrin: Paris, 1968, 2000). English version: Merleau-Ponty, M., Bjelland, A. G., & Burke, P.: *The incarnate subject: Malebranche, Biran, and Bergson on the union of body and soul.* (Amherst, N.Y: Humanity Books, 2001).

56. Judith Butler (2005), 181.

57. Ibid.

58. Biran, *De l'aperception immédiate*, (J. Vrin: Paris, 1963), 153. My translation (A.F.A).

59. Frederick Copleston, *A History of Philosophy*, Book Three, vol. IX, (New York: Bantam Doubleday Dell Publ.,1985), 26. Copleston refers on page 23 to the collection of Biran's work *Oeuvres* by Tisserand and Gouhier, 1949 and 1954. (Oeuvres III, p. 216.)

60. *Oeuvres*, III, 178. Copleston (1985), 26.

61. Maine de Biran, *Oeuvres*, II, (1954), 22. Copleston (1985), 25.

62. Copleston (1985), 30.

63. Renaud Barbaras, "A Phenomenology of Life" in *A Cambridge Companion to Merleau-Ponty*, edited by T. Carmen (Cambridge: Cambridge University Press, 2005), 208.

64. As for Mitscherling's presentation of *constitution* in Husserl, an important factor is missing, namely the constitution *for the subject*. There is no reason to believe that in Husserl constitution entails a veritable construction or creation of the object, or that "it is the subject that is solely responsible for the constitution of the object of the act." AG, 115.

65. Merleau-Ponty, *Phenomenology of Perception* (New York: Routledge, 2002), 474.

66. Maurice Merleau-Ponty, *In Praise of Philosophy and Other Essays*, (Evanston: Northwestern University Press, 1963); (EP 1953), 14–15.

67. Ibid.

68. Ibid, 28.

69. Merleau-Ponty (1988), 29.

70. On this theme see Faugstad Aarø, "Merleau-Ponty's Philosophy of Nature and the Concept of Flesh," *Biosemiotics*, Volume 3, Issue 3 (2010), 331–345.

71. Merleau-Ponty (1961), 153.

72. Ibid., 155.

73. Merleau-Ponty, *Phenomenology of Perception*, 438.

74. Ibid.

75. Ibid, 438–439.

76. Ibid, 439 (our emphasis).

77. AG, 10.

78. On this theme, see Ó Murchadha: "Reduction, Externalism and Immanence in Husserl and Heidegger," *Synthese*, vol. 160 (3), 375–395.

79. AG, 115.

80. Husserl, *The Idea of Phenomenology* (Dordrecht: Springer, 2013) see also on this issue J-L. Marion: *Reduction and Givenness*, (Evanston: Northwestern University Press, 1998), 4-76.

81. See Husserl, *The Crisis of the European Sciences* (London: Harper and Row, 1965), 302-314.

82. See Husserl, *Zur phänomenologischen Reduktion* (Dordrecht: Kluwer, 2002).

83. See Donn Welton *The Other Husserl* (Bloomington: Indiana University Press, 2001), 244.

84. Husserl, *Ideas Pertaining to a Pure Phenomenology Book II* (Dordrecht: Springer, 1990), 236

85. See Husserl, *Analyses of Passive Synthesis* (Dordrecht: Kluwer 2001), 196–8.

86. Ibid, 407.

87. See Husserl: *On the Phenomenology of the Consciousness of Internal Time (1893-1917)* (Dordrecht: Springer, 1991), 77; *Die Bernauer Manuskripte Über das Zeitbewusstsein (1917/18)* (Dordrecht: Kluwer, 2001). See too N, de Warren: *Husserl and the Promise of Time* (Cambridge: Cambridge University Press, 2008), 252–9.

88. See de Warren (2008), 235–249.

89. Husserl (2001), 407.

90. Husserl (1990), 267.

91. Husserl (1990), 268n. 1: "From a phenomenological standpoint, the habitually or the experientially has its intentional relation to circumstances . . . an implicit horizon of similar memories."

92. See, for example, *Grenzprobleme der Phänomenologie* (Dordrecht: Springer, 2014), 143

93. See AG, 115.

94. AG, 15.

95. AG, 17.

96. Husserl, *Phenomenological Psychology* (Leiden: Martinus Nijhoff, 1977), 84.

97. Ibid., 91

98. Ibid.

99. AG, 142.

100. On the influence of this movement on Marion, specifically, see T. Jones, *A Genealogy of Marion's Philosophy of Religion: Apparent Darkness* (Bloomington: Indiana UP, 2011), 15-16 and G. Ward, "Metaphysics and Phenomenology: A Summary for Theologians" in *The Postmodern God* (London: Blackwell, 1997), 289–93.

101. Indeed, as Tengelyi and Gondek show in *Neue Phänomenologie in Frankreich* (Frankfurt a M.: Suhrkamp, 2011), this is generally true of French phenomenology from Merleau-Ponty onwards.

102. Respectively, Merleau-Ponty (2002), 242; Levinas, *Otherwise than Being* (1998), 68. Although they understand this "anteriority" of the past differently, Merleau-Ponty and Levinas are true to the inner direction of Husserl's (and Heidegger's!) phenomenological understanding of time in showing how phenomenologically this never present past is revealed. This despite the claims of Meillasoux regarding "ancestrality." (*After Finitude* [London: Bloomsbury, 2009], 1–27).

Chapter Four

The Intentional Being
of Justice and the Foreseen

Kimberly Baltzer-Jaray

The foundation of Jeff Mitscherling's *Aesthetic Genesis* is its Copernican hypothesis concerning intentionality that reverses one of the most revered and fundamental tenets of phenomenology: intentionality gives rise to consciousness, rather than all consciousness is intentional. This thesis supports the notion that there are intentional entities that subsist in the real world, and their being does not require consciousness to constitute them; their being cannot be reduced solely to the operations of a conscious mind, and thus ideality. Mitscherling's thesis is rooted in the work of the realist phenomenologists, who were responding to the idealist direction Edmund Husserl's work took after 1912, and particularly the response we find in Roman Ingarden's *The Literary Work of Art* (1931). Husserl had shifted phenomenological analysis to that which is immanent to the consciousness of the cognizing subject, and thus the real world would come to be seen as constituted exclusively by the intentional mind. Mitscherling writes,

> In order to counter that idealist position, Ingarden undertook the task of constructing an argument that would demonstrate for once and for all that not all of the objects of consciousness were constituted solely through the intentionality of consciousness—in other words, that non-ideal, or 'real,' elements were also involved in the constitution of (at least some of) the objects of consciousness.[1]

This argument focused on the literary work of art, which is a non-material schema or structure that is intentional in nature, and with this Ingarden had his "realist rejoinder," since the literary work of art rested on an ontological foundation that could not be reduced to something that is purely ideal—that is, to the operations of consciousness alone.

The realist phenomenologist Adolf Reinach (1883–1917) was Husserl's student and then colleague, and later Ingarden's teacher at the University of Göttingen prior to WWI. He, too, did not take Husserl's growing idealism lightly or well; with all of its reductions and its focus on how the subject constitutes the world, he regarded this shift in philosophical thinking as dangerous. As accurately pointed out by Mitscherling, realist phenomenology is fundamentally committed to: (1) the independent existence of the real world, i.e., that which exists outside of and apart from human consciousness; and (2) the independent subsistence within the real world of intentional entities. Reinach's influence on his students was immense and manifold; he was often described as their true teacher, and I would argue that the strong commitment to these two points was the surest sign of his significance for their philosophical allegiances and mindsets. Even in the face of Reinach's death on the battlefield in WWI, Ingarden, Stein, Conrad-Martius, and others remained entrenched realist phenomenologists.

Ingarden's work on art, while novel in its description and elucidation of intentional entities found there, was not the first, nor was it the only. Reinach also worked on entities that have intentional existence in the real world, namely: (1) Legal entities (*Recht*) and (2) Foreseen entities (*Ahnungen*), especially those that pertain to impending death. His work in both these areas is neglected and misunderstood, and I believe a large reason for that pertains to the type of being these entities have and how we come to be conscious of them, something that becomes all the more clear through reading *Aesthetic Genesis*. In this article, I will describe and demonstrate how these entities exist intentionally in the world, and how we come to be conscious of them, thus providing additional support to Mitscherling's new Copernican hypothesis concerning intentionality.

LEGAL ENTITIES (*RECHT*)

Recht and *Gesetzt* are typically translated into English as "law," but they are far from being equal in meaning. When translators fail to deal with this issue, the true sense of what is intended is lost, and confusion arises. It is essential to reinforce that *Recht* is not created by, nor does it depend on humans acknowledging its presence for its existence; *Recht* is there for apprehension at any time, and will be there after the fact. *Gesetzt*, on the other hand, is *lex* (Latin) and *loi* (French), and is law in the sense of the positive or codified law, where law is a man-made rulebook or structure, and justice is the calculated outcome of following the rules. When the phrase "positive law" is used, the difference amounts to the visible (*Gesetzt*) and the invisible (*Recht*). This difference between them is crucial not only ontologically, but it also concerns their moral significance and authority. Roger Berkowitz, in his book *The Gift of Science: Leibniz and The Modern Legal Tradition*, writes:

> While blurring of the distinction in English between *ius* and *lex* may have the practical advantage of lending to law as *lex* the moral authority of law as *ius*, it has the distinctive disadvantage of concealing the significant fact that law is increasingly spoken of only in the sense of *lex*—the setting down of official rules governing behavior. This covering up of the declining significance of law as *ius*—that is, as a natural and accepted moral obligation—works to conceal the importance of what was once a meaningful part of law. [2]

In 1913, the very first issue of *Jahrbuch für Philosophie und Phänomenologische Forschung* was published, a project for which Adolf Reinach served as managing editor and contributor, and he contributed a piece called, *Die apriorischen Grundlagen des bürgerlichen Rechtes*, or what is more commonly known in English as *The a priori Foundations of Civil Law*. This article is often prized by phenomenology scholars for the theory of social acts contained in the sections on promising, claim and obligation, and the ontology of essences and *a priori* structures contained in such acts described in brilliant detail. However, the bigger picture of what Reinach is attempting to do in this article is not properly understood, and this has disastrous consequences for a true grasp of his unique contributions to realist phenomenology.

Reinach's *Jahrbuch* paper is the culmination of ideas he began contemplating around 1905: elements are present in his 1905 dissertation, *Über den Ursachenbegriff im geltenden Strafrecht* (*On the Concept of Causality in the Criminal Code*), and become more apparent in discussions with other members of the Munich *Verein* group, occurring from 1906 onwards, in a seminar he gave titled "The Philosophy of Civil Law" (SS 1912), and in rough notes on social acts dating around 1911. It seems that Reinach developed his response to the 1900 BGB (*Bürgerliches Gesetzbuch*) over several years, formulating it using his unique background in jurisprudence, descriptive psychology training under Theodor Lipps, along with his phenomenology education under Edmund Husserl. I contend that Reinach's *Jahrbuch* paper, titled *Die apriorischen Grundlagen des bürgerlichen Rechtes*, necessarily must be read as a response to the 1900 BGB. Statements contained in his introduction, along with his choice of chapter titles, clearly indicate that the content is an organized, rational, and phenomenological answer to positive law's claim that, without it, nothing in society or amongst persons would be secure and known with certainty. Without the positive law, property could not be titled and maintained; without the positive law, contracts could not be drafted and enforced; without the positive law, representation means absolutely nothing.

Previously, I have argued that misunderstandings concerning Reinach's article directly resulted from two things: (1) the translation of the German word *Recht* into English as "law" or "right," both of which are ambiguous and fail to capture the nature of the entity adequately; and (2) the lack of knowledge concerning German legal history, including the controversial 1900 German civil code (*Bürgerliches Gesetzbuch* - BGB) that changed the European landscape, which is implicit in the article.[3] Here I will also add, (3) a failure to understand and acknowledge the kind of entity *Recht* is: an independently subsisting entity with intentional being. When these are resolved, what becomes clear is that Reinach was making a philosophical, specifically phenomenological, argument for the return to and recognition of something similar to the old, natural law idea of justice (i.e., *ius, droit*)—that is, justice as the insight into a transcendent unity or harmony, an entity independently subsisting in the real world that we engage with cognitively, not something that exists purely in codification (positive law—i.e., *lex, gesetzt, loi*). This article was Reinach's attempt at demonstrating that realist phenomenology could aid in the restoration of the authority *Recht* once had, but in a new and more secure way that recognized its true ontological status as intentional and supratemporal. Reinach attempted to do for law what Ingarden did for the literary work of art, and both can be seen as realist rejoinders to Husserl's growing idealism.

At the start of the article, Reinach states his reason for going to all this effort to explore *Recht* phenomenologically: simply put, it's for philosophy. With the creation and adoption of the BGB of 1900, *Recht* was plucked from the sphere of the contemplating philosopher and placed firmly under the realm of legal science, where it was reduced to dust under the heel of codification (*Gesetz*). In fact, the evolution of *Gesetz* coincides with the complete seizure of *Recht* from philosophy, the loss of a balance, where *Recht* was firmly situated in both the legal and philosophical camps (to be contemplated, like the other grand ideas associated with freedom). This reasoning indicates that Reinach had two main aims at work: to revive and restore the importance of *Recht*, and to take it back from the legal scientists and return it to philosophy, but in a new, fresh way.

Reinach argues that the scientific approach is not appropriate for this task; rather, a philosophical approach like the phenomenological method is necessary for a clear understanding and apprehension of *Recht*, since it is rather special. He writes that his intention is to demonstrate, "that the structures which one has generally called specifically 'rechtliche' have a being of their own just as much as numbers, trees, or houses, that this being is independent of its being grasped by men, that it is in particular independent of the positive law. It is not only false but ultimately meaningless to call legal entities and structures creations of the positive law . . . "[4] Reinach states that the positive law *finds* legal concepts; it in no way creates them. Legal entities have irrefutable evidence that enables them to be known with insight, since they subsist independently of the mind that grasps them and the positive law code that utilizes them. He further adds,

> If there are legal entities and structures which in this way exist in themselves, a new realm opens up here for philosophy. Insofar as philosophy is ontology or the *a priori* theory of objects, it has to do with the analysis of all possible kinds of objects as such. We shall see that philosophy here comes across objects of quite a new kind, objects which do not belong to nature in the proper sense, which are neither physical nor psychical and which are at the same time different from all ideal objects in virtue of their temporality. The laws, too, which hold for these objects are of the greatest philosophical interest. [5]

With the mention of philosophy as ontology and this new kind of object—one that is not physical, psychical or ideal—what remains is an intentional entity. *Recht* subsists independently of the mind in the world; we become conscious of it when we engage with its intentional structure. It subsists independently of all created laws and theories of ethics; if anything, it is the foundation of these. *Recht*, subsisting through time as part of the unity of our universe and as intentional structures, makes the concretization of justice and any legal principle possible. The intentional structure of *Recht* informs or guides our experience of justice, and thus also our behavior.

On this point, it is also clear that *Recht,* as an intentional entity, is intimately related to habit. As Mitscherling so aptly clarifies, habits inform behavior; or rather, they comprise forms of behavior (i.e., habits are to actions as form is to matter), and with *Recht* we are speaking about the moral and practical sphere of behavior. [6] Habits subsist with intentional being, like the other laws of nature (e.g., gravity, force, inertia, etc.). When I cognitively grasp *Recht*—that is, when I use intuition to grasp the transcendent unity of justice that subsists in the universe as a harmony or organic unity—my potential actions and behavior take on form. It is one thing to understand that murder is unlawful according to the codified law, but it is another to understand why it is an injustice, and how the behavior of yourself and the community can bring about or prevent murder.

Speaking ontologically, if we use Mitscherling's discussion of the three kinds of being as a model, this is how Reinach's theory of *Recht* appears:

1. The law book for any nation has material being; the material ontic foundation of the physical text exists and is temporal. The laws in it can be changed at any time, and they are applicable during a time-frame to situations as they arise or to prevent situations from arising.
2. When you understand the meanings of laws (i.e., X is good, X is bad) or understand the notion of natural law in contrast to positive law

(intellectual vs. written law), you are encountering an instance of ideal being, which has atemporal (non-temporal) being.

3. When you understand the presence and meaning of justice that subsists in the world (i.e., when you have clear insight into the transcendent unity of justice) that must necessarily underlie any theory of law whatsoever, you are encountering an instance of intentional being, which is supratemporal.

Further proof that Reinach conceives of *Recht* as an entity with intentional being comes near the end of the article, when he clearly distinguishes *Recht* from natural law. The a *priori* theory of *Recht* may be utilized by both natural law and positive law; it underpins them for sure, but it itself is neither of these. To illustrate this point clearly, he writes:

> Its distinctive character lies precisely in the fact that it is independent of ALL law, from the law which is 'in force' not less than from some 'valid' law, or one which is thought of as valid. One has objected to natural law philosophers that they fill out the gaps in the positive law with the 'ideal law' or 'rational law' . . . . That they want to replace explicit positive enactments by this 'higher' law . . . Such an objection would of course not apply to us. We do not speak of higher law, but of simple laws of being. [7]

Reinach further adds, natural law philosophers were right in their search for legal structures outside of the state and positive enactments, but what they failed to see was that these structures do not amount to any "law" at all: "They need never to have entered into consciousness. There has never been a state of things in which they and only they would have positive validity."[8] Moreover, the name "natural law" is entirely inappropriate. The notion of "nature" in the name is the worst part: (1) essential laws of *Recht* do not derive their objectivity from "being implanted by nature in all men"; (2) these laws hold only for men or beings of a similar intellectual "nature" (rational mind); and (3) these entities and structures are found in the sphere of nature, meaning they are of the physical and mental. Reinach admits that as much as the essential laws involved in *Recht* are clear and present, self-evident if you will, it is quite false to say that they are actually recognized by all men; rather, all people have equal potential to do so. Essential laws also cannot and should never be grounded in the natural feelings of mankind or in the consensus of a community of people, as these are absolutely irrelevant to their being.[9]

FORESEEN ENTITIES[10]

After Germany's declaration of war on France in the summer of 1914, Reinach, like many German intellectuals, immediately volunteered for the army with great enthusiasm, even attempting to exercise pressure to be admitted as quickly as possible. He was recruited in his hometown of Mainz in mid-August, and after two weeks of training he was assigned to the reserve battery of the 21st Field Artillery Regiment of the 21st Reserve Division under the command of his younger brother, Heinrich. By February of 1915, he was fighting in the trenches against France, and later he received the Iron Cross for his efforts during this time. In November of 1915, Reinach was stationed in Belgium, serving the supply lines to the front, and in October of 1916 he was promoted to commander of the 185th Field Artillery Regiment. It was during this time at the Belgian front that he wrote a collection of rough notes (*Aufzeichnungen*), which included one very unique piece: *Zur Phänomenologie der Ahnungen* (Phenomenology of Foreseeing/Foreboding) dated July 1916.

The piece begins by detailing a conversation Reinach overheard during a break from artillery firing. A staff sergeant and an infantryman are talking about instances where fellow soldiers seemed to know they were going to die that day or very soon, and so took measures to ensure their documents and personal effects were in order. He writes,

> A young officer had fallen earlier that day; briefly before the ride, from which he never returned, he had, what he otherwise never did, given his fellow (officer) his trunk key, his classified documents and a written farewell letter. He suspected his own death. There is one (soldier) curiously displeased and distressed, before he encountered the grenade; another one (soldier) had his will/testament made; recounting quite a lot, they prophesized it firsthand, that they would not live to see forthcoming days. [11]

The infantryman is convinced by the examples he has witnessed that foreboding is something very real, something that actually happens to people. The young staff sergeant, on the other hand, stands unconvinced that foreboding is real, because there is a lack of scientific, testable evidence proving its existence. With some arrogance towards the infantryman and the general topic of the discussion, the staff sergeant says, according to Reinach,

> Certainly everyone assumes before a dangerous mission that perhaps or probably he will die. If this supposition comes true (fulfills itself), then its result is mysteriously foreboding; supposing it doesn't fulfill itself, then nobody remembers. No, there are no forebodings, only reasonable calculations are possible that acknowledge themselves with more or less probability . . . . If I am sad or ill-tempered, the world appears darker to me, and misfortune seems (to

me) impending. . . . The realization of gloomy dispositions are particularly frequent in wars, whom should that surprise?[12]

The infantryman, realizing that no matter how many instances he provides of foreboding, he will not be able to convince the staff sergeant, shrugs his shoulders and leaves the conversation. No doubt, there are many like the staff sergeant, who will treat the foreseen as pure superstition or a predictable result of the mental stresses of war; however, this not only misrepresents what the entity is, but it also places it purely in the mind of the person experiencing it, thus misunderstanding the source of it and how we come to obtain it. And so, Reinach's phenomenological investigation into foreboding begins, a task most suited for a descriptive realist phenomenologist, such as himself. After completing the storytelling, he adds:

> However, in me a world ascends, for a long time, long immersed in anything but the suffocating activity of the soldier in war. What are proper forebodings? . . . Whether foreboding carries justice or truth in itself, I do not have the means to say; it is impossible to say before I know what its proper essence is: foreboding. Still I do not know it. However, already the desire of the phenomenologist is awakened in me, to single out from the fullness of the appearance the structure, to hold it, to let it sink in and with it, what so far only the word meaning was acquainted with, henceforth it is to achieve intuitively the essence itself.[13]

The foreseen, like *Recht*, substantiates Mitscherling's Copernican intentionality thesis. The foreseen as such subsists intentionally in the world; it has an ontological foundation that is not constituted solely by consciousness. When someone experiences the foreseen, such as in Reinach's WWI story, it happens to a person as they act and live in the world, and it is not something they can ignore or un-see. It carries with it a necessity like any other law of nature, but instead of speaking to force, they speak to lived possibilities: there is no doubt that what has been obtained, what has almost been revealed to insight, *will* happen; some possibilities open and some close. In the case of Reinach's tale, death comes soon. To once again use the three types of being model Mitscherling applies, the following should illustrate the strata involved with the foreseen:

1. The material being of Reinach's story is the battlefield, with its sounds, smells and visuals of destruction, danger and death. These things exist temporally. They serve as the material foundation.
2. The ideal being present in this story is the understanding of the dangerous situation of the battlefield at hand, or the strong possibility of death at every moment of every day, or even the understanding of the stories others tell of death and fear.

3. The subsisting foreseen, when the soldier apprehends the end of his or her possibilities in life, and that it will necessarily happen (at this place, or this time, or this way, etc.). The foreseen subsists supratemporally.

Once again taking Reinach's story as the example, there are soldiers who will obtain the foreseen, and there are those who will not: the majority will engage in and experience the material existing and ideal beings present in the battle situation, but only a chosen few obtain or apprehend the foreseen. It almost "lies in wait" in the natural world to be engaged, meaning a soldier must be open to it, and also, various events must align that factor into the universal harmony (i.e., the unity of the organism in relation to the unity of the universe). Never mistake though, it is intentional and has some kind of content that engages us; we can know it, in the strictest sense. In a similar way to how Ingarden's literary work of art has strata, the real and the ideal playing important roles for understanding its intentional being, so does the foreseen have strata: the material things and the ideal beings of battle are important to the realization of the subsisting foreseen entity (i.e., the battlefield elements along with human understanding and meaning allow for the obtaining of the foreseen). It is reasonable to say that, if the soldiers who experienced the foreseen in Reinach's story had chosen not to enlist for war, if they had decided instead to work in ammunitions factories or go to another country, it is correct to think they would not have had the foreseen/foreboding experience they had (either at all or in the form they had). Reinach writes,

> That every foreseeing as such necessarily requires a related content—the "foreseen" as such—so far stretched is the boundary of its possible contents here. Not only, for example, temporally but even future forebodings can refer to something . . . . here something forms apparently timeless (atemporal)—a more or less determinate proposition (*Satz*) or state of affairs (*Sachverhalt*)—the related content of a foreseeing. But not 'this' foreseeing content, it being also identical with the content of a judgment or an apprehension, but rather the foreseeing as such . . . . Nevertheless the foreseeing adds something new to the total wealth of knowledge—in the broadest sense of knowledge spoken—; the subject here appears to grasp by means of foreseeing, correctly or incorrectly remains to be seen, something from the river of future events, which was previously not accessible to him. [14]

The foreseen is part of the laws of nature that govern human life; it subsists through time but not in time; its subsistence doesn't last long, as it comes to being and passes away with the one who experiences it. As noted by Mitscherling, several realist phenomenologists, as well as early pragmatists, relations are another example of subsisting entities. As a living organism, our existence depends on a corporeal body, but our "living" is not reducible or identical to that body. We survive by subsisting. The relations involved in the foreseen are very similar: as relations between our lived experience and the world, between life and the open possibilities available, they subsist, and they come into being at certain events or situations to rise up through lived experience, to be obtained and apprehended and then acted upon. Reinach writes,

> Certainly "knowledge" (Wissen) is taken here in the widest sense; in a narrow and proper sense one can contrast foresight and knowledge against each other. So, after this first superficial orientation, closer determinations are vital. In this sphere, we make the fundamental and far-reaching distinction between grounding and grounded structures. . . . there is no doubt that we have to account for the grounding structures it has, not the grounded ones—i.e., those which by their essence are open to a grounding. Through foreboding/foresight we grasp—or rather we believe that we grasp—something that was previously concealed. And a conviction can also be grounded in the foreboding, which in strength and inner certainty itself need be in no way inferior to the conviction based upon knowledge (Erkennen). From the foreboding of immanent death arises the certain conviction of having to die soon. [15]

This is also where we see that it engages with us from the real world as habit. As said previously, habits comprise forms of behavior; actions exhibit habits. Soldiers in Reinach's story acted after obtaining the foreseen in ways that were guided by it: they wrote their wills, gave their trunk keys to bunk mates, wrote letters home, etc. Basically, the soldiers prepared to die after they obtained the foreseen, and they weren't afraid or doubtful in any way, but rather settled in the truth and necessity of what they had grasped. These preparatory actions were only carried out because the foreseen vision revealed to them that end of their living possibilities, and thus such actions became compelling. As Reinach also indicates in the passage, convictions are formed, and thus judgments occur about the truth of the foreseen obtained, or what to do. Actions and speech acts are the matter to the form of the foreseen.

To drive this point home, Reinach differentiates the foreseen from emotions. The foreseen is not itself an emotion, it is not a state of the ego; rather, once it is grasped, it gives rise to emotions. Reinach writes, "Indeed it appears to have good sense to speak of felt foresights, of the aspect of being felt of any foreseeing. All the same, it is readily apparent that foreseeing—for example of a future event—is no feeling like joy or sorrow, no set of ego states (no state of being of the I), not in one way or another being a condition of the ego (the I) . . . ."[16] and further "What clearly stands out from foreboding is the horror of future fortunes, which as a feeling springs from this forsightful grasp, as do all aspirations and reluctance, willing and not willing, which is rooted in this feeling and knowledge (Wissen)."[17] The emotions that result from the foreseen strongly affect a person's choices and actions because of the content (death) and the sense of temporal duress (time is running out quickly), such as with the soldier who prepared a farewell letter and put his effects in order before he rode out, things he did not usually do before leaving camp to fight. The foreseen is not itself a belief, but belief arises from it.

Both *Recht* and the foreseen are intentional entities that subsist in the world; they are like Ingarden's literary work or art, a way to steer phenomenology away from Husserl's idealism. The foreseen, unlike *Recht,* is a much more difficult entity to discuss ontologically, as it is not something everyone can or will obtain. It is an obtaining for one. It can be rare, and there is no guarantee that everyone will grasp it. If there are three soldiers heading out to fight, and one apprehends the foreseen, only he knows it, only he is capable of making judgments about it, only he has a verified knowledge of it and can act on it. What does this mean for the other two? The soldier with the foresight apprehension cannot effectively show it to them, so they too can gain knowledge or clear insight: the foresight apprehension is of "his" own unique death, and it concerns only his life possibilities, not the others at all. He can only tell them about it, while they will form beliefs as to its truth or falsity. This makes the foreseen a rather unique, rare, and complex ontological entity. *Recht*, on the other hand, is something everyone has the possibility to engage with; *Recht* is in the world for all to obtain. Reinach used examples of claim and obligation, relations we engage with and understand without the positive law telling us how they work: I know that with a promise, there is an obligation to fulfill it, and when someone fails to keep their promise, there is a sense of injustice (i.e., a lack of harmony) that arises in me, and there will also be repercussions. I simply have to turn my attention to discover the intentional entity that is foundational for the positive law and everyday contracts like promises. *Recht* is available to all, just as the literary work of art is; we just need to pick up the book and read.

It is highly possible that the differences indicated here between *Recht* and the foreseen grasping boil down to one of attunement: turning one's attention to and being open to the intentionally subsisting entities we can obtain. It can be surmised that it is easier or less unsettling to apprehend the transcendent unity of justice that subsists in the world over that of our future possibilities, both good and bad. It took Reinach being at war to investigate this entity, and extreme circumstance, whereas it took only an education in law school and Husserlian realist phenomenology to open his eyes to *Recht*. So, it is entirely conceivable that were we more open to the foreseen (and other intentional entities like it that we deem elusive), we would have a better grasp of this third kind of being and all the various intentional entities that subsist in the world that we can possibly grasp.

NOTES

1. Jeff Mitscherling, *Aesthetic Genesis: The Origin of Consciousness in the Intentional Being of Nature* (Lanham: University Press of America, 2010), 17. Hereafter cited as AG.

2. Roger Berkowitz, *The Gift of Science: Leibniz and The Modern Legal Tradition,* (New York: Fordham University Press, 2010) xvii.

3. For further reading on these two points, see my *Phenomenological Jurisprudence: A Reinterpretation of Reinach's Jarhrbuch Essay* (2016). Since I have tackled (1) and (2) previously, here I will mainly touch on (3).

4. Adolf Reinach, "The A Priori Foundations of Civil Law," trans., J. F. Crosby, *Aletheia: An International Journal of Philosophy*, vol. 3: (1981), 4; cited hereafter as APF.

5. Reinach, APF, 6.

6. AG, 124.

7. Reinach, APF , 134–5.

8. Reinach, APF, 137.

9. Reinach also notes in this section, sounding rather like Mitscherling, that categories are not produced or arbitrarily applied, but rather are discovered.

10. In the past, when this piece has been translated or discussed, *Ahnungen* has been translated into English as "premonition." *Ahnungen* has a broad meaning in German; it encompasses several ideas: premonition, foresight, hunch, inkling, idea, intuitiveness, and foreboding, to name a few. In the translation that accompanies this article, you will see "foreseeing/foreboding" for the simple reason that both words have application here in the Reinach work: "foresight" or "foreseeing" are my preferred English translations for *Ahnungen*; they have less of a mystical or occult sense about them, and in the case of foreseeing one's death I think the word "foreboding" is most appropriate, as it conveys the fear felt by soldiers as Reinach describes it: foreboding can only mean something terrible or evil will happen, in its intonation it signals something dark and fearful, and has meant as much since the 1600's. Reinach speaks of *Ahnungen* in relation to the knowledge of one's own impending death, describing it at one point as the "horror of future fortunes."

11. Translation mine. German text available in Adolf Reinach, *Sämtliche Werke,* eds. Karl Schuhmann and Barry Smith (Munich: Philosophia Verlag GmbH, 1989), 589-611.

12. Ibid.

13. Ibid.

14. Adolf Reinach, *Zur Phänomenologie der Ahnungen* (1916), trans. Kimberly Baltzer-Jaray, 2; cited hereafter as PA.

15. Reinach, PA, 3-4.

16. Reinach, PA, 3.

17. Reinach, PA, 3.

Chapter Five

Mitscherling's Reading of Ingarden

Rob Luzecky

The most remarkable aspect of *Aesthetic Genesis* is Jeff Mitscherling's re-conceptualization of intentionality and his specification of how intentionality precedes consciousness. The revolutionary aspect of this claim is difficult to over-estimate: one of the great pities of contemporary discussions in phenomenology and aesthetics is how it has, thus far, fallen stillborn from the presses. An analogue to this critical blindness is found in the paucity of responses to the groundbreaking work of Roman Ingarden. Though he was one of Husserl's most gifted students, having authored volumes on the ontology, identity, and cognition of various types of artworks, and despite having given penetrating analyses into the nature of reality, Ingarden's works seem to have fallen into an abyss. The aim of the present chapter is to shed some light on Mitscherling's "Copernican Revolution" of intentionality through demonstrating how it is partially inspired by Ingarden's ontology of the literary work of art.

At the outset, I should point out that Mitscherling's concept of intentionality is not found explicitly in Ingarden, but the essential constituents of the concept can be found in Ingarden's description of the literary work of art. Ingarden describes the literary work of art as a heteronymous formation involving both "material" and "ideal" components. The literary work of art has a schematic structure that guides the reader's concretization of it; and in its concretization as an aesthetic object, the literary work of art enjoys an intentional mode of being. The literary work of art enjoys a certain sort of life in its concretizations, and it is through its concretizations that it obtains as an aesthetic object. Taken together, these claims amount to a fundamental rejection of what Ingarden refers to as the "physicalistic theory of language," which holds that only material things exist.[1] Were we to apply this claim to the literary work of art, we would be left with the emaciated (and absurd)

77

claim that the states of affairs and characters of a literary work are simply phantasmic sorts of things that we cannot speak about with any degree of precision. While such a claim is not properly within the province of aesthetics (claims about the identity and reality of literary entities are, by nature, within the purview of metaphysics), we find that the conclusions of the physicalistic approach to language rob discussions of literary aesthetics of all substantive content. How, for instance, can we say that we enjoy or have been struck by the tragedy of a given literary work of art, if we have consigned it to an ill-defined non-existence?

Both Mitscherling and Ingarden maintain that literary works of art live and die. As sad as it may be, your favourite literary character and the world they inhabit will one day cease to be. One of Mitscherling's most vexing statements is that the words in a literary text are "supratemporal" entities that exist outside the temporal continuum. This concept becomes much less obscure when we examine Ingarden's extensive elaboration of the nature of supratemporal entities. In the first and second sections, I will elaborate on the claim that an element of the meaning of words (and, by extension, higher linguistic formations—i.e., sentential structures) is not extended over any period of the history of the real world, despite the fact that literary works may be read at any time (after their creation) and enjoy a form of intentional life.

But what does it mean to assert that literary works of art enjoy intentional life, or that the literary work of art is not just a passive object (i.e., an artifact) that is solely constituted by the author's intent? In the final section, I elaborate on Ingarden's concept that the literary work of art enjoys an intentional existence as an aesthetic object. Reducible to neither material being nor ideal being, the literary work of art is a type of organic being that enjoys an intentional existence.

THE "IDEAL" NATURE OF THE SOUNDING MOMENTS IN MUSICAL WORKS OF ART AND LITERARY WORKS OF ART

Perhaps one of the most vexing statements contained in *Aesthetic Genesis* is the claim that "when you understand the meaning of an individual word in a sentence, you are encountering an instance of ideal being, which is atemporal (or non-temporal)."[2] The suggestion here is that words have the same metaphysical status as the ideal elements of the sounding elements of musical works, in the sense that they enjoy a sort of being that is not dependent on any sort of spatio-temporal location. Mitscherling elaborates on this description of word meanings when he notes that: "The meaning of a word, after all, does not come into being or pass away, although the words themselves undeniably do just that over the course of a living language."[3] If word meanings were simply and solely social entities, then we would have to reject one of the most oft-repeated and substantive claims of *Aesthetic Genesis*. In order to clarify why the meanings of words (conceived of as sounding entities which have the strange property of having many meanings but which retain their identity of meaning) are not simply socially determined, we have to turn to Mitscherling's analysis of Roman Ingarden's identification of the musical work to unpack the quite complex (and very limited) analogy that exists between musical works of art and literary works of art.[4]

When we read a novel or a poem (i.e., works specifically designed by the author to be concretized as literary works of art), we are encountering something that is analogous to the musical work of art in two relevant respects. Like the musical work of art, the literary work of art 1) is composed of sounding units (i.e., phonemes, phonetic structures of a higher order—diphthongs, words, etc.—and, in musical works, differently sounding notes—flats, sharps, etc.) and; 2) appears as a temporally complete composition (i.e., with a temporal "beginning" and "end") that "does not enter into the time-continuum of the real world,"[5] in that the meaning of the sounding elements exists independently of the temporally-determined real world. Ingarden strengthens this analogy by pointing out that musical works of art (like literary works of art) have a physical ontic base, which is produced by psycho-social individuals who enjoy a particular spatio-temporal location. Finally, and most importantly, both literary works of art and musical works of art have a "quasi-temporal" structure that is immanent to them, through which their content is presented in a certain order of succession; however, the particular "meaning" of this content is partially dependent on "supratemporal" ideal meaning units. The analysis of the peculiar temporal structure of these works will assuage the concerns that the meanings of sounding elements of these works are socially determined.

While we may imagine Chopin huddled in his room scribbling the notes and treble clefs of a prelude on parchment in Majorca in 1836, these actions would not constitute the beginning of a musical work of art. As Mitscherling points out, "the most powerful of the arguments that Ingarden marshals . . . against the identification of the musical work as a 'real [physically extended] object'"[6] is based on the observation that a physical object obtains in its entirety in a particular time and place. Ingarden points out that, in terms of its content, it is absurd to conceive of a musical work of art as located in a particular place at a particular time:

> What is it supposed to mean, for example, that Beethoven's sonata, opus 13, is 'here'? Where is 'here'? In this room, or in the piano, or in the section of space over the piano? And if the sonata is performed at the same time in ten different cities, is one and the same sonata then supposed to be in ten different places? That is an obvious absurdity. In the *proper content* of the musical work, in its individual tone formations, and the *Gestalts* built upon them, there are no traits

or elements which in any way indicate that it is located in a definite place and in real space.[7]

In terms of its content (i.e., the sound "colouring" of it is tone formations) the musical work of art cannot be localized to any particular spatio-temporal location. Ingarden amplifies this point by observing that through its performances the musical work "acquires a unique colouring that it would never have if anything at all in this environment were modified."[8] This is not to say that the musical work has no temporality in any sense of the term. The quasi-temporal structure of the musical work reveals itself in that its various tone clusters have an ordinal arrangement. From the sounding of its first notes, the musical work manifests a temporality, in the sense that its tonal structures form a sequence of before and after.[9]

That a musical work manifests a temporal structure indicates that it is the sort of thing that is temporally determined, but this raises the question of what sort of temporal determination applies to it as a whole. Mitscherling points out that Ingarden distinguishes among 1) objects enduring in time, 2) processes, and 3) events.[10] We can safely exclude the musical work from the category of objects enduring in time for two reasons: Ingarden explicitly notes that musical compositions "are nothing mental and nothing 'subjective'"[11] and, in addition, they are not to be identified with their (temporally-enduring) score.[12] We can also see that the musical work of art is neither simply a process nor an event. Elaborating on these concepts, Ingarden writes:

> Every process not only develops through its phases in time, but also requires time in order to constitute itself. This does not apply to an event. It appears in being *at once* as a *ready* creation, coming into existence and vanishing from it as if *in one sweep*. An event does not take place in a succession of phases. Even the briefest process is an entity in transition, in change, in flux. The phases of a process form a *continuous* whole that is neither a fragmented manifold nor a *Gestalt* of a higher order, composed of separate, stationary elements that are distinct and merely contiguous.[13]

We cannot think of the temporality of the musical work as a process, because the sounding elements do come together to form a whole of a higher order that is something other than a mere aggregate of discrete sounding elements. Were we to break the musical work apart (i.e., attempt to conceive of it as merely a process constituted by discrete sounding elements), we would lose any awareness of the way these sounding elements modulate one another. The modulation of the sounding elements produces a *Gestalt* that typifies a particular piece of music (e.g., the sadness and overwhelming longing of the theme from *Raging Bull* cannot be identified with any single note, and yet it permeates the entirety of piece). On the other hand, were we to conceive of the musical work as an event, we would have to resign ourselves to the (counter-factual) claim that the musical work does not have any sort of time progression (i.e., that it has no perceptible temporal progression from one sounding moment to the next). Both alternatives are inadequate.

When we hear a musical work, the quasi-temporal ordering of the sounding elements forms a continuum of musically-coloured moments, which (quite literally) resonate with one another and define the work's meaning without reference to any temporally given moment in the world of spatio-temporally located entities. "[A] continuum," Mitscherling highlights, "is characterized by *completeness*."[14] Unlike a process, which is essentially incomplete, a continuum is the sort of temporal form which is of a different order than that which can be considered as incomplete—the predicate "incomplete" cannot apply to a continuum—and "[i]t is this completeness of its continuum of phases that most clearly points to the supratemporality of the musical work."[15] The supratemporal character of the musical work reveals itself when we recognize that this continuum is "filled out in advance" of any particular hearing of the musical work in its performance. Referring to the supratemporal character of the musical work, Ingarden writes:

> It means that the continuum of the temporal colourations of the work's phases, a continuum immanent to the work, is determined exclusively by the elements of the work itself. Or, more precisely, only the elements of the work, above all those of a tonal nature fill out the individual phases of the work (the places in its time continuum); and no objectivities, processes, or the like, which are alien to the work, have a part in filling out the work's phases. The temporal structure of the musical work itself is complete proof, so to speak, against all events and processes of the real world taking place outside the musical work.[16]

That the meaning of musical works has its ontic foundation in this supratemporal continuum is evidenced by the fact that various tempi of musical works (e.g., a *largo*, an *adagio*, a *grave*, etc.) mark very specific temporal rhythms that are not at all determined by the temporal rhythms of the world that is extrinsic to the musical work.[17] Were the musical work and its various tempi simply reflective of the extra-musical reality, and if the meaning of the musical work were simply reflective of the extra-musical reality, then we would not have any means by which to distinguish particularly poor performances of musical works from great performances in which the musical work expresses its true meaning.

Both musical works and literary works have the common feature that they are composed of sounding elements that (when placed in order) take on a certain melodic character. In a literary work, the combinations of phonemes reflect various types of tempi which give it certain mood qualities. This rhythmic quality of sounding elements is particularly evident and used to great effect in poetic verse. Analyzing Edgar Allen Poe's "The Raven,"

Mitscherling notes that the sonorous qualities of the poem produce a trochaic rhythm, in which "each foot (trochee) consists of a stressed followed by an unstressed syllable,"[18] and this particular rhythmic quality of the sounding elements establishes a melody that is essential in the creation of mood qualities (i.e., the senses of dread and foreboding) that are evident in the poem. Ingarden elaborates:

> At issue are characters which in themselves are not purely phonic but have their basis in the purely phonic properties of the word-sound sequence and formations arising in it (the kind of rhythm, tempo, melody, timbre of individual word sounds) and also achieve their appearance through them. These are the many and various 'emotional' or 'mood' qualities: 'sad,' 'melancholy,' merry,' 'powerful,' etc. Their appearance can also be conditioned and influenced by the meaning that is bound to the word sound. But, as is clearly shown in musical works, they can also be produced solely by the phonic material. For example, we frequently do not need to understand at all a poem read in a foreign language in order to apprehend clearly the characters here in question.[19]

The emotional qualities (and their associated meanings) are not entirely dependent on the socially determined meanings that emerge when we understand a given language. This aspect of their meaning (which is divested from our own lived reality) indicates that the meaning of these may be considered to be ideal. The ideal aspect of word meaning is further evidenced when we note that the combination of sounding elements (i.e., word sounds) in a literary text demands a particular type of reading (i.e., reading slowly or quickly), and this imparts a certain emotional colouration to the text that is not entirely subject to our understanding of the socially determined meanings of words.[20]

At this point, one might object that this analogy among the sounding elements of musical works and literary works leaves us with a type of meaning that is, at best, vague. To alleviate this concern, we have to discuss the concretization of the literary work of art, a discussion which I postpone to the third section. First, we must turn to the multiple senses of meaning which can be discerned in various words.

THE "IDEAL" PARTS OF WORD MEANING

The claim that words have an ideal meaning is derived from the observation that a word can be used in different situations, and its meaning seems to vary in these situations.[21] In order to understand why Ingarden and Mitscherling assert that words have an ideal meaning, we have to review Ingarden's threefold negative argument against competing claims that putatively explain why the meaning of the same word can change in various situations. Ingarden points out that: 1) the similar meanings of words are *not* merely a case of equivalence of meanings; 2) we cannot resolve the difference in meaning with the claim that both expressions of meaning refer to the same formal object and; 3) the variability of meanings of a term cannot be explained by asserting that the meaning of a word in one instance of its use "contains implicitly 'the same thing' that is explicitly meant"[22] in other expressions of its meaning. We can safely dismiss the first of these as inadequate, because though two expressions may refer to the same object, the meaning of these expressions is different. (E.g., though the expressions "that which is the capital of Poland" and "that which is inhabited by about two-million people" both refer to Warsaw, the identity of the object of reference does not imply an equivalence of meaning between the two expressions.) The other two claims, however, require a bit more work.

It does not seem that we can resolve the question of why a single term has different meanings by asserting that these meanings point to the same formal object. Using the example of a nominal term that has various similar meanings, it cannot be argued that this similarity is due to the fact that these point to the same formal object. Reflecting on the word "square," Ingarden notes:

> While the formal object of the word 'square' is something constituted exclusively by squareness as the qualitative element of its nature, the 'equilateral rectangular parallelogram' is constituted by an entirely different 'immediate *morphē*' (namely, by the 'parallelogramness'), and, moreover, it is distinguished by two features: its equilateralness and its rectangularity. It is true that if anything is constituted by squareness, then in itself, due to the a priori references between the corresponding essences, it must also be a parallelogram and be distinguished by both of the above features. But this is an ontological circumstance which exists independently of the purely meaning-oriented manner of determination of the intentional object projected by the meaning. The *formal* object of the first meaning [i.e., squareness], on the other hand, is conceived differently (with respect to both its qualitative property and its formal structure) from that of the second meaning [i.e., paraellogramness], and in this respect the two formal objects differ from each other. For this reason, the alleged 'sameness' of the meanings in question cannot be reduced to the sameness of their formal objects.[23]

Each definition has a different formal object. That the meanings of a single term are different, and that these meanings are each correlated to distinct formal objects, indicate that the difference in meaning cannot be resolved by asserting that different meanings of the same term refer to the same formal object. There are as many formal objects as there are meanings, and, therefore, an appeal to an identity of formal objects does nothing to explain how a given word may at the same time have different meanings.

Finally, it is inaccurate to claim that the different meanings of a single term can be resolved by asserting that these different meanings are either

implicit or explicit. Were we to say that one meaning of a word is implicit or
explicit in another (slightly different) meaning of the same term, then we
would have to determine in what sense the two meanings reflect one another,
and such a specification is simply not given in the definition of the terms
"implicit" or "explicit." Due to these ambiguities, we cannot appeal to implication or explication to resolve the difficulty posed by the different meanings
of a term. When one meaning of a nominal term—say "city," defined as "a
large grouping of people in a particular spatio-temporal location"—is said to
make explicit or be implicit in a second definition—say "a large grouping of
inhabited buildings in a particular spatio-temporal location"—the assumption
is that the former meaning is somehow "transferred" to the latter. But Ingarden points out that it is utterly unclear how the first meaning of the nominal
term shifts to another, or even if such a transference of meaning is possible,
even though these sorts of transitions are necessary to our understanding the
words and sentences of a work of literature.[24]

The inadequacy of these three attempts to explain the special ability of
(nominal) words to have multiple meanings yields the conclusion that their
meaning is ideal, in the sense that for any given nominal term that has two or
more meanings, these meanings "belong to one and the same ideal concept of
the same object and, on the other hand, two different ways in which the
elements of one and the same meaning can appear"[25] in different "actualiza-
tions" of the term. In order to make sense of this claim that word meanings
are (in a limited sense) ideal, we have to note that the meanings of a word are
merely its potential, held in readiness, waiting be actualized as meaningful
elements of a work of literature. Mitscherling explains:

> The word meaning of a determinate name, when used in a particular situation,
> is an *actualization* of a *part* of the *ideal sense* (*des idealen Sinnes*) contained in
> the concept that 'corresponds' to the intentional object. It is this actualization,
> as determined in the word sound, that creates (*ausmacht*) the material and
> formal content of the meaning. Thus each 'ideal concept' has a number of
> word meanings for the same object. That part of the ideal sense of the concept
> which is to be actualized constitutes the *potential stock* of the meaning.[26]

When we encounter a word in a literary text, this word has (from the outset)
multiple potential meanings which are contained within its concept. A
word's concept is not dependent on a word's particular placement in the
context of the sentence. In this sense, the word's meaning is ideal. As we
progress along the sentence, the suggested meaning of the word becomes
more perspicuous. That is, the potential stock of meanings gets winnowed as
we read the text. This reduction of the ideal meanings identified with the
concept is precisely the process of the word's meaning being actualized.
Elaborating on the process of actualization of meaning, Ingarden observes
that taken in isolation, the word conceals within itself a manifold of possible

meanings (i.e., its ideal parts), which are "selected" by the reader's consciousness, until the word's meaning

> . . . stands before us as something finished and no longer in the state of production, and, in conjunction with the word sound, forms a 'word' which we can use as frequently as we wish, in various situations as identically the same, i.e., as having, to put it more precisely, the same word sound and the same meaning content.[27]

That this process of actualizing the meaning of words occurs every time we read a text, and that the meaning of these words does change while still retaining a general identity of meaning, indicates that while the meaning of words is partially conditioned (i.e., refined) by social determinations, these are dependent on the existence of word's meaning in an ideal sense.

STRATIFICATION OF THE LITERARY WORK OF ART AND INTENTIONAL BEING

The above discussions of the ideal meaning of the sounding elements of musical works and the words of literary works do not imply that literary works *only* have meaning in an ideal sense. While it is the case that monosyllabic nominal terms do have a general meaning that is indicated by their sound, many nominal terms are polysyllabic, and the determination of what general meaning they might have becomes quite obscure if we were to simply remain at the level of ideal meaning.[28] Moreover, were we to simply remain at the level of ideal meaning, we would deprive ourselves of any possibility of explaining the means by which a literary work of art becomes a meaningful part of the living world (that is quite far removed from the ideal, in the senses in which it has been discussed in the previous sections). In order to resolve these difficulties, Ingarden introduces the process of concretization of a literary work of art, by which its meaning becomes more refined as the reader progresses through the text.

Perhaps the most direct way to understand Ingarden's influence on Mitscherling's thought is 1) to recall Ingarden's claim that literary works of art are stratiform entities; and 2) to clarify Ingarden's description of the processes of their concretization as aesthetic objects. The literary work of art is an ontologically stratified formation in which the strata differ from each other in terms of both "their characteristic material" and "the role each stratum plays in relation to other strata and the work of art."[29] To qualify as a stratified structure, a work of art must satisfy four necessary and sufficient conditions. First, the "work of art is composed of "heterogeneous elements that appear in it."[30] (I.e., a literary work of art has phonetic elements, represented characters and states of affairs, etc.) Second, the heterogeneous elements of a work of art "unite together into formations of a higher order that ultimately pervades the whole of its structure."[31] (For example, the various words form sentences and chapters, and the represented characters and states of affairs form a "plot.") Third, these elements do not lose their "relative independence and delimitation in the whole of the work."[32] Finally, Ingarden notes that "an organic union obtains"[33] among the constituent elements of the work. The stratified structure of a work of art is what designates the relations of the various elements to each other, and these relations are necessary to the unity of the description of the work of art as a whole. When we speak of the strata of a work of art, we are referring to the relations of the elements. Literary works of art are constituted by four strata: (1) the "linguistic stratum" of phonological elements. This stratum is constituted by the inscribed words of a text, their requisite sounds, and the higher linguistic and phonetic formations built on the words and word sounds in a given piece of literature (i.e., the sentences and paragraphs); (2) the stratum of "meaning units," which involve ideal elements that are actualized through the reading of the text; (3) the stratum of represented objects; and (4) the stratum of schematized aspects.

The nature and function of the stratum of schematized aspects is as complex as it is important to the process of a literary work of art's concretization. Ingarden notes that "to the represented objects of a literary work 'belong' *all* the schematized aspects in which these objects may generally be given"[34] and that through the process of fulfilling these aspects, the represented objects take on a particular meaning. Mitscherling summarizes:

> When consciousness attends to (or 'intends') a particular object, it is usually the case that only some of the 'aspects' of that object are presented immediately to consciousness, and these aspects are said to be fulfilled or unfulfilled. For example, when we look at a table from above, the table presents us with aspect of 'table-top' and 'table-bottom,' and the former is fulfilled while the latter remains unfulfilled . . . A similar situation obtains in the literary work of art, but here the reader is often forced to fulfill for herself many of those aspects that are presented by the author as unfulfilled, and she does so with regard to those aspects that are presented more fully, i.e., as fulfilled. The latter provide the reader with a direction to follow in her conscious activity of fulfilling these unfulfilled aspects, which are said to have been 'schematized.' This intentional activity of fulfillment of schematized aspects is a central component of the general activity of 'concretization.' As no character, for example, can ever be exhaustively presented by an author—no character, that is to say can ever be portrayed fully and completely determined—the manner in which this concretization is to proceed can only be schematically determined by a literary work of art through its stratum of schematized aspects.[35]

These elements are schematic aspects, because they are presented to the reader as part of a schematized whole; they achieve their realization through their presentation to the reader. For example, when a person reads a literary text, they concretize the schematic aspects that have been presented in the various passages, but which are incomplete in the sense that there are things that are simply not presented in the text—i.e., how a character gets from a particular represented location *A* to another represented location *B*, when the text indicates that a character makes such a voyage, but does not give any specification of the mode of transportation. To the extent that these are not fully determined in a work of art, they are "schematized," and their fulfillment is one of the ways the text gets concretized as an aesthetic object.

The aesthetic object (in which its represented objects, processes, and states of affairs obtain as parts of an object with aesthetic values) is distinct from the material physical text. Were we to simply identify the literary work of art with its material ontic base, it seems that we would be condemned to accepting the absurdity that various copies of the same edition of a particular text are, in fact, different literary works of art, and this plurality of works would preclude any identification of a single work of art—thereby rejecting a claim that serves as the basis of literary criticism, as well as any non-subjectivist account of the meaning and metaphysical status of a literary work. The most important outcome of the observation that the literary work of art is not to be identified with its material substrate is that it enjoys a type of "intentional being"; it cannot be tied to any particular spatio-temporal location, and this mode of intentional being is crucial to an understanding of its identity as an aesthetic object. [36]

CONCLUSION

Through his readings of Ingarden, Mitscherling elaborates three distinct features of the literary work of art which inform his re-conceptualization of intentionality. The literary work of art has its material ontic foundation in its physical pages and covers, but it cannot be reduced simply to this. In the sense that it has ideal meaning elements as one of its ontological parts, the literary work of art is analogous to the musical work of art. The vague ideal meaning of musical and literary works of art (i.e. that meaning we experience before their concretization) is a consequent of the supratemporal nature of their meaning units. Finally, the literary work of art comes to life, in the sense that its ideal meanings are winnowed by the reader through the process of concretizing the literary work as an aesthetic object.

NOTES

1. Roman Ingarden, "The Physicalistic Theory of Language and The Work of Literature," in *Problems of Literary Evaluation*, ed. Joseph Strelka (University Park: Pennsylvania State University Press, 1969), 90.

2. Jeff Mitscherling, *Aesthetic Genesis: The Origin of Consciousness in the Intentional Being of Nature* (Lanham: University Press of America, 2010), 27. Hereafter cited as AG.

3. AG, 70.

4. Ingarden explicitly notes the limit of this analogy: "A composition of (pure) music is not a literary work, and despite certain features that appear in both of them, (e.g., both have a quasi-temporal structure) the musical work is not in its characteristic structure, similar to a literary work of art" (Roman Ingarden, *The Work of Music and the Problem of Its Identity*, trans. Adam Czerniawski, ed. Jean G. Harrell [Berkeley: University of California Press, 1986], 49). The principle structural difference among musical works and literary works is that the latter have four distinct ontological strata, including the stratum of represented objectivities (represented persons, places, and states of affairs), but this stratum is wholly lacking in musical works. A symphony, for instance, does not "represent" various persons, places, or states of affairs in a way that is similar to how they are presented as aspects of the fictional realities of literary works. This structural difference does not imply that musical works are without meaning. The peculiar emotional and temporal "meaning" of musical works is found in their phonetic stratum, and this stratum is the foundational stratum of literary works of art. For excellent summaries of the function of the various strata of literary works of art, see Jeff Mitscherling, *Roman Ingarden's Ontology and Aesthetics* (Ottawa: University of Ottawa Press,1997), 129–139, Jeff Mitscherling, "Concretization, Literary Criticism, and the Life of the Literary Work of Art," in *Existence, Culture and Persons: the Ontology of Roman Ingarden*, ed. Arkadiusz Chrudzimski (New Brunswick: Ontos Verlag, 2005), 137–158 (esp. 138–139), and Anita Szczepańska, "The Structure of Artworks," in *On the Aesthetics of Roman Ingarden: Interpretations and Assessments*, eds. Bohdan Dziemidok and Peter J. McCormick (Dordrecht: Kluwer, 1989), 21–54. For Ingarden's remarks on the non-stratiform structure of musical works, see Ingarden, *The Work of Music and the Problem of Its Identity*, 50–54 and Roman Ingarden, *Ontology of the Work of Art: The Musical Work, the Picture, the Architectural Work, the Film*, trans. Raymond Meyer and John T. Goldthwait (Athens: University of Ohio Press, 1989) 30-34.

5. Ingarden, *The Work of Music and the Problem of Its Identity*, 77. Ingarden strengthens this analogy by pointing out that (like literary works of art) musical works of art have a physical ontic base (ibid., 22) which is produced by real individuals who enjoy a spatio-temporal location (ibid., 56).

6. Mitscherling, *Roman Ingarden's Ontology and Aesthetics*, 169.

7. Ingarden, *Ontology of the Work of Art: The Musical Work, the Picture, the Architectural Work, the Film*, 35–36.

8. Ibid., 36.

9. Ingarden, *The Work of Music and the Problem of Its Identity*, 74: "This initial cluster [of sounded notes] is also the first member of a system of 'moments' of the work, comprising the members of the whole temporal or quasi-temporal structure of a musical work—a structure unique to every composition. In strictly formal terms, these members succeed one another in a definite sequence of 'before' and 'after,' but in this relationship they are at the same time qualitatively determined by the above-mentioned temporal colouring."

10. Mitscherling, *Roman Ingarden's Ontology and Aesthetics*, 172.

11. Ingarden, *Ontology of the Work of Art: The Musical Work, the Picture, the Architectural Work, the Film*, 22.

12. Ibid., 26.

13. Roman Ingarden, *Time and Modes of Being*, trans. Helen R. Michejda (Springfield: Charles C. Thomas, 1964), 123–124.

14. Mitscherling, *Roman Ingarden's Ontology and Aesthetics*, 173.

15. Ibid.

16. Ingarden, *Ontology of the Work of Art: The Musical Work, the Picture, the Architectural Work, the Film*, 42–43.

17. A *largo* is a temporal progression of forty to sixty beats per minute, a *grave* is a temporal progression of twenty-five to forty-five beats per minute, and an *adagio* has a temporal progression of sixty-six to seventy-six beats per minute.

18. Mitscherling, *Roman Ingarden's Ontology and Aesthetics*, 161, fn. 20.

19. Roman Ingarden, *The Literary Work of Art*, trans. George G. Grabowicz (Evanston: Northwestern University Press, 1973), 51–52.

20. Mitscherling amplifies this point when, with reference to the opening lines of James Joyce's "The Dead," he notes were we to read these "while remaining ignorant of the word meanings, themselves, the mood would to some extent be made manifest" (Mitscherling, *Roman Ingarden's Ontology and Aesthetics*, 141) simply by virtue of the sounds contained in the sentences.

21. Ingarden, *The Literary Work of Art*, 84–85: "the same word, with indeed identically the same meaning, can be used in different situations in different ways, so that, despite the identity of meaning a distinct change can be ascertained in it." Ingarden uses the example of the word "square" which "means (i.e., in our terminology has the following material content) an 'equilateral rectangular parallelogram' (1). We can also say, however: an equilateral rectangular parallelogram with sides of any length (2); or: an equilateral rectangular quadrangle with two pairs of parallel sides of any length (3)" (ibid., 85). While Ingarden restricts his analysis to very particular nominal terms, this does not imply that his conclusions do not apply to other types of words. Transitive verbs have nominal terms as their object, so to determine their meaning we end up analyzing the meaning of nouns. Intransitive verbs, on the other hand, have no noun as their object, and are naming of actions. Adverbs and adjectives respectively function to a modify verbs and nouns, so their meaning element is dependent on the meanings of nouns and verbs. Further, syncategorematica (commonly referred to as grammatical conjunctions, and also including the verb "be") have meaning only insofar as they denote relations among various grammatical and logical elements, and if we are to understand the specific nature of their meaning, we have to first understand the meaning of nominal terms that they relate or identify.

22. Ibid., 86.

23. Ibid.

24. Ibid., 86–87.

25. Ibid., 87.

26. Mitscherling, *Roman Ingarden's Ontology and Aesthetics*, 133–134.

27. Ingarden, *The Literary Work of Art*, 101.

28. Mitscherling amplifies this when he notes: "The most striking difference between the word and the sentence is that while the former is 'characterized' by word sound, which exists as a uniform whole, there is not, in the same sense, any such thing as a 'sentence sound.'" (Mitscherling, *Roman Ingarden's Ontology and Aesthetics*, 131).

29. Ingarden, *The Literary Work of Art*, 29. Ingarden's rather odd use of the term "material" in his elaboration of the strata of literary works of art invites misinterpretation and demands clarification. The term "material" does not refer to material in any physical sense (i.e., the material of the various strata does not have physical extension). Rather, the matter of a stratum is its ontological elements. In this sense, the material of the schematized stratum is the particular ways by which meanings are schematized (i.e., the material is schematization itself). Similarly, the material of the stratum of represented objectivities is the particular represented objects in a text, none of which have any particular spatio-temporal location in the physically extended world. This use of the term "material" gets a bit confounded when we try to apply it to the phonetic stratum, which has physical signs (i.e., the inscribed text on the pages of a book) as one of its ontological elements. Ingarden repeatedly points out that the phonetic stratum cannot be reduced to the inscribed text. Though the phonetic stratum involves physical graphic representations, it also involves the non-physical sounds of phonemes. It is the interrelation of these elements that constitutes the characteristic material of the phonetic stratum.

30. Ingarden, *Ontology of the Work of Art: The Musical Work, the Picture, the Architectural Work, the Film*, 32.

31. Ibid.

32. Ibid.

33. Ibid. Ingarden elaborates on the organic structure in *The Cognition of the Literary Work of Art*. In order to be considered "organic" an entity must fulfill three conditions: 1) the entity should "perform a particular main function, to which various other functions, performed by its individual organs, are subordinated" (Roman Ingarden, *The Cognition of the Literary Work of Art*, trans. Ruth Ann Crowley and Kenneth R. Olson [Evanston: Northwestern University

Press,1973], 74); 2) this system of functions is "closely related to the structure of the organism, which is adapted to them" (ibid.) and ; 3) the entity has "a certain typical course of life [that] is manifested in all organisms" (ibid., 76). The strata of a literary work of art each have certain aesthetic value qualities, and these coalesce to form a "polyphonic harmony" of values which define the literary work of art as an aesthetic object (Mitscherling, *Roman Ingarden's Ontology and Aesthetics*, 139). In this sense, the literary work of art fulfills the first of the conditions of being organic. The function of the literary work of art is to obtain its realization as an aesthetic object, and the particular value it has as an aesthetic object is dependent on the ontological structure of the literary work of art. The literary work of art meets the second of these conditions, in the sense that it fulfils a function that is identical to that of other literary works of art. This point is amplified when we recognize that the literary work of art's function is derived from an ontological structure that is identical with the ontological structure of other literary works of art. Finally, the literary work of art meets the third condition, in the sense that it enjoys a peculiar form of "life" as an aesthetic object. Mitscherling clarifies: "it [the literary work of art] both i) 'comes to life' through the reader's individual actives of apprehension and concretization and ii) exerts an ongoing influence in the creation and preservation of the cultural life-world of its readers" (Mitscherling, "Concretization, Literary Criticism, and the Life of the Literary Work of Art," 141).

34. Ingarden, *The Literary Work of Art*, 265.

35. AG, 143–144, fn. 10.

36. Mitscherling illustrates: "To take the literary work of art as an example, the positivist analytic approach has to maintain that the physical object—for example, my copy of *Huckleberry Finn*—is identical with the work of art. But if this were the case, there would be as many works of art as there are copies of *Huckleberry Finn*; that is, there would be millions of *Huckleberry Finn*s. Yet we in fact acknowledge that there exists only one *Huckleberry Finn*; namely, that unique individual work of art created by Mark Twain, which is indeed to be distinguished from the physical, 'real,' mass-produced copy of that work." Mitscherling, "The Identity of the Architectural Work of Art," in Jane Forsey, ed., *Contemporary Issues in Aesthetics* [supplemental volume of *Symposium*, vol. 8, no. 3 (Fall 2004)], 494, 491–518.

Chapter Six

Being That Can Be Understood Is (Not Just) Language

On Linguisticality and Intentionality

Jason C. Robinson

The now famous hermeneutical discussion of language takes centre stage in "Part Three: The Ontological Shift of Hermeneutics Guided by Language," of Gadamer's *Truth and Method*.[1] After almost 400 pages of what might be described as context, he turns his attention to language as the cornerstone that holds his project in place. The discovery of language, or rather, the rediscovery for Gadamer (following St. Augustine), means nothing less than a new start for philosophy and science. In his ontological description of language, Gadamer finds the means to describe human understanding and our very mode of being. We are linguistic, our reason is linguistic, and therefore our known world is linguistic.

As one of the pioneers of the broadly defined "linguistic turn" in philosophy, Gadamer's philosophy of language remains both relevant and challenging. If we dismantle this element in his hermeneutics, or substantially revise it in almost any manner, the risk to his entire project is nothing less than apocalyptic. In *Aesthetic Genesis*, Mitscherling proposes precisely such a revision.[2] Mitscherling argues that there is something fundamentally wrong with Gadamer's claim regarding being and language—something that does not align with a closer examination of human experience and reality, and therefore, something that needs to be replaced if we wish to articulate a realist phenomenology.

Gadamer's too often decontextualized phrase, "Being that can be understood is language," is opposed by Mitscherling on the grounds that language is a utility, not a description of our way of being.[3] Instead of language,

Mitscherling argues for the intentionality of all being—reality—as something that makes understanding (indeed life) possible. Intentionality is prior to language, even bodily sensation. This intentionality exists at the heart of all nature, rather than merely the consciousness of humans. There is meaning and understanding before there is language, he argues. Given that so much of Gadamer's project relies on language, we must take Mitscherling's stance as very provocative, if not outright antagonistic.

The "not just" in the title of this chapter is meant in two main ways. The first way, a relatively modest endeavour, is the way of affirming. I will interpret Gadamer's philosophy of language in a way that attempts to do justice to its intended universal scope—arguing that language as signs and symbols, as lexical[4] and semiotic[5] (words), is not "language" as Gadamer understands it, but the limited concretizing of a much broader linguisticality of understanding in which being—reality—presents itself. I hope to show that "language" is not "linguisticality,"[6] and that important notions such as freedom, reason, and self-understanding are involved in the linguistic.

The second "not just" is more ambitious, for it tries to situate the pre-linguistic and rational in Gadamer's hermeneutics. Gadamer's recognition of the pre-linguistic and reason as a guiding (pre-linguistic) *telos* or force is often either ignored or misunderstood by commentators.[7] Gadamer recognizes, as does Mitscherling, that there exists a pre-linguistic experience of reality, but the two draw radically different conclusions. The great difficulty here is talking, or rather writing, about something that cannot be captured in words, for it is the pre-word or pre-linguistic. One may very well wonder why such a discussion is even attempted. The answer is that such a discussion about the unsaid, perhaps the unsayable, is of great value—as I hope to show—even if opaque in nature.[8]

As someone who reads Mitscherling and Gadamer eagerly, drawing insight and affirmation about the nature of being and language from both, the argument that these two philosophers are offering something fundamentally oppositional is difficult to accept. However, that is Mitscherling's confessed starting point for *Aesthetic Genesis*. My instinct, contrary to Mitscherling, is that these two are in conversation, highlighting stresses and gaps the other has not been able to address fully. I have faith that Gadamer and Mitscherling may be reconciled, at least in part. In the end, I sympathize with Mitscherling's frustration that the "language" of Gadamer's hermeneutics fails to satisfy, in so much as it fails to offer a robust realist phenomenology—as Mitscherling seems to envision it. But this, as I see it, is not a failure of Gadamer's description, but an inevitability of our linguistic understanding. Once we accept that not all being is linguistic or understood, as does Gadamer, then the perceived failure of Gadamer becomes, instead, an acceptance of the nature of language and thought.

GADAMER AND LANGUAGE

While Gadamer's writing is far more accessible than that of his teacher, Heidegger, there is nevertheless ample terminology to decode, e.g., "dialogue," "tradition," "effective-historical consciousness," "prejudice," "understanding," and "self-understanding." A basic understanding of these terms is necessary before Gadamer's controversial discussion of language is more readily understood.

Objectivity, Dialogue, and Tradition

The big fight motivating Gadamer's *Truth and Method* is with the distorted scientific *ethos*, specifically the role of method, said to yield a certain kind of superior objective knowledge. The basic starting point of objectivity is that there is a world that exists independently of the human mind and that the "knowing" mind must stand as a detached observer (without bias, pre-judgment, or interest, e.g., in a specific truth/result that might cloud reality). Gadamer asks, rather simply, why it is that we take this position as the ideal. Is this not some weirdly ironic prejudice against prejudice?

Gadamer's response is to argue that objectivity and similar concepts of distance (between subject and object), which are said to increase understanding through methods and techniques (and related epistemologies), rely on a devastatingly bad misunderstanding of human experience. It is not merely that objectivity is a poor description of human understanding, but that its application may yield disastrous results, for it is based on illusion and a perverted form of self-denial. Instead, Gadamer argues that we are participants in an ongoing conversation between ourselves and the world—subject and object are dissolved in the dialogue. As a conversation, or dialogue, we are not merely employing a tool or strategy for understanding, but living "as" a conversation. It is the nature of our awareness of the world to be in interaction, give and take, questioning and answering with the other—text, work of art, person, etc. We have not chosen this particular path toward understanding; nevertheless, we are on it. "Dialogue" describes the basic structure and activity of our understanding, to give and take, to question and answer, to interact. Understanding is an action best characterized as "a fusion of horizons" rather than a distancing (objectivity).

When does the individual become an objective (detached) observer? From what great vantage point does one gain a God's-eye-view such that "Truth" (universal, necessary, and certain) is grasped? Never and nowhere, he argues. The nature of human understanding is always situated, historically conditioned, and finite. The personal and social implications of the acceptance of objectivity—especially in so much as we give up personal choice to so-called experts—is potentially vast.[9] Objectivity is not the erasure, destruc-

tion or bracketing of prejudice and bias. Rather, objectivity harbours prejudice (pre-judgment) behind a dismissiveness toward all other forms of
thought and reason. Having set itself up as absolute, objectivity—realized
most fully in the natural sciences, emulated by most others—is dangerous. In
its place, a hermeneutics of understanding, reason, and knowledge (however
we choose to label thinking and thought) promises more. As we shall see,
replacing objectivity with a hermeneutical consciousness, something living
within a linguistic being that finds freedom through a particular sort of reflection, is the only legitimate birthplace of reason and enlightenment.

We are, for Gadamer, living embodiments of tradition and history, and
language acts as a medium (and application) of its existence. Gadamer's
famous term for this is "effective-historical consciousness." The simplest
explanation of this consciousness is that it is a description of the influence of
past experience. Prior experiences (including social, cultural ideas, esp. traditions) have contributed to what we are today; our beliefs, concepts, values,
dreams and, obviously, our memories. However, the term "contributed" is
too weak for Gadamer. There is a significant difference between saying past
experience has influenced or contributed to one's present (as if the past and
present were at a discernable distance of some kind), and saying that past
experience is active and living in the present—making us who we are in the
present. Tradition does not merely contribute, it creates and sustains our very
being—reality as we know it.

A consequence of such an active and ever-living past is, for Gadamer,
that it takes the form of hidden prejudices and biases, for no one is fully
aware of themselves—i.e., no one is able to critique themselves as if under a
microscope. As historical beings, the world as we experience it is not present
to us as a detached object to be interrogated and read, i.e., as a book of
nature. We are everywhere and always within the horizon of history and
tradition (culture, language, etc.). Effected in this way, we are no more able
to free ourselves from our past than we are able to free ourselves from our
present mode of being (thinking, feeling, acting, etc.). While we are not
complete slaves to tradition, for Gadamer, we are hardly its masters.

In a fairly obvious way, the basic argument that we are the ongoing
products of history seems oddly uncontroversial—even common sense. I am
obviously related, even dependent upon my past. It would be difficult to
argue the contrary, namely, that I am untouched by my past experiences,
uninfluenced by culture's spirit, or that I may ignore the vast web of ideas
presented to me without my asking. The more difficult reality to accept is
that the seemingly infinite diversity of thoughts and ideas that manifest in my
own voice—presenting themselves as if they are my own ideas—may indeed
belong to culture, to a world and language that I did not choose freely. That
is, I am not really me, in the sense of being an autonomous, fully self-created
being. I belong to my culture and tradition in ways I cannot fully conceive or

anticipate. It is a simple, but telling experiment on this issue to travel. It does not take long for one's hidden assumptions and biases about even the simplest practices to be challenged by the foreign, the other.[10]

For Gadamer, the language we speak is not a private language, but a language that belongs to another.[11] Language is a realm of many realms (horizons, spheres, worldviews, perspectives, etc.), some of which we know, most of which we do not. As a consequence of understanding through language, of knowing the world as well as ourselves through its nature, we cannot even say that we know ourselves fully and completely. Who would claim to know themselves, or even more audacious, (aspects of) the world completely? Such would be a strange and difficult thing to argue. And yet, this is precisely the spirit of our times—if not in practice perhaps then as a living ideology embodied in objectivity. It is not until we take Enlightenment ideals seriously that Gadamer's view begins to look more antagonistic, especially to the natural sciences. Hermeneutics is controversial because it opposes the modern view of the superior person as a rational self, able to use language and reason to sit above the profane (subjective, relative).

Freedom and the Historical Self

New readers of Gadamer may see him as pushing for an anti-science or an anti-enlightenment. He is not. On the contrary, he is in pursuit of a genuine science that allows for a different ideal of knowledge and truth, one upon which present sciences rest, i.e., a hermeneutical science.[12] There is much at stake in this discussion, for this is a debate about the very nature and possibility of understanding and freedom of thought.

Consider the popular conception of freedom idealized in an individual, living in the moment, being able to pick and choose among clear life options, to decide through reason a way forward in accordance with deliberate thought. This person is free of significant baggage (internal and inhibiting concepts, ideals, beliefs or external forces) clouding his judgment and preventing autonomous choice. In other words, this person is free, in so much as he is unaffected by his past—he is above history and tradition—literally free of it, except in so much as it may be selectively used as a tool or utility. If he is not making the judgment call, if tradition is making choices for him, then he is not free. In other words, I am not really me if I am they (my culture, language, tradition). Distance between myself and the world makes freedom and truth possible in the modern world. Gadamer disagrees with this popular conception.

For Gadamer, the harsh reality is that there is no isolated "me" making a neutral or detached judgment. "Me" is something far more relative, conditioned, and controlled. Freedom, the absence of control on my thought, is an illusion, according to Gadamer. We are our histories. Or, rather, we are in constant dialogue with our histories and the present. Each of us is a conversation, for Gadamer. We are our understanding, an effective-historical consciousness that no method or technique may dissolve, thereby separating dialogue partners (us/world, past/present, text/interpreter). The big question then becomes whether or not we acknowledge this control and enter into critical conversation with it, or attempt to hide it under blankets of method and technique—tools to control thought.

It is important to note, before anyone is tempted to interpret Gadamer as abandoning us to the relativities of history and tradition (or language), that this "conditioned me" is not the whole story. This is only the starting point for a discussion of understanding and language. Optimistically, Gadamer believes that we are partially able to rise above history, or tradition—our prejudices and pre-judgments—and to know truth despite the force of an ever-authoritative past carving out the path before us.

Self-Understanding, Prejudice and Progress

As Gadamer presents it, understanding is always self-understanding. The dialogical (back and forth, give and take) relationship we have with tradition, a mutual speaking in which truth emerges that belongs neither solely to tradition nor to us, is self-understanding. In our understanding of the world, we are coming to an understanding (of ourselves) from within tradition (culture, etc.)—both being made by tradition and making it ourselves. Self-understanding is not a self-awareness, as if looking in the mirror and reflecting upon oneself clearly, but a living out of the changing conversation between oneself and one's tradition. We do not know ourselves or the world from a distance. Gadamer writes, "The self-awareness of the individual is only a flickering in the closed circuits of historical life. *That is why the prejudices of the individual, far more than his judgments, constitute the historical reality of his being.*"[13] The movement of reason, the freedom of thought, resides not in thinking of ourselves as distanced from the world (to assume that there is a knowing subject and its object) but as fully immersed within it.

I have often found Gadamer's description of prejudice challenging and also vague. One of the best passages to help me in this regard is this one:

> [T]he historicity of our existence entails that prejudices, in the literal sense of the word, constitute the initial directedness of our whole ability to experience. Prejudices are biases of our openness to the world. They are simply conditions whereby we experience something—whereby what we encounter says something to us.[14]

It may seem like an over-generalization, but in a very real way I am my prejudices, my pre-judgments. In so far as my thinking happens, it is not happening in a vacuum but in the fertile ground of all prior experience and thought. This ground makes it possible for me to experience something new. In a sense I am programmed, not like a machine that is no greater than the sum of its parts, calculating numbers, a series of 1s and 0s on a screen, but a living creature full of beliefs, assumptions, concepts—"mind things," and so much more than I realize. My programming includes a uniquely human linguisticality, and prejudices that no programmer controls or even fully recognizes. Such prejudices do not belong to me, as if I might take them off a shelf and polish them before presentation to another person. They are my instincts and thoughts before I even know them as thoughts. They are moving me to see, hear, taste, and feel. Their sphere of influence is universal but not total.

As counter-intuitive as it may seem, Gadamer argues that hermeneutical understanding as situated self-understanding represents an overcoming of illusion through the acceptance of unavoidable ambiguity. The acceptance of prejudice as the primordial ingredient of awareness (historically effective consciousness, in language, shaping thought), is the beginning of freedom, not captivity. Self-understanding makes the idea of progress feasible, albeit awkward. Let me quote Gadamer at length:

> Hermeneutics achieves its actual productivity only when it musters sufficient self-reflection to reflect simultaneously about its own critical endeavors, that is, about its own limitations and the relativity of its own position. Hermeneutical reflection that does that seems to me to come closer to the real ideal of knowledge, because it also makes us aware of the illusion of reflection. A critical consciousness [natural science] that points to all sorts of prejudices and dependency, but one that considers itself absolutely free of prejudice and independent, necessarily remains ensnared in illusions. For it is motivated in the first place by that of which it is critical. Its dependency on that which it destroys is inescapable. The claim to be completely free of prejudice is naïve whether that naïvete be the delusion of an absolute enlightenment or the delusion of an empiricism free of all previous opinions in the tradition of metaphysics or the delusion of getting beyond science through ideological criticism. In any case, the hermeneutically enlightened consciousness seems to me to establish a higher truth in that it draws itself into its own reflection. Its truth, namely, is that of translation. It is higher because it allows the foreign to become one's own, not by destroying it critically or reproducing it uncritically, but by explicating it within one's own horizons with one's own concepts and thus giving it new validity.
>
> . . . In this process of finite thought ever moving forward while allowing the other to have its way in opposition to oneself, the power of reason is demonstrated. Reason is aware that human knowledge is limited and will remain limited, even if it is conscious of its own limit. [15]

These are dense passages. Hermeneutical progress—understanding—occurs within situated or contextualized (controlled) reflection. More importantly, it occurs when one recognizes himself as bound to higher authorities. Illusion does not belong first and foremost to one possessed of subjectivities, but one believing himself free of them and able to be free of them (those that linger). The hermeneutical ideal of knowledge, a higher truth, for Gadamer, is something achieved through translation (ultimately the same thing as understanding).[16] By modern scientific standards, this is an insane logic. The so-called enlightened hermeneutical consciousness must seem backward, dogmatic, and ignorant to the world of today. And yet Gadamer is arguing that this is the best form of human understanding, namely, translation. What then, might we make of translation? How might we argue that this human-hermeneutical understanding is progressive, i.e., an ideal worth striving after? The answer to both, for Gadamer, has something to do with the nature of language, which also presents something of an insane logic by contemporary standards.

Language in Philosophical Hermeneutics

Admittedly, the discussion of language in contemporary hermeneutics is something of a muddied subject. Language has proven to be something of a mysterious activity and/or thing. Gadamer famously claims that "Being that can be understood is language."[17] This description of language and being is almost as ambiguous as it is important to his hermeneutics. What is language, for Gadamer? Why does it matter? What is "Being that can be understood"?

As a confrontation with what he sees as a narrow description of understanding—a "naïve" and "delusional" form, best exemplified in the natural sciences—Gadamer wishes to describe language as it is, historically and ontologically.[18] As a descriptive phenomenological approach, Gadamer believes he is bringing attention to what is the case, how things are in our experience of the world. The point is not to show us how we might do things better, but first and foremost to explain how understanding unfolds, how it happens to us.

What we find in language is surprising, he argues. Most philosophers, following Plato's inspiration, have tended to see language as a set of signs and symbols that merely act as vessels of thought. Language is said to be the vast system of exterior signs and symbols we use to describe the world. These signs and symbols (conventions of language) follow after thought has emerged, after meaning and understanding has been achieved to a discernible degree. Language is representational, for it literally re-presents thought, and it is referential, connecting thought and world through its spoken and written elements. Is this not our common sense experience of language? Do we not use it to express ourselves, our ideas, whether spoken or written? Gadamer argues, "No."

Language, or rather, the linguisticality of understanding, turns out to be far more dynamic and entangling than common sense admits. Gadamer recognizes that it is difficult to see, for language hides itself behind the subject matter (reality we understand), but if we are discerning, we will soon see that everything is linguistic in character—the world, ourselves, all being is linguistic—at least in so much as it is the human person experiencing the world. Gadamer writes:

> Language, by the way, is not only the language of words. There is language of the eyes, the language of hands, pointing and naming, all this is language and confirms that language is constantly present in our transactions with-one-another [*im Miteinander*]. Words are always answers, even when they are questions.[19]

I prefer to use the term "linguisticality" or "linguistic" to bring attention to Gadamer's controversial description of language, as evident in this passage. Language is something present in our encounters with the other, e.g., world, person, work of art. Are we to think of language as the presence of intelligibility? Are we to equate the presence of language with the presence of understanding, believing that wherever there is thinking, even in the silent dialogue with oneself, there is language? The answers, for Gadamer, seem to be, "Yes." The moment we do away with language chained to words, a vast new world opens up in which all "pointing and naming," all "transactions with-one-another," all actions (e.g., hands, eyes), are linguistic.

Assuming for the moment that we allow Gadamer to make such a bold move, the consequences may be troubling. This is a claim that all understanding—all being (reality)—all truth, is linguistic in some inseparable fashion (we cannot divide the linguistic from thought; therefore we cannot divide the object from subject, knower from known, for all are linguistic). Thus, when we turn to a discussion of Mitscherling's intentionality, Gadamer argues that it too must be bound to the linguistic. Mitscherling disagrees. Language is a tool, he argues. Thought and language may be close, but they are hardly inseparable.

The Instrumentalization of Language

For Gadamer, a re-thinking of language in the context of modern thought allows us to combat the continued instrumentalization of language, and the ongoing leveling of language to technical sign-systems. We live in an era of ever-diminishing language, he argues. Widespread technical language is one "[t]hat is not speaking, for it does not have the infinity of the act that is linguistically creative and world experiencing."[20] Is our culture less able to speak, to creatively speak, and therefore to experience the world? To take language as a tool, to think of it as a utility for an end, signals this danger of speechlessness. The external form of language in semiotics, language signs, is not language or speaking, as Gadamer sees it. For Gadamer:

> Signs . . . are a means to an end. They are put to use as one desires and then
> laid aside just as are all other means to the ends of human activity. . . . But
> actual speaking is more than the choice of means to achieve some purpose in
> communication. The language one masters is such that one lives within it, that
> is, "knows" what one wishes to communicate in no other way than in linguistic
> form. "Choosing" one's words is an appearance or effect created in communi-
> cation when speaking is inhibited. "Free" speaking flows forward in forgetful-
> ness of oneself and in self-surrender to the subject matter made present in the
> medium of language. . . . Hermeneutical inquiry is based on the fact that
> language always leads behind itself and behind the façade of overt verbal
> expression that it first presents. [21]

We have forgotten, and therefore neglected, the important connection between language and thought in the Western world (with the exception of St.
Augustine, for Gadamer). The widespread emphasis on a subject coming in
contact with an object—a mind coming in contact with a world—forgets
language; it forgets that language "leads behind itself and behind . . . the
overt verbal expression." Speaking of this forgetfulness of the unity of
thought and language, Gadamer writes:

> This is to say that thought is so independent of the being of words—which
> thought takes as mere signs through which what is referred to, the idea, the
> thing, is brought into view—that the word is reduced to a wholly secondary
> relation to the thing. It is a mere instrument of communication, the bringing
> forth (*ekpherein*) and uttering (*logos prophorikos*) of what is meant in the
> medium of the voice. [22]

This instrumentalization of language manifests as an emphasis on the logical
priority of thought over linguistic expression. For example, this priority is
said to be evident in the routine experience when one lacks the right words to
speak—when one has difficulty picking just the right word to express a
thought. In such a moment, there is a realization that perhaps language obscures thought, baffles understanding. Placing method over language, to
strain thought of impurities, the new era of objectivity and linguistic instrumentalization has attempted a standardization of language so that, through a
pure sign-symbol system, we might have a better vehicle for thought. The
instrumental standardization is merely one way of overcoming the subjectivity and relativity of language—especially when knowledge is to be shared
across cultures (including labs and disciplines).

Gadamer believes that such a view of language fails to describe our
hermeneutical experience, that is, our common sense, everyday experience of
thinking, acting, being. We cannot draw a meaningful distinction between
thinking and its linguistic being, or manifestation. There is no great gap in
which to say, "Here is thinking, inside the mind," and "There is language,
outside of the mind." The thinking mind is a linguistic mind. Grondin de-

scribes this well when he states that for " . . . Gadamer, thought cannot be situated before or beyond the boundaries of language. The materiality of language is the space, the element wherein all thought can and must bring itself into being."[23]

What is linguistic? All thought is linguistic. While not all experience is linguistic, anything approaching the level of reason and reflection is brought about in language—living, adapting, malleable language. Instrumental language is said to help reduce error and misunderstanding, to stabilize the ambiguous and vague, but it is a dead language, lacking the infinite creativity necessary for experience. Born of a disdain for ambiguity, instrumental language fails to appreciate the nature of human understanding, Gadamer argues. Ambiguity is not a weakness but a strength, for language remains open to the other, rather than closed by the weight of its own dogmatism, i.e., that its truth is complete. There is no room for reflection if the truth is beyond question. It is the nature of language to possess an openness, an unsaid, that leaves us hesitant, waiting for more to complete the thought.

In Gadamer's account, the instrumental failure is evident, in so much as the scientist remains dominated by his language—his time, its concepts and prejudices.[24] If we grant that objectivity is characterized by the ultimate pursuit of closure, i.e., the final fact or truth by which to clear away alternatives, then Gadamer is correct that it is dangerous. More than this, he argues that it is "not only impossible but manifestly absurd."[25] By contrast, the hermeneutical consciousness accepts that it cannot fully escape language, and yet acts as a corrective by which reason (thought) may find greater clarity and truth.[26]

Universality of Hermeneutics: Language as Medium

Gadamer states, "For language is not only an object in our hands, it is the reservoir of tradition and the medium in and through which we exist and perceive our world."[27] It is difficult to imagine a stronger claim for language than to say that in it "we exist and perceive the world." This is his logical conclusion. If we are creatures of tradition, and language is the medium (application) of that tradition, then it follows that we meet the world linguistically. However we decide to describe the activities of thinking, understanding, and knowing, that description must have a linguistic character. Meaning comes to us through language—all meaning[28] —hence Gadamer's declaration, "Being that can be understood is language."[29]

A point sometimes overlooked in Gadamer's argument is that of solidarity. In language, we share in what is common, what connects us to one another in understanding. Language as communication draws on a sense of communing, of affirming the interconnectedness of our being (together). In language, we meet the other (person, work of art, nature, etc.); we do not merely express information "about" the other. An emphasis on language is an emphasis on our social relatedness—the activity of being-in-the-world-with-others. May we therefore conclude that everything "is" language, for Gadamer? Here are four (decontextualized but interesting) Gadamer passages:

1. "Not only is the world world only insofar as it comes into language, but language, too, has its real being only in the fact that the world is presented in it."[30]
2. "Language is the fundamental mode of operation of our being-in-the-world and the all-embracing form of the constitution of the world."[31]
3. "In language the reality beyond every individual consciousness becomes visible."[32]
4. "[I]n language the order and structure of our experience itself is originally formed and constantly changed."[33]

So, is everything language? While it may seem so, based on the above passages, Gadamer's answer is actually "No." Language is not everything. Not all being is language. Gadamer's connection between thought, world, and language is so strong that he has, since the initial publication of *Truth and Method*, needed to repeatedly affirm that he did not mean everything is language. In an interview with Jean Grondin, Gadamer clarifies his position:

> No, no, I never meant and also have never said that everything is language. Being that can be understood is language. In this is hidden a limitation. So what cannot be understood can become an infinite task, the task of finding the right word that at least comes near to this 'thing,'—*Sache*.[34]

Being is not language. Being "that can be understood" is language. Understanding is linguistic. Language is not a vehicle by which thought travels, only to disembark when it has arrived at its destination. "The linguisticality of understanding is *the concretion of historically effected consciousness*."[35] Thought is always linguistically created, challenged, and shared. We are beings that understand—think—in language. The vagaries of metaphors only go so far. The point is that any attempt to understanding the nature of our being from behind or before language is meaningless. One must think and speak such an understanding within language—the "infinite task . . . of finding the right word."

To return to our discussion of the scientist, then, we find that the universal character of understanding as linguistic prevents the universal grasp of anything objectively, instrumentally. All objects are linguistically understood and therefore not really objects at all. They are partners in an evolving conversation about truth and reality, what it means and what it looks like.

In addition, the scientific-instrumental view of language supposes a starting point for language. Let us return to our previous example of searching for the right word to express thought. Is that not an example of the failure of language to convey pre-linguistic thought? Is the failure of words proof that thought takes precedence? Gadamer argues that, before the spoken word, there is already a linguistic understanding (an inner word, if you will). In the search for the right word, one has simply failed to arrive at the right verbalization of an inner dialogue. Not yet expressing (arriving upon) the concrete word does not show a pre-linguistic source, on the contrary. Words are the manifestation of the conversation we already are, not the source of language. Words routinely fail us. The more we focus on the words, the less they mean, the less they act as living language. Our (linguistic) understanding gets lost in the word if we tarry too long on it. We must move forward, finding new words in a new relationship if we wish to continue meaning something. There is no identifiable beginning to the linguistic. It is speaking as us long before we know it externally in words.

Intentionality of Language, Freedom and Reflection

For Gadamer, in our examination of the linguistic, we also gain a sense of the movement of rationality and enlightenment.[36] The linguistic as a tool misses the power of language in at least two important respects. First, it misses that in the linguistic there is a *telos*, a hidden force moving us along with its ambitions (to answer, to know). And second, it misses the nature of our freedom, found in reflection. Having shown that the linguistic is something that speaks us more than we speak it, Gadamer's discussion of these two features of the linguistic come as welcome reprieve.

According to Gadamer, the truth that emerges in language is not that of an autonomous mind caught up in relativities and blind change (swept up in the ignorance of prejudice and whim of culture, etc.). Rather, there is something largely outside one's control. It is a product (if one may speak in such an objectivist tone) of conversation and dialogue, of one's living life with others. Gadamer repeatedly emphasizes that language is about something, namely the subject matter (reality). Language is not merely an endless loop of tradition and experience feeding inward (a vicious hermeneutical circle). It is directed toward something. There is an invisible hand at play in language, a purpose working itself out. It is the truth of the subject matter—what is the case. One, might, as Gadamer does, go so far as to claim a *telos*, a guiding force at play. "We can learn from the sensitive student of language that language, in its life and occurrence, must not be thought of as merely changing, but rather as something that has a teleology operating within it."[37] The linguistic, then, possesses a guiding force. This is important because, as

Mitscherling will argue, to make sense of experience, we need to see it as guided somehow.

In his *Enigma of Health*, Gadamer considers the nature of intelligence and reflection. He argues that today's view of intelligence is one of performance, a tool to be employed.[38] Intelligence and reflection, like language, have been leveled down, instrumentalized. "Reflection, the free process of turning in on oneself, appears to be the highest form of freedom that exists at all."[39] Reflection, for Gadamer, the ability to stand back from oneself, is freedom. This freedom is a linguistic freedom, for it is pursued in language, like all thinking. "To pursue this freedom is not itself in turn a free act but is rather something motivated, with conditions and intentional grounds which are not themselves under the control of the free exercise of one's ability."[40] The linguistic, then, is the medium of reflection and freedom.

Intelligence is the ability to reflect—in language, in life, in action. Through reflection, something new is brought into being (language) that did not exist before. This is important, for the point of hermeneutics, as Gadamer sees it, is not language as language (semiotics, words) but "the coming into language of what has been said in tradition: an event that is at once appropriation and interpretation."[41]

Speaking of the infinity of language(s), Gadamer says, "Precisely through our finitude, the particularity of our being, which is evident even in the variety of languages, the infinite dialogue is opened in the direction of the truth that we are."[42] We are, for Gadamer, an "inner infinity of . . . dialogue."[43] Our intelligence manifests in this context, through this structure. The hermeneutical discipline of reflection extols, among other things, this great activity of "uninterrupted listening."[44] The lasting importance of reason and reflection is realized in a great power, for Gadamer. "The real power of hermeneutical consciousness is our ability to see what is questionable."[45]

The Limits of Language and the Pre-linguistic

We are probably all familiar with that moment when language seems inadequate for the job of describing experience. I have no substantial words to describe the feeling of watching my first child, a boy, laying in an incubator for the first three weeks of his life. The dreadful wondering felt every day if he would live is an experience without adequate words. I have no meaningful phrase to describe my annoyance, just a moment ago, four years after his birth, at his refusal to brush his teeth for the millionth time. My mind fails to grasp, to label, even though these are my experiences. I could meditate on these experiences and come up with numerous different ways of assigning words, but such would be secondary to the experiences themselves, experiences that were meaningful without words.

Gadamer recognizes that, because our desire to understand often goes beyond any statement we make, this might seem like a critique of the linguistic.[46] Indeed, this unsayable seems to frustrate his argument about the universality of language. But are my experiences truly unsayable, or are these experiences sayable infinitely, without end? I am able to speak of them without ever exhausting the meaning, never having fully captured feeling in speech or in writing, but all of this, while infinite, is still linguistic. Moreover, I am finite, and my own language (English) is limited. The limits of "words" or "language" reflect my limits and vice versa. There is perhaps a more persuasive experience that might prove that the linguistic is not all that may be understood, that of the pre-linguistic.

There are numerous examples that we might intuitively take as non-linguistic experiences, such as gestures, laughter, dance, sense perception, ritual, imagination, non-verbal art, and music. For surely music is to be understood musically, and pain is understood . . . however pain is understood. These are not language *per se*. When I stub my toe or hear an engaging song on the radio, I am experiencing something pre-linguistic (a beat, a nerve stimuli, etc.). In the raw sensation of pain, have I not begun to understand something dispossessed of language? Have we, therefore, arrived at evidence that Gadamer's position is untenable? Not quite. For the claim of "understanding" does not seem to apply until something else emerges in my experience. Upon hitting my toe—as close to the initial moment as is reasonable to measure—thinking takes hold, language and understanding emerge, "Damn, that hurt. Why do I keep doing that on that particular door? I hope I didn't break that toe. I should wear shoes inside from now on." My thinking and language are for all practical purposes, instantaneous with the sensation. Without hesitation or reflection, I am uttering and thinking, chastising myself for doing something I have done before. To be sure, I am technically feeling pain (if I am just a nervous system) before I am speaking it, but it makes no sense to say this is a pre-linguistic experience. It is immediately linguistic (a millisecond after the pain receptors do their job), precisely because I am more than my nerves and senses.

I turned on the car radio the other day, and I was immediately grasped by a beat. It was somehow familiar and yet unknown, predictable but unnameable. Without reflection or even a conscious decision about the song, I was singing parts of it, anticipating lyrics I did not know, filling in gaps as best I could. I didn't know the song, consciously, fully, and yet I was able to sing it. After the words were out of my mouth, memories flashed a vague impulse of a by-gone era, and I recalled—after what seemed like an eternity—the name of the song, when I first learned it, and why I liked it. It is EMF's "Unbelievable." Though slow, my mind has been at work from the first sound of the song to place it, to name it (to use words to concretize my linguistic need to understand). This was a form of thinking that followed the words, for the words were simply a partial manifestation of my linguisticality, my conversation with history. Along with the song come memories of my past, a school bus trip during which one of the teachers had an emotional meltdown in frustration, trying to keep teens organized, quiet on the bus. I like the song, but I felt bad remembering its context, specifically the teacher. With EMF comes a whole world, not just a song. The pre-linguistic in both cases is but a fleeting blip in my experience, the historic and linguistic rush to fill the demands of understanding left by the stimulus.

Gadamer describes the world of language as something built up, "a process that works as if guided and one that we can always observe in children who are learning to speak."[47] Gadamer asks, "When does a child know its mother for the first time?"[48] He argues that we cannot identify a single point or event of sudden knowledge or understanding. We experience the pre-linguistic and the building up of a linguistic world without a precise event to demarcate pre-linguistic and linguistic. For Gadamer, a conversation between mother and child exists long before a word is spoken.[49] Language includes the entirety of our socialization. Reflecting on the beginning(lessness) of language and the pre-linguistic, Gadamer writes, "In his first apperception, a sensuously equipped being finds himself in a surging sea of stimuli, and finally one day he begins, as we say, to know something. Clearly we do not mean that he was previously blind."[50] What we mean is that he has, until then, not yet recognized or picked out something from the sea of stimuli. The illusion at work in the understanding is that, as Gadamer puts it, "things precede their manifestation in language."[51] The pre-linguistic perhaps feels more common than it is, for we intuitively think of thought (of things) as preceding language. Indeed, " . . . the illusion of the possibility of the universal objectification of everything and anything completely obscures this universality itself."[52]

To bring this into the context of our previous discussion, Gadamer claims that every utterance should be understood as a response to a question. To understand something is to know it within its web of questionability, the many different voices, horizons, truths, that have given an utterance or subject matter being, existence. In other words, we understand what is said by hearing what is unsaid. If all we have before us are propositions on paper, letters strewn about in order, we have very little. Such signs exist as meaningful when we know them because of an already real rationality, a world, a movement toward truth. In this way, the pre-linguistic never remains pre-, for it is always pulled into the moving river of intelligibility and meaningfulness.

Does Gadamer ignore the pre-linguistic as an unknowable realm? Yes and no. He does nothing of substance with it, but he accepts that there is a pre-linguistic. Gadamer writes:

I acknowledge that these phenomena demonstrate that behind all the relativities of language and convention there is something in common which is no longer language, but which looks to an ever-possible verbalization, and for which the well-tried word "reason" is, perhaps, not the worst.[53]

MITSCHERLING'S REALIST PHENOMENOLOGY

On the very first page of *Aesthetic Genesis*, we learn of a new "philosophy of the organism," that signals a clear departure from Gadamer's hermeneutics. Mitscherling writes:

All human experience entails and arises from our sensitive existence. In other words, all of the "higher" cognitive and perceptual activities arise from and are informed by sensation. And further: sensation itself is already "meaningful"— it too is already informed . . . .[54]

The origins of consciousness already exist, he argues, at the moment of sense perception. In the pre-linguistic, we find a world of meaning and significance, for it is already understandable, contrary to Gadamer. What we will find before language, he argues, is an "ontologically prior intentionality."[55] Even beneath (or behind, or whatever metaphor one chooses) the sensational exists the deeper origin of reality, the intentional structure of nature. Mitscherling says, "I shall be speaking of the origin in intentionality of 'reality' itself, of the 'object' as well as the 'subject.'"[56]

Mitscherling's "Copernican hypothesis" of realist phenomenology argues that it is misleading to say that consciousness is always intentional. It makes more sense, he argues, to say that out of the structure of living bodily intention, consciousness emerges. Mitscherling's emphasis throughout his book is on intentionality as a distinct kind of activity, not as material stuff (e.g., structured material) or ideal (mind) stuff.

He describes an intentional mind as something that become conscious when it "operates intentionally"—a specific kind of activity—yet intentionality remains independent of the mind.[57]

Intentionality, from which consciousness emerges, tends to be relational, he argues.[58] Intentionality is a guiding force. Experience is not structured in any logical or epistemological sense. It is guided. It makes more sense to speak of consciousness as tending to something in the present, rather than the future, as is so often done in phenomenology. Consciousness does not "intend" in the future-oriented manner we assume. Rather, consciousness attends to the present—to the dynamic activities of the moment. Mitscherling argues that consciousness has intentional being, in that it exists as the activity of relating to other bodies. Consciousness is not full of content (knowledge bits or factoids) but exists as tending to this or that—it arises out of intention-al relations.

If intentionality, which is inherent in nature, gives rise to consciousness, then, Mitscherling argues, intentionality is not unique to humans. Conscious-ness does not exist as a thing to be observed, but as, in, and through the activity of relating—which is everywhere, including the nonhuman. The be-haviour of plants and animals, all creatures (simple or complex), may be described as intentional. Are plants conscious? In a qualified sense, yes. In so much as a plant is relational, tending to this (sunlight) or away from that (acidic soil, rocks, etc.), it reveals intentionality. Mitscherling identifies a spectrum or scale of consciousness, with the more complex creature possess-ing (or being possessed) by the more obvious sense of consciousness.

Critical reflection has its foundation in a pre-linguistic—nonlinguistic—experience of bodily sensation, for Mitscherling.[59] However, even deeper than the sensational is the intentional. Sensation, as well as critical reflection, are born of the intentional structure of nature. In reflection (something that happens more to us than we make happen, according to Mitscherling), "what we have is a relation happening between or among acts of intending, which are themselves relations."[60] Conscious reflection is not constituted by the mind but follows the intentional being. It seems then, that Mitscherling is arguing that it is not "we that reflect" so much as "we who are caught up in the reflection." We are guided, moved, in some ontological manner. Mits-cherling believes that " . . . the presence of some sort of guiding force does seem to be necessary to account for my experiences."[61] The source of this guiding force needs to be external to natural activities, such as in a mind or consciousness, he believes. The *telos* of an activity belongs to the activity itself.[62]

Common Ground

Mitscherling wishes to resist the anthropocentrism of Heidegger, and pre-sumably Gadamer as well. In intentional being, we find something universal and distinctly pre-human, for while we may depend upon it, it does not depend upon us for existence.[63] The origin of meaning and value is not language but the intentional structure of nature—which is neither ideal nor material. Intentional being, not linguistic being, is constitutive of our world. Mitscherling argues for a pre-conceptual and pre-linguistic view of our expe-rience of the world:

> . . . it is not the case that we think only in words—indeed, strictly speaking, we
> do not 'think' in words at all. We use words to communicate our thoughts to
> ourselves and to others, to follow our thinking and slow it down, to record it
> and to analyze it. Language, that is, always comes after the fact of thinking.
> That is the reason behind the difficulty we so often experience in attempting to

clearly express our thoughts to others, and how it is that we might find ourselves searching for a word that's 'on the tip of our tongue.'[64]

Later on, he writes:

> The words, however, are just the vehicle of this understanding, they are not its
> content or its object. When I am speaking to the reader, the 'being' that is
> being understood is not, in short, my words, or even the meaning of my
> words—it is what the words are 'about.'[65]

And then a couple of pages later:

> Again, there is already meaning at the most primal stage of cognition—that is,
> we already 'know' perceptually what the table is as soon as we organize our
> sensations of it.[66]

The difference between Mitscherling and Gadamer on language seems obvious enough, for Mitscherling sees language as an instrument of subjectivity.
Indeed, there seems to be little room for reconciliation—unless, that is, we
accept Mitscherling's description of "words" but reject his clear implication
that words represent the entirety of the linguistic. Agreeably, words are used
to communicate, and we do not (always) think words *per se*. "Words" may
be seen as vehicles for thought, but that thought is linguistic, not bare
thought. It is thought clothed fully in the garments of one's life (pre-judgments, culture, specific language, etc.).

It seems strange to claim that I know a table the moment I see it, and that
my sensations are organized. However, it is not strange to say, with Mitscherling, that no one walks around all the time putting words on the things,
which "then" become thinkable because they have names. When I walk into
my dining room I do not think specific words "carpet," "wall," "light," etc. It
would be hopelessly inefficient and confusing to do so. This is not Gadamer's position either, as I understand him. Gadamer's argument is that the
table is intelligible, understandable, because of the web of understandings
that pre-exist words. It is a table in so much as I am applying my historically
effected consciousness (awareness), itself having the shape and form of language, in an instantaneous moment of awareness. At one time in the past, I
have named the things in my dining room, and I will do so again, but that is
only one part of my linguistic experience, and one typically done when I
must attend to a specific thing in detail. The inner word "table" does not
sound like the spoken word, so we should not expect it to. The inner word
has no sound at all, but that does not mean there is no conversation.

In response to Mitscherling, it is tempting to say that bare sensation tells
me little about the table, but, if I am honest to my experience of the table, I
do not have a recognizable experience of bare sensation—me knowing a

table, free of the linguistic (historically-informed reality). The moment I look at the table, especially in this scholarly context of thinking about it, I am swept up in its history-with-me, e.g., place of purchase, time of purchase, its reason for existence, its materiality, its physical appearance. I cannot really look at the table with my eyes alone . . . I have tried. Perhaps this is a personal failure, e.g., a lack of attunement to what is happening.

A better test is to look at something new, something never before translated and appropriated into my world. I have done this with the hopes of describing my perception of the object as pre-linguistically as possible—to judge when the linguistic takes hold. Of course, such a discernment has the character of reflection and language, but this is the best scenario I can imagine. To do this, I watched a few segments of "This Old House," specifically the "What is it?" section of the show.[67] Random objects are presented for viewers to try to figure out, e.g., what they do, what they are for, why they exist. These are generally either old, new, or very limitedly employed items, so very few people would have a context for informed guessing.

A phenomenological analysis of my experience boils down to basically this. There is a moment of perception in which I see something entirely new. I know it is new because it does not make sense. I see its colour and shape, and I am instantly curious as to how it fits into the world—what it does and why. My instinct is not to pause on my perception but to know its purpose. The naming begins right away: it is blue and red, flat and round, tall and has poles, etc. I am employing as many concepts and words as I have to make sense of the thing. There is meaning in a way, before the words, but that meaning is simply that there is something questionable before me, something that must be understood; thus it seems that even this brand new thing I am sensing is being pulled into a pre-existing dialogue. "Pulled" implies a temporal distance that does not exist. It is perhaps better to simply say that I am translating and appropriating from the moment of my first impulse.

I have an overwhelming sense that I understand that I do not understand. Of course, I already know it is an object with a *telos*; it has a purpose, that is the basis of the show, but I have not discovered it yet. My sensations are useful insomuch as I use that information. My perception is a tool for thinking. Or so it feels. Even if I assume this thing is a work of art and that it has no purpose, I am still driven to place it, to appreciate it, for it must, I assume, have meaning—it must answer a question. Until I am told what it is, there are many versions of what the thing might be, a bird house, a hat, a tackle box . . . . Upon the final reveal regarding the nature of the object, I am more often than not shocked by the true nature of the thing.

Mitscherling would disagree. Indeed, he must disagree, if he wishes to have intentionality that is free of tradition, language—anything but intentionality itself. The point of identifying intentionality is to show something that guides life throughout all nature, not merely the *telos* or guide of language and tradition for human consciousness. My account is missing an essential consideration, for it begins after the intentional.

Mitscherling discusses intentionality in the context of action—of relating to things. This is similar to Gadamer's dialogue—an activity of relating to the other. The structure of relating is a guiding structure for Mitscherling and Gadamer. Both recognize an intentionality and *telos* in the activity that we do not control—we are swept up in it. Moreover, consciousness for both Gadamer and Mitscherling arises from a certain kind of complexity. Gadamer would call it linguistic, while Mitscherling would not; yet the claims are similar, in so much as a distinct kind of being exists (unlike plants and animals). Gadamer claims:

> The power of nature flows through all living beings, including the human. Nevertheless, a separation from being controlled by nature and their so-called freedom is a fundamental characteristic of humans, by virtue of which the human world is lifted above the animal world by its rituals and capacity of showing or pointing and naming [*des Zeigens und Nennens*].[68]

Gadamer's argument, which I believe complements Mitscherling's, is that there is a degree of freedom realized in language that does not exist elsewhere, and yet "the power of nature [intentionality] flows through all living beings." I am, of course, putting words in Gadamer's mouth. Might there be room in Gadamer's account to broaden the linguistic to include all forms of intentionality, including those outside the human? Gadamer has already moved us very close to this position by admitting that there exists something behind language—reason, perhaps.

Failure of Language and Thought

Mitscherling and Gadamer share the same great foes: idealism and materialism. The failure of Gadamer's "language" as Mitscherling sees it, is that thought and language rely on a still more fundamental and ignored reality—intentionality. As exemplified through Mitscherling's own account, we find not only the failure of language to describe a realist phenomenology, something Mitscherling reminds us of repeatedly, but also the failure of thought. For every failure of language, we find a co-related failure of thought to penetrate more deeply, to describe more fully, to understand more clearly. What would it look like to understand the nature of being and intentionality without language—to think the understanding without speaking/writing the understanding? It would be to live it, to experience it, as both Mitscherling and Gadamer recognize.

Still, there is something unsatisfactory at hand. Notice that the phenomenology at play in both Mitscherling and Gadamer is one of describing what is the case. Neither offers a new method or science of method. Neither prescribes new systems of thought. Rather, both are trying to articulate what it means to experience, to live, to be a being. The success or failure of either project must be determined by whether or not there is agreement between experience and thought. What is most unsatisfactory is that both Gadamer and Mitscherling cannot be right. At base, they are describing two different versions of understanding.

To put words in Mitscherling's mouth, Gadamer gives us false hope by encouraging an infinitude of language, i.e., he claims that we are able to reach beyond our finite, historical understandings, through language, upon the back of language—not in spite of language. For all its inhibiting features (historical baggage), language is, indeed, inhibiting. Thus, Mitscherling offers a new conversation that, while steeped in language, attempts to think beyond its limitations by appeal to experience. Moreover, to couch a realist phenomenology in anything other than experience—to try to think it, speak it, write it—is to go beyond what seems possible. The great argument in Mitscherling's work is his appeal to everyday, common experience as the basis of identifying the intentionality of life. Yet even there, something is missing, something Gadamer's account may help clarify in my personal examples already discussed.

On the one hand, we have Gadamer, who argues that there is no substantial understanding aside from language, although there is experience and pre-linguistic something . . . whatever that might be. Language is the key to understanding being. On the other hand, we have Mitscherling, who argues that there is understanding separate from language. Mitscherling sweeps away the emphasis on historical consciousness, self-understanding and language, for he believes intentionality is the key to understanding being. By drawing out the notion of reason, *telos*, and even hinting at the pre-linguistic in Gadamer, I hope to have shone light on similarities with Mitscherling. By extending language to linguisticality, in the spirit of Gadamer, I have also hoped to draw out something unlike Mitscherling's "words," with the hope of perhaps finding in the linguistic something close to Mitscherling's intentionality. Of course, I cannot, for these are different, far too different. While the stark contrasts remain, a more nuanced account of Gadamer's "language" is perhaps not as stark an opponent as it initially appears. In Gadamer, we find a sympathy for the pre-linguistic, a complimentary sense that there must be a guiding *telos* to experience (that we might call "reason"), and the recognition that higher forms of consciousness may have language and reason to achieve some sense of freedom.

NOTES

1. Hans-Georg Gadamer, *Truth and Method*, 2nd rev. ed., trans. Joel Weinsheimer and and Donald G. Marshall (New York: Continuum, 2006).

2. Jeff Mitscherling, *Aesthetic Genesis: The Origin of Consciousness in the Intentional Being of Nature* (Lanham: University Press of America, 2010). Hereafter cited as AG.

3. Gadamer, *Truth and Method*, 474.

4. Relating to words in a language's vocabulary, e.g., a dictionary.

5. Relating to signs and meaning.

6. I am using "linguisticality" to emphasize the activity of language in its many different forms. "Language," especially the English vernacular, implies a static thing one possesses.

7. This is probably for good reason, because Gadamer does almost nothing with them.

8. An example that comes to mind is the discussion of nothing, which finds roots throughout philosophy (and, today, in modern cosmology). Whether one is contemplating the existence and nature of matter, God, thought, etc., the concept of nothing plays a role. In a similar fashion, the pursuit of the pre-linguistic, pursued in language, has value.

9. Gadamer: "The method of modern science is characterized from the start by a refusal: namely, to exclude all that which actually eludes its own methodology and procedures. Precisely in this way it would prove to itself that it is without limits and never wanting for self-justification. Thus it gives the appearance of being total in its knowledge and in this way provides a defense behind which social prejudices and interests lie hidden and thus protected. One need only think of the role of experts in contemporary society and of the way economics, politics, war, and the implementation of justice are more strongly influenced by the voice of experts than by the political bodies that represent the will of the society." Hans-Georg Gadamer, "The Scope of Hermeneutical Reflection," in *Philosophical Hermeneutics*, trans. and ed. David E. Linge (Berkley: University of California Press, 1977), 93.

10. One of my first experiences of this was while waiting to board a ship in Civitavecchia, just outside Rome. Standing in line, waiting patiently like everyone else, someone came and, as we I would call it here, "butted in line." The absurdity of the logic and the shaming of social convention baffled me. I was stunned. Later it became evident that this was a fairly common practice. To this day I cannot understand why it is socially permitted. This is not a valuation of either practice but an example of one's world being questioned by the other in a way that could not and would not be done at home. Having had that experience I am, in some very small way, more aware of myself than before.

11. Gadamer: "[T]he fact that one can never depart too far from linguistic conventions is clearly basic to the life of language: he who speaks a private language understood by no one else, does not speak at all. But on the other hand, he who only speaks a language in which conventionality has become total in the choice of words, in syntax, and in style forfeits the power of address and evocation that comes solely with the individualization of a language's vocabulary and of its means of communication." *Philosophical Hermeneutics*, 85–86.

12. Gadamer: "What hermeneutics legitimates is something completely different, and it stands in no tension whatever with the strictest ethos of science. No productive scientist can really doubt that methodical purity is indispensable in science; but what constitutes the essence of research is much less merely applying the usual methods than discovering new ones—and underlying that, the creative imagination of the scientist." *Truth and Method*, 551–552.

13. Gadamer, *Truth and Method*, 276–277. Cf., "Self-understanding refers to a historical decision and not to something one possesses and controls" (Ibid. 524).

14. Gadamer, *Philosophical Hermeneutics*, 9.

15. Gadamer, *Philosophical Hermeneutics*, 93–94.

16. Gadamer, *Truth and Method*, 388.

17. Gadamer: ". . . the coming into language of meaning, points to a universal ontological structure, namely to the basic nature of everything toward which understanding can be directed. *Being that can be understood is language.*" *Truth and Method*, 474.

18. Gadamer, *Philosophical Hermeneutics*, 93–94.

19. Hans-Georg Gadamer, "Zur Phänomenologie von Ritual und Sprache," as cited and translated in Richard E. Palmer "Gadamer's recent work on language and philosophy: On 'Zur Phänomenologie von Ritual und Sprache'" *Continental Philosophy Review* 33 (2000): 384. Palmer's paper is both a summarizing and interpreting essay on Gadamer's work.

20. Gadamer, *Philosophical Hermeneutics*, 16.

21. Gadamer, *Philosophical Hermeneutics*, 87–88.

22. Gadamer, *Truth and Method*, 414.

23. Jean Grondin, "The Universality of Hermeneutics and Rhetoric in the thought of Gadamer" *Symposium* 8 (2004): 330.

24. Gadamer, *Truth and Method*, 396.

25. Gadamer, *Truth and Method*, 397.

26. Gadamer, *Truth and Method*, 402.

27. Gadamer, *Philosophical Hermeneutics*, 29.

28. It would be a mistake to say that the world creates language. Equally, it is a mistake to say that we create language. The given subject matter—reality—is a product of interpretation, itself manifest in and through language, with the structure of dialogue (question and answer).

29. Gadamer: "The phenomenon of understanding, then, shows the universality of human linguisticality as a limitless medium that carries *everything* within in—not only the "culture" that has been handed down to us through language, but absolutely everything—because everything (in the world and out of it) is included in the realm of 'understandings' and understandability in which we move." *Philosophical Hermeneutics*, 25.

30. Gadamer, *Truth and Method*, 443.

31. Gadamer, *Philosophical Hermeneutics*, 3.

32. Gadamer, *Truth and Method*, 449.

33. Gadamer, *Truth and Method*, 457.

34. Gadamer, in an interview with Jean Grondin, "A Look Back over the Collected Works and Their Effective History" in *The Gadamer Reader: A Bouquet of the Later Writings*, trans. Richard E. Palmer (Evanston: Northwestern University Press, 2007), 417.

35. Gadamer, *Truth and Method*, 389.

36. Gadamer, *Philosophical Hermeneutics*, 93–94.

37. Gadamer, *Philosophical Hermeneutics*, 13.

38. Hans-Georg Gadamer, *The Enigma of Health: The Art of Healing in a Scientific Age*, trans. Jason Gaiger and Nicholas Walker (Stanford: Stanford University Press, 1996).

39. Gadamer, *The Enigma of Health*, 50.

40. Gadamer, *The Enigma of Health*, 53.

41. Gadamer, *Truth and Method*, 463.

42. Gadamer, *Philosophical Hermeneutics*, 16.

43. Gadamer, *Philosophical Hermeneutics*, 17.

44. Gadamer, *Truth and Method*, 465.

45. Gadamer, *Philosophical Hermeneutics*, 13.

46. Gadamer, *Truth and Method*, 401.

47. Gadamer, *Philosophical Hermeneutics*, 14.

48. Gadamer, *Philosophical Hermeneutics*, 14.

49. Palmer, "Gadamer's recent work on language and philosophy," 384.

50. Gadamer, *Philosophical Hermeneutics*, 14.

51. Gadamer, *Philosophical Hermeneutics*, 77.

52. Gadamer, *Philosophical Hermeneutics*, 77.

53. Gadamer, *Truth and Method*, 547.

54. AG, 1.

55. AG, 6.

56. AG, 7.

57. AG, 47.

58. AG, 51.

59. AG, 6.

60. AG, 115.

61. AG, 51.

62. AG, 52.

63. "We don't need human consciousness in order to have intentionality in this world . . . ." AG, 19.

64. AG, 129.

65. AG, 130.

66. AG, 132.

67. For an example, try "What Is It? | Two Metal Poles (with Jimmy Fallon)" https://www.youtube.com/watch?v=ca3Wp1APXeI

68. Palmer, "Gadamer's recent work on language and philosophy," 385.

Contemporary Discussion

Chapter Seven

Overcoming Husserl's Mind-World Split

Jeff Mitscherling's Aesthetic Genesis
and the Birth of Consciousness through Intentionality

Antonio Calcagno

FOR JEFF MITSCHERLING, TEACHER AND FRIEND

Jeff Mitscherling's *Aesthetic Genesis* reverses our traditional thinking about the relationship between intentionality and consciousness: Intentionality is not simply a feature of consciousness; rather, it is a "feature of the natural world."[1] Mitscherling draws upon the insights of Alfred North Whitehead and Roman Ingarden, ultimately arguing that his own view of intentionality overcomes the subjective mind-external object (world) split that dominates present-day theories of consciousness.[2] Chapter Three of *Aesthetic Genesis*, "Intentionality," introduces a Copernican hypothesis: intentionality or the directionality of reality gives rise to consciousness.

> Intentionality . . . subsists independently of the human mind. The operations of the mind, as operations of consciousness, are indeed characterized as intentionality, but this intentionality does not derive from the mind or consciousness. Our mind becomes conscious when it operates intentionally, and it does so by engaging with the intentional structures of the world of which it is part . . . [I]ntentions—operations of intentionality and structures of these operations—subsist 'objectively,' independently of the human mind. The mind operates, becoming 'conscious,' so to speak, when it engages with and in these operations.[3]

Edmund Husserl, by contrast, views intentional consciousness as bestowing sense upon, and thus constructing, objectivities. It would seem that his
view of consciousness suffers from the uni-directionality and egological dependency that Mitscherling finds untenable in classic phenomenology. In this
essay, I address his criticisms and try to show how his view of intentionality
can be applied to Husserl's phenomenology, albeit in a "heretical fashion," to
draw upon the words of Edith Stein.[4]

INTENTIONALITY AND NATURE

Edith Stein had unprecedented access to Husserl's philosophical work as it
was developing. As his first academic assistant, she understood her work to
be a collaboration with Husserl that would refine and develop what they
together understood phenomenology to be. Stein worked tirelessly on prepar-
ing Husserl's manuscripts for publication, but Husserl was always unsatis-
fied with the progress Stein had made, as he kept changing his mind on
various issues. Stein would engage Husserl in long discussions about his
work, sometimes urging him to change his mind about certain idealist ten-
dencies in his thought. One of Stein's important critiques of Husserl (and we
see the result of this critique in how she organized his *Ideas II* and *III*) was
that Husserl had to give a more foundational account of nature before he
could claim what he did about the the transcendental structure of phenomenological consciousness.[5] Though Husserl wrote much on the theme of nature,
especially in his *Nachlass*, there is little sustained treatment of the topic in his
published work. Mitscherling's framing of intentionality within the natural,
physical structure of the world in many ways takes up Stein's project and
critique of Husserl, albeit Mitscherling and Stein somewhat differ on the
precise essence of intentionality, with Stein ultimately defending a view of
intentionality rooted in consciousness.

How does Mitscherling re-inscribe intentionality into nature? He begins
with embodiment and claims that "The material body is the center of the
various intentional relations engaged in by the organism, and consciousness
arises out of these intentional relations. As the complexity of these relations
increases, so does the 'level' of consciousness. The natural intentionality that
gives rise to consciousness seems always to be relational."[6] If we read Mitscherling's philosophical claim closely, we discover that embodied beings in
nature are intentional prior to their being conscious. Their intentionality
stems from their interrelationships. All beings are embodied in one form or
another, and nature consists of a series of complex material and spiritual
relations. These relations imply interactions between the embodied things of
nature. Natural, embodied relations between things elicit consciousness, and

not the other way around, according to Mitscherling. In fact, consciousness need not always be intentional, as the early Husserl used to claim.

> To intend is, quite simply, to tend towards, or away, or with. The verb indicates an activity of 'directionally' relating. This tells us something not only about intention, but also about relation: all relations are actual instances of intention, and all instances of intention are relations, either potentially or actually. Again . . . it is misleading to say that consciousness is always intentional. Consciousness doesn't 'intend' at all. The word 'intention' as we commonly employ it has a futural, purposive or anticipatory connotation, but the act that is consciousness is always *now*. Consciousness consists in the relation, the tension between entities, so we might better say that consciousness is always 'tending' to this or that. Out of the living structure of organic intention, consciousness merges.[7]

Mitscherling displaces consciousness from its usual human center, for in nature the varied and diverse relations between nature's embodied beings could in effect produce consciousness. "The behavior of dogs, cats, insects, plants, and even single-celled organisms must be described as intentional."[8] But could not this description of consciousness simply be called sentience, and is not consciousness different from sentience? If there is a distinction between sentience and consciousness, then we inevitably and largely preserve consciousness as belonging to higher, more complex living beings. But Mitscherling notes that the tending or "stretching toward" that marks intentionality is found in all natural beings. For example, purposiveness in the natural world can be read as a sign of the intentionality we find in nature. He clarifies the aforementioned distinction between sentience and consciousness by arguing that the consciousness of higher living beings is simply a more complex and intense form of sentience:

> But there must certainly be a spectrum, or graduated scale, here, so it would be more precise to regard and locate what we call consciousness as at the 'higher' end of the spectrum of complexity of sentience . . . For example, it may or may not be the case that human consciousness is different from other sorts of consciousness in that it's guided by some peculiar sort of intelligence, but the presence of some sort of guiding force does seem to be necessary to account for my experience.[9]

If we follow Mitscherling's analysis thus far, we have a view of interrelating entities that interact and sense one another, therefore causing them to be conscious of each other. One entity stretches out to another, and consciousness is produced. Consciousness is not part of the life of an I, nor is it something that perdures; rather, consciousness is localized and becomes situated within the time frame of a specific encounter between entities. Mitscherling displaces the traditional Husserlian view of transcendental time, under-

stood as retentive, protentive, and present duration. The time of consciousness is determined by the relationality between things. Mitscherling observes:

> Consciousness does not 'really' exist at any given moment: it consists in the
> activity of a peculiar relating to one another of entities—or more precisely, it
> *subsists* in and throughout the activity of relating. This activity proceeds in
> accordance with (and may be said to 'exhibit') a form, which is distinct from
> both the 'matter' and what we call the 'content' of this activity of conscious-
> ness. The 'matter' of the activity of consciousness is the 'stuff' of which the
> act is made. It is the material foundation of the embodiment of consciousness,
> or, quite simply, the body of the organism engaged in the act of cognition. This
> is the necessary material condition (or at least one of the material conditions)
> of the possibility of cognition. [10]

This punctuated and relational view of consciousness departs from the more
traditional view of an egological consciousness that simply intends objects
before itself. The problem with this traditional view is that it cannot explain
how it is that we can be changed—more precisely, that I-consciousness itself
can be altered, by the very object it supposedly intends. Mitscherling's introduction of a natural intentionality or relationality between entities better
accounts for how consciousness itself can be altered by the relations from
which it extends.

> . . . [T]he claim of realist phenomenology is that the act of consciousness itself
> consists in the mutual creation of its two poles: constitutive elements of the act
> itself. To speak of the 'priority' of one or the other, of 'ideal' mind or 'materi-
> al' external world, is wrongheaded according to this realist phenomenology.
> But it is equally wrongheaded to deny the existence of either, or to 'reduce' the
> one to the other. Both mind and world exist, and they exist independently of
> each other—but they do not exist independently of the subsisting relation that
> gives rise to and (dialectically) maintains each of them. This subsisting rela-
> tion is intentionality at work, and we find intentionality at work everywhere. [11]

It is the relation between things, as they are found in nature, which gives
birth to consciousness. Entities of the natural world reach out and stretch out
to one another, usually in a purposive fashion. Consciousness is located
between the stretching out and touching of entities. Mitscherling gives an
example of reading or interpreting a text. The reader and the text stretch
toward one another, and intentionality subsists in the relations between the
two: consciousness of the reader as reader, consciousness of the text as text,
consciousness of meaning and interpretation, all of these ensue from the
interrelation between the reader and the text. Conscious awareness of content, forms, critique, insights, similarities, differences, etc., all manifest
themselves. The reading is guided by a kind of *logos* [12] or purposiveness,

which Mitscherling says is not to be understood in teleological terms, but more in the sense of a relatedness or possibility of relatedness between entities in nature.

INTERSUBJECTIVITY AND EMPATHY

One of the standard critiques of the phenomenological account of intersubjectivity, achieved primarily through empathy or *Einfühlung*, is its inherent solipsism: it seems that the ego constitutes the sense or meaning of the alter ego as it appears in I-consciousness. The other is never really allowed to manifest itself in her or his alterity. The reason this critique is powerful and continues to haunt phenomenology is that there is a thick egological framework that surrounds the question of intersubjectivity, a framework that sees intentionality as the unique character of consciousness. It is the consciousness of the I that is primary, and through its intentional rays it constitutes the who and the what of others. But what happens if we introduce Mitscherling's notions of intentionality and consciousness as discussed above? I believe that a relational model as proposed by Mitscherling, especially within the framework of embodiment, can overcome the problem of solipsism that we find in classical phenomenology. I propose we test the foregoing claim by turning to the account of empathy that we find in Husserl's work.

HUSSERL ON EMPATHY

Husserl claims that, in the natural attitude, one knows that one lives in an intersubjective world, and that a mutual understanding between people exists.[13] In Section 48 of the *Logical Investigations,* he maintains that we cannot have empathy or "intimate comprehension" with everyone, including those spirits that live in other stellar worlds. Empathy is described as a "mutual understanding." But how is mutual understanding possible?

On the empirical view, that is, in the natural attitude, consciousness is seen as mixed with the world through the body and through perception.[14] It is only through its empirical relation to the body that consciousness becomes a human consciousness and truly animate. It is only through the body that consciousness takes its place within the space and time (time understood as physically measured) of nature. Here, we see in Husserl what Mitscherling understands by embodiment. Husserl claims in Section 53 of *Ideas I* that a mutual understanding between animated beings belonging to one world is possible through the unique relation of the body to consciousness in a natural unity given in empirical intuition. Moreover, this unique relation of body and consciousness makes it possible for each knowing subject to discover the total world as englobing the subject and his or her fellow subjects. And it is this unique relation that permits subjects to recognize the world as being the same and only environment that belongs commonly to all subjects. In order to understand how this unique relation between body and consciousness occurs, an original apprehension, grasping or apperception (*Apperzeption*) must occur. Husserl maintains that consciousness does not lose anything in this interweaving of body and consciousness, which happens in the original grasping of the unique body-consciousness unity. Consciousness as embodied becomes an integral part of nature. This unique relation between body and consciousness can also be understood in an eidetic sense, and hence will serve as the eidetic basis for the possibility of empathy or mutual understanding, which will be treated later.[15]

Furthermore, for Husserl, the universality of essences implies that an essence is available not only to my own individual consciousness, but it is also constituted intersubjectively as an identical objective reality.[16] Hence, my individual experience of the other in empathy can become an objective reality; that is, one can also speak of subjectivity *generaliter* as an object. According to Husserl, the understanding of the other in empathy is not given as an originary act of intuition like perception. Empathy is described as a presentification (*Vergegenwärtigung*). Presentifications and *Gegenwärtigungen* (like perception) are two types of representation (*Vorstellen*). As the root etymology of both types of representation suggest, both have to do with how objects of consciousness come to present themselves in consciousness. If something is *gegenwärtig*, then the "object" of consciousness presents itself immediately, whereas in presentifications the object is made present in a secondary fashion. Take the example of memory: I remember an event of my youth. The remembering itself is an act of consciousness, but the intentional correlate of the act of remembering is not immediately present as in perception. It is recalled from a past experience. We literally make the content of memory present again (as is suggested by the German prefix *ver*). In presentifications, as in empathy, the objects of empathy, namely, the consciousness of the other, is not present to me immediately as in a perception. The consciousness of the other is not given to me like the intentional object of a perception. It becomes present through an act of empathy. It is represented in my consciousness in a non-originary fashion.

Ultimately, for Husserl, the intersubjective world is the correlate of intersubjective experience; that is, it is mediated by empathy. Empathy has a twofold goal for Husserl. First, it is an act that permits understanding of the other's consciousness. Second, if the intersubjective world is the correlate of experience as described by empathy, then it is up to the phenomenologist to describe the objectivities of the intersubjective or social world—in other words, to show how they are constituted in consciousness.[17]

EMPATHY IN *IDEAS II*

Husserl's early analyses of empathy in *Ideas I* and *II* assume many things. The discussion, therefore, will focus mainly on empathy proper and its most immediate assumption or precondition, namely, the embodied psycho-spiritual person. The goal, then, is to show how the embodied psycho-spiritual person is constituted, with particular reference to the discussion of empathy.

Husserl maintains that in the sphere of original constitution there is a certain givenness of *animalia*. Originally given is a multiplicity of things in space and time in a manifold of appearances. Also given originally are *zoa*, including human beings, understood as "rational living beings." *Zoa* are twofold unities wherein two different strata can be distinguished: unities of things and subjects, along with the subjects' psychic life. Given that human beings are given originally in the sphere of original constitution, and this being human implies mutual relations and communication between human beings,[18] one must also note that common to all human beings is a human nature. The lowest level of human being is bodily. My body is given to myself originarily.

Chapter Three of Section Two of *Ideas II* is devoted to the constitution of psychic reality through the body. The body (*Leib*, understood as lived-body and not *Körper*) is described as the medium of all perception; it is the organ of perception and is necessarily involved in all perception.[19] "We have seen that in all experience of spatio-thingly Objects, the Body is involved as the perceptual organ of the experiencing subject, and now we must investigate the constitution of this Corporeality."[20] The body is the bearer of localized sensations. One ascertains this through perception. Perception gives things immediately in their originality. Husserl gives the example of sight and touch. I can look at and touch a body just as I would touch and see any other thing, "and in this respect the appearances have entirely the same nexus as do other appearances of things."[21] I can touch my hand and I have touch sensations, but I also have touch-appearances. "I do not just sense, but I perceive and have appearances of a soft, smooth hand, with such a form." My sensation is not only a sensation but is also localized in a body. "All the sensations thus produced have their localization, i.e., they are distinguished by means of their place on the appearing Corporeality, and they belong phenomenally to it."[22] That one can have touch sensations and touch appearances means that the body for Husserl is constituted in a double way.[23] It should be noted that, "the localized sensations are not properties of the Body as a physical thing, but on the other hand, they *are* properties of the thing, Body, and indeed they are effect properties."[24]

The body can also come into contact with other material things through touch. In touching a table, I not only sense it in my hand, but I also apprehend something about the thing touched, namely, the table. I can feel whether it is hard, smooth, rough, etc. "Moving my hand over the table, I get an experience of it and its thingly determinations."[25] Husserl calls these experiences of the thing and its thingly determinations "sensings." There is a doubleness to touch in that I may touch something and acquire a sensing, but I may also have a sensation. For example, I may touch the table and feel it as smooth. When I remove my fingers and with a "different direction of attention," I feel the touch-effects or the lingering touch sensations in my fingers." . . . [My] body as a touched Body is something touching which is touched."[26]

The visual realm is distinguished from the tactual realm of sensations. In the tactual realm, one finds the external object and the body as a second object, both as tactually constituted. Hence, when I touch the table, I sense the table as smooth, but I also find myself as a touching body. In seeing, I do not see myself as seeing as I would in touching, where I sense myself as touching-touched.[27] It should be noted that Husserl also comments on hearing, but not to the extent that he does on touch and sight. Hearing, unlike touching, does not have any localized sensings. So in touching the table, the "smoothness" becomes localized in the fingers. In the case of the ear, "[t]he ear is 'involved,' but the sensed tone is not localized in the ear."[28]

It was mentioned earlier that the body is involved in all perception. One can see this also in kinaesthesis. In sense perception, the body is presupposed. Perception is not a purely psycho-spiritual phenomenon. For example, when I see something, my eyes are directed upon the seen. If I do not hear something, I move my body closer to the speaker or incline my ear in order to hear better.[29] The body moves as an "organ of sensation" in order to help the individual sense organ sense or perceive better. There is a co-movement, as it were, which occurs between the rest of the body and the particular sense organ.

Husserl also sees other types of sensations as being localized in the body: sensuous feelings, feelings of pleasure and pain, the feeling of well being that can permeate a whole body, and the sensation of general malaise of "corporeal indisposition."[30] The feeling of pleasure aroused by the touch of another's hand causes one to smile, the smile being an indication of the sensation of pleasure. The feelings are immediately localized in the body.[31] Husserl concludes his treatment of sensation by clarifying a vital point. The body is a physical-aesthesiological unity. Hence, one cannot separate the physical body from the field of sensation.[32]

In addition to the bearer of localized sensation, the body is also described as an organ of the will and a seat of free movement. "'I can' move my body immediately and spontaneously. I can will to move my hand in a circular fashion. Moreover, in moving my body spontaneously and immediately, I can cause other material things to move. I can strike the table, causing the glass of wine to tumble to the floor. The Ego has the 'faculty' (the 'I can')"[33] to move freely its body and to perceive the external world by means of it. In freedom, in the "I can" of the ego, I can choose to turn my eye to look on the table. There is a fundamental sense of freedom articulated as the "I can," which is fundamental to the constitution of the body—a bodily "I can."[34] It is in Husserl's treatment of the body, therefore, that one finds the more basic form of the "I can" as a bodily "I can." Freedom is not something that is only found in consciousness or higher social objectivities; it is also bodily.

Just as the body can be freely moved by the will of the ego in a spontaneous and immediate way, the body can also be moved; it can "be done to." It has a certain passivity.[35] I can find my hand moved or my foot struck. The body itself is apprehended as something that affects others in free spontaneous movement and upon which others have effects in its passivity. The apprehension of this affectivity of the body in terms of passivity and activity shows that the body is an integral part of a natural causal nexus. The body, in apperceiving that it is struck, recognizes that this hit causes the foot to move, and as such is aware of the body as part of a causal nexus.

In addition to being constituted as a bearer of localized sensations, an organ of the will and seat of free movement, and as internal part of the causal nexus, the body is also seen as a center of orientation. All spatial being necessarily appears as nearer or farther, below or above, right or left, etc. It appears in relation to my body. The "far" is far from me; my "above" just as the "below" stands in relation to my body. Husserl says that one can affirm that I perceive that my body is "here" and all things over and against me are "there." "The Body then has, for its particular Ego, the unique distinction of bearing in itself the zero point of all these orientations."[36]

The preceding description of the body is vital for Husserl's understanding of empathy. Why? First, it points to the fact that phenomenology is not only concerned with consciousness but also with the body, and that the body plays an important role in the constitution of objects. This is definitely the case with empathy. The body receives and acts on objects in order that sense experiences may arise. Second, the body serves as the most basic level of mediation and contact with the external world. The world outside of us is sensed and felt through bodily perceptions. The body serves as a locus for the reception of sense data and experiences. The body also causes experiences and phenomena to occur. Such is the case with the aforementioned touching-touched example. The activity and passivity (read receptivity) of the body make the body capable of receiving and transmitting sense perceptions, including the givenness of the other's body as a sensual, lived body. Finally, it is the very data and experiences acquired through the medium of the active and receptive body that one comes into contact not only with external objects but also with other bodies like the embodied "I." The body alone does not constitute the other. Rather, it serves as the most fundamental layer through which the body of another becomes sensed. Consciousness will ultimately constitute and give sense to the other, but in order for consciousness to do so, it needs the basic and vital data given by perception as delivered through the body. The body itself is not capable of empathy. Nonetheless, it provides a fundamental locus and serves as a vital medium of ground material necessary for consciousness to give sense to objects.

Immediately following his treatment of the body, Husserl introduces his discussion of empathy. Recall that the body is a physico-psychic unity, insofar as it is corporeal and also sentient (and therefore, psychic). Both Husserl and Stein give the term *Einfühlung* to the act of consciousness that permits consciousness to know or become inwardly aware of foreign or other consciousnesses. For Husserl and Stein, *Einfühlung* never means that the consciousness of the ego and that of the other are identical, an *Einsfühlung*. Rather, both philosophers see *Einfühlung* as an act of consciousness that allows the ego to recognize the other ego as an other ego and to understand, in some part, the consciousness of the other, both *qua* his or her activity and content. Yet, the consciousness of the ego is not reducible to the consciousness of the other and vice versa. The ego literally "enters into" (*ein*) the life of the alter ego. Yet, entering into the life of the other ego does not necessarily imply knowing or understanding the consciousness of the other completely, totally or absolutely.[37] There is a coincidence and a non-coincidence between the ego and the alter ego, but never a relation of identity between the ego and the alter ego. This is significant because both Husserl and Stein will want to preserve the integrity and dignity of the individual ego, while at the same time allowing this very individual ego the capacity to comprehend and interact with the other.

In order to describe what empathy is as an act, Husserl makes the distinction between primal presence and apprece. The latter refers to the former. "If we give the name *original perception* to the lived experience in which a subject has the perceived object given in original presence, then that means the object is there 'actually,' 'in the original,' and is not merely co-presented. Hence, there is a difference between primal presence and apprece."[38] Primal presence does not mean that an object has to present all of its inner determinations or proper attributes. Husserl affirms two things about the nature of primary-presencing objects of original perception. First, that which primally presences, presences *idealiter* not only for one subject, but also to all other subjects as well. Husserl clarifies what exactly can be given primally by calling it "nature in the first and original sense."

> The totality of objects that can be given as primally present and that make up a domain of common primal presence for all communicating subjects is *nature in the first and original sense*. It is spatio-temporal-material nature: the one space, the one time, the one world of things for all: the one that can be given as primally present to all.[39]

Second, Husserl affirms that one can make the distinction between what is properly subjective to the subject, and the objective, which lies over and against the subject. Hence,

> . . . the subjective is the individual-unique, the temporal, the total content of original presence that can be given to only one subject in primal presence. Each subject belongs here itself along with all its acts, states, noematic corre-lates, and, furthermore, with the Corporeality and the properties, or faculties, constituted in it in the inner attitude. [40]

In original perception, the subject primally presences to itself and is distin-guished from that which stands over and against it—namely, the objective. Husserl sees the subject as having immediate access to itself through original perception.

For Husserl, human beings as components of the external world are origi-nally given, in so far as they are apprehended as unities of corporeal bodies and souls. I experience the bodies standing over and against me in primal presence just as I would any other things. The interiority of the other's psyche is experienced in appresence. How do I know that the object before me is a unity of corporeal body and psyche similar to mine as described previously? The previous description of the psychic body is solipsistic, in that the description revolves around the experience of the ego's own body. In other words, how do I know that the object before me in primary presence is another psycho-bodily unity? Empathy is the act that allows me to do so. Empathy is described as a kind of apprehension where I understand the object of my perception not as any object, but as a body similar to mine. Husserl says that he "feels" by empathy that the object is a body similar to mine. Moreover, I also feel that in this body there is an ego-subject similar to mine. There is also a transference of the localization that I accomplish in sense-fields and the indirect localization of the ego's spiritual activities. [41] I understand that the object becomes an embodied psycho-spiritual ego-subject similar to myself through empathy. Husserl says that this other embodied psycho-spiritual ego-subject is given to me as a primary presence.

Just as I experience my body as the localization of sense, so too through empathy I can experience the other's body as a localization of sense. This is given in primary presence. Husserl reminds us that with experienced local-ization, there is always continual coordination of the physical and the psychi-cal. This co-ordination is called a co-presencing. [42] All of this coordination is seen as belonging together and, therefore, as co-presencing. This is given immediately to the ego in originary experience. How do I understand this co-presencing in the other ego-subject? I see the other ego-subject's co-presenc-ing immediately as originarily given, and I know it is similar to mine through the transference over in empathy. "Yet to the appearance of the other person there also belongs, in addition to what has been mentioned, the interiority of psychic acts."[43] What appresences to me is the interiority of the other's experience of the co-presence. Hence, I can see in primary presence that the other has a similar co-presencing of coordination between body and psyche (through an understanding of causality), and therefore, a psychic interiority similar to mine; however, the other's experience of the coordination is appresented to me "in presentified co-presence." The other's interior experience of co-presence is not immediately present (*Gegenwärtigung*) to me. Rather, it appresences to me as a representation (*Vergegenwärtigung*) of the other's interiority based on my own immediate experience. I do not have immediate access to the other's interiority; it is appresented to me through empathy.

Body and psyche are coordinated and immediately seized as such through co-presence. Empathy makes me understand this coordination of the other as similar to my own experience of coordination, and yet I understand the other's experience in his or her own interiority. Thus, a system of signs develops that expresses certain psychic events. For example, a frown may reveal the other's state of mind as somewhat sad or depressed. Husserl tries to account for the fact that we have a grammar of psychic expression through a mutual understanding of bodily and psychic coordination.[44] This mutual understanding is achieved through empathy. Husserl's point regarding the possibility of a grammar of expression may seem banal today, but Husserl's insight is relevant, since empathy (in its most basic form) is shown as being valuable for other sciences. The grammar of psychic expression certainly is part of psychology. Empathy is shown as being vital for one's understanding of the other within the framework of a grammar of psychic expression. This grammar of psychic expression is also relevant, because it is an intimation of Husserl's greater project, which is to show how other sciences are grounded in phenomenology.

To recapitulate, we have seen that empathy is a "polysemantic" act, in that it achieves different things. Essentially, it achieves understanding between the ego-subject and another ego-subject. As an act of understanding, it achieves many types of understanding through presence and appresence. It allows for the understanding of the object of consciousness to be seen as an embodied psycho-spiritual (unity) ego-subject like the solipsistic ego. It makes the ego-subject understand the other ego-subject as a similar ego-subject, in terms of bodily, psychic and spiritual (unity) constitution through a transferred co-presence. The ego-subject sees the other ego-subject as possessing a psychic interiority similar to the ego-subject's. Finally, empathy allows one to understand the interiority of the other through appresence. The consequence of this last meaning of empathic understanding is that empathy has larger ramifications for mutual understanding in other sciences, as testified by the grammar of expression being possibly considered part of a science (albeit in a seminal form). Moreover, empathy as understanding of the psychic interiority of the other in appresence is vital for an understanding of larger social objectivities composed of a multiplicity of ego-subjects.

It seems that the other is constituted from the viewpoint of the ego. The ego appears to constitute the other, and hence, the other seems to be reduced to the sphere of the ego's immanence, which leads to the charge of solipsism that has plagued Husserl. Husserl would respond to the charge by reminding us that the ego is universal, and therefore, is also a "we." Second, for Husserl, all that is subjective about the ego is not only encountered in solipsistic experience; the other also helps form the subjectivity of the ego through empathy. "It is only with empathy and the constant orientation of empirical reflection onto the psychic life that is appresented along with the other's Body and that is continually taken Objectively, together with the Body, that the closed unity, man, is constituted, and I transfer this unity subsequently to myself."[45] Empathy, then, may be reciprocal. It is not simply a one-directional (unilateral) act emanating from the life of the ego. The other, who is also an ego, can influence my ego, in that I can learn something about my subjectivity through the other.

Because both the ego and the other are embodied psycho-spiritual unities (or body-soul unities), and because such unities are embodied in space, empathy must also be viewed from the vantage point of space. "In order to establish a mutual relationship between myself and an other, in order to communicate something to him, a Bodily relation, a Bodily connection by means of physical occurrences, must be instituted. I have to go over and speak to him. Thus space plays a major role here . . . "[46] I am given to myself as a "here," whereas the other is given as a "there," standing over and against me. Yet in empathy, the other is understood as a "here" as well, in that the other is understood in my interiority that is primordially given as a "here." The question then becomes, how does one conceive of space, especially the space of the other, in empathy. It should be noted that Husserl, having achieved an act of empathy, calls the similar body-psyche unities "analogons." The ego is the analogon of the alter ego. Empathy allows the ego to understand the space of the other as "there" but also as a "here" in so far as the ego can "trade places" with the other—all of course, within the realm of consciousness. Likewise from the perspective of the other's place, I can view myself as an object.[47] Space and the trading places it implies means that empathy may also be reciprocal; that is, it is not a unilateral act. I can learn about my subjectivity by trading places with the other, thereby seeing myself as an object. My subjectivity is not constituted solipsistically, but concomitantly with the other, understood in and through empathy.[48] Finally, it is this trading places of analogons in space that permits one to have an idea of "Man as Object." Standing from a "there" and looking at my "here," I become an object. Moreover, Husserl notes that this object "Man" is not exclusively immanent, but becomes transcendent in that space, and the trading places in space makes it possible to experience the object "Man" as two strata.

In short, the human becomes an object of nature that can be examined intersubjectively, however, "human" is not understood in a full sense. Rather, "human" refers to the basic psychic-bodily unity. "Empathy then leads, as we saw earlier, to the constitution of the intersubjective Objectivity of the thing and also that of [hu]man, since now the physical Body is a natural scientific object."[49] As an object, "man" as a physico-psychic unity can be examined in scientific terms, in phenomenological terms, through which one can acquire insight into the essence of man. Empathy not only describes the act whereby one individual ego understands another ego, but it also delivers an object of scientific inquiry, namely, man. The psycho-physical unity of the human is considered to be a part of nature, a nature that is intersubjectively constituted. "Then there are constituted the other subjects, apperceived as analogons of oneself and, at the same time, as natural Objects; nature is constituted as intersubjectively common and as determinable Objectively (exactly), and oneself as subject is constituted as member of this 'Objective nature.'"[50] Husserl is quick to point out that object "human," the object of nature that can be investigated scientifically, is not disconnected from the mutual understanding that occurs between psycho-physical ego-subjects. Husserl uses the term "index" to describe the relation between the two. One literally points to the other, and they are relative to one another.[51]

Empathy, for Husserl, has revealed an intersubjective world of psycho-physical ego-subjects (unities) that can understand one another as ego-subjects, both in appresence and primal presencing, but also as objects that can be studied scientifically. Hence, possible through empathy is an object called "subjectivity." Up until this point, subjectivity has been described in its most rudimentary or natural form as psycho-physical unity. We must now consider the spiritual dimension that elevates the constitution of the natural unity "Human" to a "Person." Again, empathy will be considered in two senses. Empathy will be seen as the act that permits the mutual understanding of one person by another as person. Like in the preceding discussion of nature, however, the other's spiritual interiority can only be experienced in appresence. Empathy is also vital for allowing us to understand what the essence of the "Person" or "Spiritual subject" is as an object of inquiry. In other words, we can also posit an essence of "spiritual Subject."

NEGOTIATING THE NATURAL AND THE PHENOMENOLOGICAL ATTITUDES: RETURN TO MITSCHERLING'S WORK

Had Husserl not insisted on such a radical split between the phenomenological attitude and the natural attitude, further complicated by his turn from a realism (*Logical Investigations*) to a transcendental idealism (*Ideas I* and *Cartesian Meditations*)—a turn which Mitscherling discusses at various points in *Aesthetic Genesis*—one can find in Husserl a view of "natural" (that is, phenomenologically non-reduced) consciousness that is mixed with the world. It would seem that in the opening sections of *Ideas I*, Husserl is willing to admit that a natural view of consciousness is possible. On this view, consciousness is described as a kind of sentience, and it seems to be dependent upon other entities for it to arise. There is a natural intentionality (albeit it is still described as an intentionality) that belongs to consciousness and that is marked by an awareness of things. We do not find in Husserl the kind of intentionality that Mitscherling advocates, but we find intimations of a consciousness dependent upon nature for its function. The description of natural consciousness that Husserl puts forward stresses relationality, dependency, but intentionality is not central; rather, it would seem that the mixed relations of things in nature seem to be conditions for human consciousness. Though we must ascribe a more direct intentionality to consciousness as Husserl describes it, I wonder if we can also infer a more oblique form of intentionality that we can attribute as existing between things, as they sense one another, a kind of natural and sensate interrelating that gives rise to the natural, mixed form of consciousness described at the beginning of *Ideas I*? It is obvious from Husserl's descriptions at the beginning of *Ideas I* that there are different kinds and grades of consciousness. If this is the case, then why can we not also accord the same kind of grades and intensities to intentionality in Husserl's description, the very grades and intensities that Mitscherling argues are constitutive of his view of intentionality? If we admit an oblique form of intentionality, which we find in nature while we live in it in the natural attitude, then we find in Husserl some room for the kind of intentionality that Mitscherling sees as originary of consciousness.

Furthermore, Husserl makes the distinction between straight and oblique empathy. [52] In straight or direct empathy, there is an understanding of the other's experience as original and direct, whereas in oblique empathy the understanding is based on reproduced experience, recalled from the past, which is not seized in immediate reflection on the other's experience. The foregoing distinction opens up the discussion of empathy to being one of grades and intensities. Also, Husserl describes different kinds of empathy, as we saw with our earlier discussion of the grasping of the psychological and spiritual content of acts of empathy, which imply grades of complexity of understanding. Though Husserl insisted on the split between the natural and the phenomenologically reduced world, if we follow Stein's and Mitscherling's notions that these two realms are interdependent and condition one another, then we can see in Husserl's oblique and lower level descriptions of empathy, especially when it comes to sensation and the body, as discussed above, a kind of consciousness that ensues and thickens—that is, a consciousness that becomes more aware of itself as it relates to other entities with which it finds itself immersed in the natural world.

Mitscherling proposes a more grounding and originary understanding of the genesis of consciousness through a natural and relational intentionality, an intentionality that gives rises to sensation, an aesthetic genesis. Husserl, though he cannot admit the originary possibility that Mitscherling offers us, as he wishes to preserve the purity and apodicticity of his essences, nevertheless intimates aspects of Mitscherling's project in his analysis of the arising of consciousness in nature, in the natural attitude, and in his account of empathy. Edith Stein sees the need to connect nature and the ideal world of phenomenology, hence her reluctance to speak of the *epoché* and her attempts to weave a way through the nettling world of realist and transcendental phenomenology, always trying to be faithful, yet critical, of her beloved Husserl's project. Mitscherling's unique contribution to phenomenology is that he pushes us back to a more originary understanding of consciousness and intentionality, which ultimately undoes the mind-world, ideal-real, split that has haunted much of modern philosophy.

NOTES

1. Jeff Mitscherling, *Aesthetic Genesis: The Origin of Consciousness in the Intentional Being of Nature* (New York: University Press of America, 2010), 26. Hereafter cited as AG.
   2. AG, 26.
   3. AG, 48.
   4. Edith Stein, *Letters to Roman Ingarden*, trans. Hugh Chandler Hunt (Washington, D.C.: ICS Publications, 2014), Letter 6, February 3, 1917, 40.
   5. Ibid.
   6. AG, 50–1.
   7. AG, 51.
   8. AG, 51.
   9. AG, 51.
   10. AG, 52.
   11. AG, 53.
   12. AG, 56.
   13. Edmund Husserl, *Ideas Pertaining to a Pure Phenomenology and a Phenomenological Philosophy: General Introduction to a Pure Phenomenology*, trans. F. Kersten (Dordrecht: Springer, 1982), §28. Hereafter cited as Ideas I.
   14. Ideas I, §39.
   15. Ideas I, §53.
   16. Ideas I, §135.
   17. Ideas I, 363.

18. Edmund Husserl, *Ideas Pertaining to a Pure Phenomenology and a Phenomenological Philosophy: Second Book Studies in the Phenomenology of Constitution,* trans. R. Rojcewicz and A. Schuwer (Dordrecht: Springer, 1989), 170. Hereafter cited as Ideas II.

19. Ideas II, 61.
20. Ideas II, 152.
21. Ideas II, 152.
22. Ideas II, 153.
23. Ideas II, 153.
24. Ideas II, 154.
25. Ideas II, 153.
26. Ideas II, 155–56.
27. Ideas II, 155–56.
28. Ideas II, 156.
29. Ideas II, 61.
30. Ideas II, 160.
31. Ideas II, 160.
32. Ideas II, 163.
33. Ideas II, 159.
34. Ideas II, 159–60.
35. Ideas II, 167.
36. Ideas II, 166.
37. Rudolf A. Makkreel, "How is Empathy Related to Understanding?," in *Issues in Husserl's Ideas II,* eds. T. Nenon, L. Embree (Dordrecht: Kluwer, 1996), 203.
38. Ideas II, 170–71.
39. Ideas II, 171.
40. Ideas II, 171.
41. Ideas II, 172.
42. Ideas II, 173–74.
43. Ideas II, 174.
44. Ideas II, 175.
45. Ideas II, 175.
46. Ideas II, 176.
47. Ideas II, 177.
48. Ideas II, 177–78.
49. Ideas II, 178.
50. Ideas II, 179.
51. Ideas II, 180.
52. Edmund Husserl, *Zur Phänomenologie der Intersubjektivität. Texte aus dem Nachlass. Erster Teil (1905–1920),* ed. Iso Kern (The Hague: Martinus Nijhoff, 1973), in *Husserliana,* volume 13, 401–402.

Chapter Eight

Artistic Creation

On Mitscherling and Dylan

Paul Fairfield

The term "aesthetic genesis," as Jeff Mitscherling defines it in his remarkable book of that title, connotes at once aesthetic experience and artistic creation. These two phenomena, he argues, are structurally similar and, in the case of the latter, somewhat less mystifying than has traditionally been supposed. "The topic of artistic creativity," he writes, "is most definitely the black sheep of the aesthetic-theory flock. Nobody wants to talk about it." The virtually orthodox view on the matter has long been that the process by which a work of art comes into being is so utterly unanalyzable that only fools rush in with interpretations and theories with which more prudent scholars wish nothing to do. Perhaps the explanation for this silence is that the creative process is "buried so deep in the soul" that it is simply impenetrable; then again, perhaps it is "because it's too 'subjective,' maybe because it's so obviously 'mysterious'—or maybe because we're all just waiting for somebody else to talk about it."[1] Whatever the explanation, the topic permits and indeed requires phenomenological interpretation. My aim in what follows is twofold: to analyze Mitscherling's account of artistic creation in *Aesthetic Genesis* and *The Author's Intention* and to test this account by bringing it into contact with the autobiographical reflections of an artist who has been called "the Shakespeare of songwriting," Bob Dylan. For all his famed mystique, no contemporary artist has offered more insight into the creative process than this one, nor has any had their work more frequently analyzed and dissected, for better or for worse. This chapter takes a close look at Dylan's infrequent but illuminating descriptions of his own songwriting process, descriptions that in important ways afford a test case and, in some ways, corroboration of some themes in Mitscherling's account.

FOLLOWING THE *LOGOS*

That our theme is elusive—indeed, highly elusive—is a self-evident fact. That it defies description utterly, however, is another matter. In an interview with 60 Minutes in 2004, Dylan responded to Ed Bradley's question, "Where did ['Blowin' in the Wind'] come from?" in these words: "It just came. It came from right out of that wellspring of creativity, I would think." Asked further about some of the era-defining songs of his early period, he remarked:

> I don't know how I got to write those songs. Well, those early songs were like almost magically written.... Well, try to sit down and write something like ["It's Alright, Ma (I'm Only Bleeding)"]. There's a magic to that, and it's not Siegfried and Roy kind of magic, you know, it's a different kind of a penetrating magic.

Artists have always struggled to explain the creative process, and philosophers have struggled along with them, often resorting to otherworldly explanations that are little preferable to a shrug of the shoulders. How does one write a song, a poem, a novel, or accomplish any manner of creative work? What is the process like, and from a first-person point of view? Mitscherling's hypothesis is that "perhaps it's not really all that mysterious after all," that artistic creation is largely identical in structure to the activity of the listener, in the case of music, or to aesthetic experience in general. Creative work, as he conceives of it, is "not so much creation as it is apprehension, or recognition. Perhaps artistic creativity has to do less with creation *ex nihilo* than with the discovery of what's already there, of what's just sitting there, waiting to come into being. Michelangelo said of his later sculpture that he freed the figures from the stone. And isn't this really closer to the truth of all 'creative' endeavour?"[2]

There is more than an element of mystery here, as artists and philosophers since ancient times have never ceased to remark. There is no formula, no tidy set of procedures to consult, but to say that the matter is mysterious is not quite to say that it is mystical or wholly beyond the reach of experience. Our theme is not ineffable; it is merely elusive. No appeal need be made to any conception of "genius" that suggests a capacity not found in the mental equipment of ordinary human beings, or to equally otherworldly notions of "inspiration" and so on. Artists, according to Mitscherling, are not unlike the rest of us. They are merely good—on occasion superlatively good—at doing what we all do every day. But what is that? Mitscherling speaks of it as a mode of following; the artist is imaginatively following, for want of a better term, the *logos*. So too in the encounter with the work of art, "[w]e're actively *following* the reception of these bits of data [in the case of the visual work of art], these colours, this visual *stuff*. We're tracing the progress of our gaze, and adjusting our sight as we proceed. We're establishing relations, getting familiar with the lay of the painted land." Following, apprehending, recognizing, and discovering are all apposite verbs here. In the account that he provides, "[t]he familiar hermeneutic dictum that 'you see yourself in art' is no longer an empty romantic pronouncement—it here assumes a much richer and far more profound *ontological* significance."[3]

It is nothing less than a wholesale revision of hermeneutical ontology and indeed phenomenology that Mitscherling attempts, with much influence from Roman Ingarden and other proponents of realist phenomenology. The basic point of his "Copernican hypothesis" is that "intentionality is found to reside in the structures of the natural world itself, and that the human consciousness that we have long privileged as the origin of intentionality appears now to find its own origin in the intentional being of nature."[4] Mitscherling reverses the standard phenomenological hypothesis regarding the intentionality of consciousness, instead locating intentional structures at least partly beyond the realm of subjectivity. In realist phenomenology, there is intentionality in the world, which minds do not constitute so much as apprehend. "[W]hat we call consciousness arises from intentionality," he and his co-authors state in *The Author's Intention*; consciousness "is indeed an emergent feature of organisms comprising complex intentional structures, just as 'sentience' is an emergent feature of organisms comprising less complex intentional structures."[5] Intentions, then, "subsist 'objectively,' independently of the human mind. The mind operates, becoming 'conscious,' so to speak, when it engages with and in these operations."[6]

Mitscherling formulates the point as follows:

> [T]he claim of realist phenomenology is that the act of consciousness itself consists in the mutual creation of its two poles: the subject and the object of the act of consciousness both arise within and as constitutive elements of the act itself. To speak of the 'priority' of one or the other, of 'ideal' mind or 'material' external world, is wrongheaded according to this realist phenomenology. But it is equally wrongheaded to deny the existence of either, or to 'reduce' the one to the other. Both mind and world exist, and they exist independently of each other—but they do not exist independently of the subsisting relation that gives rise to and (dialectically) maintains each of them. This subsisting relation is intentionality at work, and we find intentionality at work everywhere.[7]

We find it, to take one of his examples, in material bodies such as the paramecium which, when viewed under a microscope, does not merely lie inert. It tends this way and that, displays movement and directionality which is not an imposition of mind or "a determination of the subject," as Martin Heidegger put it, but belongs to the thing itself.[8] Organisms are continually responding to their environment, and in more complex ways as their material structures become more complex. An intention is most fundamentally an affair of tending, being in motion, and being directed by what he calls a *logos*. The notion of substance as well, "(like Heidegger's 'being,' *Sein*), refers to nothing other than a kind of activity" rather than a thingly entity which subsequently becomes directed toward an end.[9]

In this ontology, a substance may *be* in any of three ways. Natural objects, such as bodies, exist "materially"; concepts, meanings, and numbers exist "ideally"; while the third category is designated as "intentional being." The three categories of substance are "ontologically distinct kinds of *activity*" rather than categories of "stuff," and the third on this list is of particular importance to our theme. The items that fall under the heading of intentional being include, along with works of art, minds, consciousness, relations, traditions, behaviour, and habits, among other things. On this view, it is this "third mode of being, neither material nor ideal, that in fact grounds the possibility of minds and bodies." Whereas material and ideal beings are said to exist, intentional beings subsist. Consciousness, for instance, "doesn't 'really' exist at any given moment: it consists in the activity of a peculiar relating to one another of entities—or more precisely, it *subsists* in and throughout that activity of relating."[10] It is the nature of intentional entities to direct activity and awareness in a certain way, to provide them with a bent or direction that is specific, in the way that a conversation or a game directs our thoughts and actions in a particular manner. To act here is to respond or follow along in the trajectory that the intentional structure sets forth, a description that applies to aesthetic activity as well as the lion's share of what human beings do.

The notion of habit is especially important here. Returning, as he frequently does, to Plato and (especially) Aristotle, Mitscherling characterizes a habit as a behavioural structure as well as "a manner in which one 'is' in the world." To form a habit is not merely to repeat a given course of action but to acquire or participate in a way of being. Plato famously worried about the imitation of the child, on grounds that children become what they imitate; that is, they come to participate in the same form of life as their models, for better or for worse. The worry is entirely reasonable, Mitscherling believes, as both the arguments of Plato and Aristotle as well as evidence from contemporary psychology show that environmental factors have a profoundly formative influence on the young: "a good part of a child's earliest education consists precisely in imitating the actions of her elders, and were the child to imitate a bad example, she might easily herself become bad." Education in the form of repeated imitation and habit formation forms the soul. It is not only actions that are habitual in this way but consciousness itself, which tends one way or another as a consequence of the way of being in which it has participated with others. Learning how to speak a language, for instance, involves acquiring through imitation particular patterns of speech, which become habitual. Consciousness itself is learned in this way; it is a habitual mode of action which invariably exhibits some form of learned directedness. All human action and cognition develop like this, Mitscherling holds; they are governed one and all by habits which are themselves examples of intentional being.[11]

The heart of Mitscherling's conception of artistic creation is the notion of apprehending intentional structures that are in the world. Artists do not create works or meanings *ex nihilo*, nor are they "inspired" in the ancient sense of the word. Plato was perhaps the most important ancient proponent of the inspiration theory of art, according to which the creative act is "a power divine, impelling you like the power in the stone Euripides called the magnet." As Plato expressed it in the *Ion*,

> [T]he Muse . . . first makes men inspired, and then through these inspired ones others share in the enthusiasm, and a chain is formed, for the epic poets, all the good ones, have their excellence, not from art, but are inspired, possessed, and thus they utter all these admirable poems. So it is also with the good lyric poets; as the worshiping Corybantes are not in their senses when they dance, so the lyric poets are not in their senses when they make these lovely lyric poems. No, when once they launch into harmony and rhythm, they are seized with the Bacchic transport, and are possessed—as the bacchants, when possessed, draw milk and honey from the rivers, but not when in their senses. So the spirit of the lyric poet works, according to their report.

What artists report, Socrates observes, is that they do not know how it is that they do what they do. Something comes over them, takes hold of them and works through them, something that is not the artist him- or herself and that is of a divine nature: "the deity has bereft them of their senses, and uses them as ministers, along with soothsayers and godly seers; . . . it is not they who utter these precious revelations while their mind is not within them, but . . . it is the god himself who speaks, and through them becomes articulate to us."[12] Assuming their work is of some merit—"and only [great] art is under consideration here"—the artist's voice is not their own.[13] They are Hermes-like messengers of the gods. This, according to the ancient theory, is the meaning of inspiration and the logic of artistic creation.

As one might expect, Mitscherling does not regard artists in quite such a religious light. They are not "conduit[s] of communications from the divine," but conduits of a more worldly kind they may well be. Above all, they are followers. The act of following here is nothing as simple as a dog picking up on a scent and tracking it to its source, but the image is not wholly inapt. There is something going on in the world—Mitscherling calls it an "intention"—that the artist in their creative moments tunes into and pursues. Phenomenologically speaking, there is an experience of following along which, while involving a certain relinquishing of self-possession, is no mere passivity. One does not know what the outcome will be, nor is one altogether in control of the process. Rather, one is led—one allows oneself to be led—by an intention that holds a kind of authority over the artist. This is not an intention in the sense of a psychological state, or intended meaning originating in someone's mind, but what he terms an "'energic' intention or *logos*" external to the mind.[14] The work of art itself contains a *logos* or internal logic, which the artist follows along in the very act of creating it. "When the author writes the novel," as he puts it, "she's following the current as she swims, and we readers swim in her wake (and thereby follow the same current, the same *logos*)."[15] There is nothing uncomplicated about this; immersing oneself in intentional structures can call upon resources of mind and body that are of the highest order of complexity, yet it remains that the only conception of artistic inspiration that is phenomenologically adequate is one in which the artist takes direction from an intention that originates without. In his words,

> Without knowing what the final product will be like, the author, as well as the reader, becomes completely drawn in by a movement that seems to flow beyond one's own initiative and control. Similar to the feeling of encountering the sublime, we begin our excursion into an artistic piece of work through a sense that we are being controlled by a movement greater than ourselves. And this is what is meant by inspiration . . . . Inspiration signifies nothing else but this movement that one undergoes only through opening oneself to being guided by an other.[16]

One allows oneself—artist and audience alike—to be swept up in a process one does not control so much as creatively follow.

While there is a long tradition of speaking of the artist as a kind of authority over their work and its meaning, the only authority here is "this movement that one undergoes." Artists no more simply "make it up" than wait for lightning to strike. In a very real sense, they take direction. Creative thinking is a responding to, a thinking together with, something that comes before, on the model of call and response. Mitscherling mentions, as an example outside the province of art, medieval philosophers whose manner of thinking was invariably a "*thinking with* . . . cited authorities" in searching for a solution to a problem:

> These authors were not 'relying on authorities'—they were trying to *think with* the authorities. They were attempting to enter into the same way of seeing and analyzing that was engaged in by these earlier authors, and they were at the same time *critically evaluating* these authors, testing their modes of thinking to see which was the most logically suitable to the task at hand.[17]

In much the way that a reader follows where the author leads, the author follows where a line of thought leads, or a question, until some manner of conclusion is reached. The author or artist, without any unimaginative defer-ence, is guided by something that is experienced as having authority over one's activity.

The *daimon* of Socrates is another instance of an authority that was trusted and followed, but in a way that can scarcely be described as unthink-ing or abject. This is an authority that is non-discursive and immediate. The *daimon* did not proffer reasons, but prescribed a directionality to Socrates' conduct that was invariably prohibitive. Do not do this, it commanded, and in a way that appears to have been apprehended as at once unreasoning and authoritative. Socrates, in this respect, resembled the inspired poets whom Plato, for all his famous reservations, also greatly esteemed:

> [W]e must not forget that Socrates, too, was said to be 'inspired' in his own way. In the *Apology*, for example, Plato has Socrates tell us that, throughout his life, whenever he was about to make a wrong decision, his *daimon* in-formed him of the error he was about to commit . . . . Socrates received instruction from his *daimon* much in the same way that the poets he mentions, in *Apology* and elsewhere, received their instruction from the gods via the muses: this was not an intellectual instruction, for it could not be reformulated discursively—neither the poets nor Socrates could give a rational account of the source or nature of this information. Yet its overwhelming authority re-mained indisputable.[18]

There is an immediacy to this authority; reasons, if they arrive on the scene at all, do so late in the day. The experience is one of being guided, directed, or indeed commanded in a certain way, and there is a corresponding relinquish-ing of control. Following your nose, or your instincts, is how artists often speak of this, in much the way that a detective follows a hunch, or a moral agent follows their conscience, even when no arguments can be produced. The examples here are many, and what they are examples of are intentions which themselves are "fundamentally a matter of 'tending towards'"; indeed, "all *intentionality* consists in such a 'tending towards,' or a *directed move-ment* that one undergoes prior to the activity of conscious deliberation," an activity that he describes "*nonmetaphorically* as being directed by a *logos*."[19]

Intentions of this order, then, are substantial; they have being, but again in the manner of actions rather than thingly entities. In the case of sculpture, the shape slumbers within the stone and is freed by the work of the artist. This is more than a metaphor. There is something there that the artist must, in a sense, get right, apprehend, and allow to speak. In responding to an inter-viewer's question in 1991, "Until you record a song, no matter how heroic it is, it doesn't really exist. Do you ever feel that way?" Dylan answered: "No. If it's there, it exists."[20] Mitscherling's way of putting this is that it subsists or possesses intentional being. The work of the artist is not to create some-thing out of nothing, but to track an intention that is already there, or "out there" as it were. One way this is accomplished is by a kind of perceptual matchmaking, where a given sound or musical element is found to harmonize with another; or in the case of painting, one color is seen to cohere with another, not on any kind of rational basis, but because it works—it follows along in a process where one thing leads to another, and the work itself takes shape in the way that it must. There is necessity here. An author who knows what they are doing writes the book that needs to be written, and in the way it needs to be written; they are following a line of thinking or the course of a narrative and are in no way making it up. So is the painter, songwriter, or poet taking direction from the work itself and what it needs, matching and synthesizing elements into an arrangement that makes sense and indeed that is true.

There is also an incompleteness about the work of art which plays an important role in Mitscherling's account of aesthetic experience. The audience carries to completion the very process in which the artist engaged, allowing the work to wash over them, while also participating in what they see, hear, or read. The work of the artist precedes and makes possible the work of the experiencer, but also underdetermines it. Aesthetic experience is a response in much the way that artistic creation is, one that is not strictly an effect of what the artist has done but that follows its trajectory a while further. The experiencer completes the work in the sense of concretizing or actualizing it, in a way that is ontologically significant. Unlike a natural object, such as a river, that may be regarded aesthetically, a work of art is created for the purpose of producing an experience of this kind; and the work of art is, in this way, incomplete. The act of reception fulfills the being of the work itself. "The work of art, that is to say, is *essentially* something that is created in order to become an aesthetic object. That is the 'essence' of the work of art that Anglo-American philosophers of art, committed to analyzing our language and logic instead of our experience, have managed so successfully to ignore for the past several decades."[21] Art lovers engage in this kind of process habitually—indulging the senses in ways that the senses themselves come to long for, after repeated exposure to a given form of art. One develops a felt need to listen to a piece of music that one completes again and again, perhaps in varying ways, and perhaps in collaboration with other listeners. There are people who need art in a profound sense—usually a specific art and perhaps by a specific artist—and for whom the experience is a condition of their existence. "Without music," Friedrich Nietzsche wrote, "life would be a mistake."[22] These are the words not of an eccentric but of someone with a cultivated love of music and a will to listen to it repeatedly, a phenomenon that Mitscherling terms "aesthetic gluttony." The work itself calls upon us to experience it and to complete it; this is why it exists and "[i]t seems the natural thing to do"—to listen with an appreciative ear to a piece of music, to touch the contours of a sculpture, or to follow with the eye the inherent directionality of a painting. Our sensory apparatus becomes attuned to specific forms of aesthetic stimuli which are craved and habitually delighted in for its own sake. The mystery novel is an obvious and, in Mitscherling's view, "the *best* example of aesthetic gluttony," although the examples one could mention are many.

> Some people have read every mystery novel ever written—twice—and they still crave more. They're insatiable. This might at first seem puzzling, especially given the formulaic nature of the genre. But when we pause to think about it for a moment, we see that it's precisely this formulaic nature that *explains* the addiction: it's the *form*—or rather, the *identity* of the form. It's the *same form* . . . the butler did it. [23]

The senses too have their habits and crave repeated exposure to the same form of stimuli. To others not so inclined this can seem a mystery indeed—try explaining your love of nineteenth-century Russian literature to one who has limited exposure to the form and, not coincidentally, does not share your enthusiasm—but it is a commonplace phenomenon and not limited to the domain of art.

In *The Author's Intention*, Mitscherling and his co-authors illustrate the general phenomenon of artistic creation with an important example from literature. Mark Twain offered some compelling observations of his own creative process, which the authors cite at some length, and it is important to do so here as well. Twain wrote in the prefatory remarks to "Those Extraordinary Twins" in *Pudd'nhead Wilson*,

> A man who is not born with the novel-writing gift has a troublesome time of it when he tries to build a novel. I know this from experience. He has no clear idea of his story; in fact he has no story. He merely has some people in his mind, and an incident or two, also a locality. He knows these people, he knows the selected locality, and he trusts that he can plunge those people into those incidents with interesting results. So he goes to work. To write a novel? No— that is a thought which comes later; in the beginning he is only proposing to tell a little tale; a very little tale; a six-page tale. But as it is a tale which he is not acquainted with, and can only find out what it is by listening as it goes along telling itself, it is more than apt to go on and on and on till it spreads itself into a book. I know about this, because it has happened to me so many times. And I have noticed another thing: that as the short tale grows into the long tale, the original intention (or motif) is apt to get abolished and find itself superseded by a quite different one. [24]

Of course, no one is born with the novel-writing gift, and it is not a gift. The notions of giftedness and innate abilities not shared by others of the species are as mystifying as genius and divine inspiration, each of which amounts to saying one has no idea how a particular form of work is accomplished. It is the work of tracking a specific kind of intention, and it comes not from the skies but from habit. One learns to follow this particular *logos* by following it, and for years or decades. One is not born with it—unless some team of scientists manages to prove one day that the brain of a Dostoevsky or a Twain is different at birth than yours or mine. The explanation is not "brain-based." Twain's point is that the artist becomes habituated to a form of "listening"—listening to the story itself "as it goes along telling itself." The experience is that the narrative "goes along" and "spreads itself into a book," and in a way that the artist does not quite anticipate. The accent on receptivity is essential here, just as, as Heidegger expressed it, "We never come to thoughts. They come to us"; also, "The greater the master, the more completely his person vanishes behind his work."[25] This is not an experience of command but of receiving, apprehending, and following in the wake of something as it withdraws. It is not a matter of mere passivity either; some swimming is involved, but we are swimming in a wake or a current that pulls us along. Our work is to stay on track, find out where it leads, and prepare to be surprised.

INVENTION AND TRADITION

Enter a stranger from Minnesota. Among the epithets that have been directed toward this artist over the decades, he has been called everything from a genius (of course) to an enigma, the original singer-songwriter, and "the poet of our time."[26] Enormous legend has surrounded Bob Dylan for over half a century: 36 studio albums and counting (not including various bootleg, best of, and live albums), writer of well over 600 songs in nearly every genre of American music, author of a best-selling and critically lauded memoir in 2004, recipient of the Presidential Medal of Freedom and the Pulitzer Prize along with awards and honors too numerous to mention, this artist continues to draw legions of fans and sell out concert venues the world over while performing largely newer music and fronting a band of remarkable musicians. In the words of a recent biographer (and not one, by any means, who is inclined to uncritical praise), "his art is his life. It is, profoundly, who he is. Dylan doesn't control the art; the art controls 'Bob Dylan,' and remakes him time after time."[27] Another biographer echoes the point: "What he says and what he does are the same thing. His expression is precisely what he is."[28] This is one complex individual. His songwriting, his lyrical poetry, his vocal phrasing, his voice, his demeanor on stage and off—all of it, and by all accounts, is nothing short of strange, and exactly what one would hope for in an artist.

There is a species of human beings who are known as the Dylanologists. A book about them has recently appeared (naturally); there are fan websites, on which all the citizens of Expecting Rain Nation can find news items, concert reviews, set lists, and so on and so forth. On the artist's official site, one can find about all the information one could wish for, from a complete inventory of his music to the number of times he has performed a given song in concert ("Scarlet Town," 219 at time of writing; "Hurricane," 33). Every recording artist has a website, of course, and some kind of popular following, but if one is looking for an example of aesthetic gluttony, one need look no further than the Dylanologists. Learned and unlearned commentary on his work is a veritable industry. His music has never been described, including by the artist, as mainstream, unlike some other musical entertainers who have attracted a comparable following, and has resisted classification from the beginning. That he was signed at all in 1961, and by Columbia Records no less, was mystifying, and was widely considered so at the time. "The folk labels had all turned me down," he writes in *Chronicles*, volume one.[29] From the beginning, there was nothing commercial about his sound. He was barely twenty, a difficult sell, and a singer-songwriter before the term existed. The norm in popular music at the time was that performers did not write their own songs, and the exceptions to this were few. No one mistook him for Johnny Mathis or Bing Crosby. When he was signed by John Hammond, the corporate executives at Columbia and Dylan's musical peers in Greenwich Village were likewise mystified. What did this famous record producer, credited with having discovered and signed Billie Holiday, Count Basie, Lena Horne, Blind Boy Fuller, Pete Seeger, and Aretha Franklin, among others, see in this artist? The whole episode was, at the time, being spoken of as "Hammond's folly." As biographer Ian Bell writes, "Hammond knows the blues. Yet here he is producing an act turned down by every label in town with even the slightest interest in folk or blues."[30] To make matters worse, Dylan's self-titled debut album in 1962 was not great and included only two original songs. His second album, released the following year, would be called *The Freewheelin' Bob Dylan* and included "Blowin' in the Wind," "Girl from the North Country," "Masters of War," "A Hard Rain's A-Gonna Fall," and nine other self-written songs. Hammond, according to his own account, was acting on instinct, and so was his artist.

Instinct, mystery, and destiny are words regularly used by this artist in speaking of his musical career from his first recordings to the present. When an interviewer once assured him that "A genius can't be a genius on instinct alone," Dylan responded with "Well, I disagree. I believe that instinct is what makes a genius a genius."[31] The early songs often came quickly, with an assurance and fearlessness that was seemingly absolute, and by a process that the writer did not claim to understand. Speaking nearly four decades after writing "Like a Rolling Stone," he remarked: "It's like a ghost is writing a song like that. It gives you the song and it goes away, it goes away. You don't know what it means. Except that the ghost picked me to write the song."[32] There have been periods in his career when the ghost visited often and other times, equally mysteriously, when it did not.

Dylan's own understanding of his talent appears to be, once again, complex. He has long been known to balk at interviewers' questions on a host of matters, from his creative process to "what the songs mean," what life itself means, the existence of God, and other issues on which he has long and widely been believed to have the inside track, all denials from the man himself notwithstanding. Yet in other moments the artist is more forthcoming. In such moments, he speaks invariably and at length about influences. The list of these is long and is not limited to songwriters, folk singers, and poets. Especially well known is the early and decisive influence of Woody Guthrie. Recalling his first hearing of songs such as "Ludlow Massacre," "Pastures of Plenty," "Talkin' Dust Bowl Blues," and "This Land is Your Land," Dylan writes in *Chronicles*:

> All these songs together, one after another made my head spin. It made me want to gasp . . . . Guthrie had such a grip on things. He was so poetic and tough and rhythmic. There was so much intensity, and his voice was like a stiletto. He was like none of the other singers I ever heard, and neither were his songs. His mannerisms, the way everything just rolled off his tongue, it all just about knocked me down . . . . I was listening to his diction too . . . . He would throw in the sound of the last letter of a word whenever he felt like it and it would come like a punch. The songs themselves, his repertoire, were really beyond category. They had the infinite sweep of humanity in them.

Before the release of his first album, Dylan's reputation was that of a Guthrie clone, and for a time his were the only songs Dylan would perform in the clubs of Greenwich Village. "It's almost like I didn't have any choice."[33]

An artist, however, is not a disciple, and the number and range of influences grew. Some are household names—Elvis Presley, Chuck Berry, Buddy Holly, Hank Williams, the Kingston Trio, Lead Belly, Joan Baez, Pete Seeger, Johnny Cash—others perhaps not—Stephen Foster, the New Lost City Ramblers, John Jacob Niles, Len Chandler, Robert Johnson, Dave Van Ronk, to give a partial list. Dylan often speaks in a reverential tone of such artists:

> Johnny Cash's records . . . weren't what you expected. Johnny didn't have a piercing yell, but ten thousand years of culture fell from him. He could have been a cave dweller. He sounds like he's at the edge of the fire, or in the deep snow, or in a ghostly forest, the coolness of conscious obvious strength, full tilt and vibrant with danger. 'I keep a close watch on this heart of mine.' Indeed. I must have recited those lines to myself a million times . . . . Words that were the rule of law and backed by the power of God. When I first heard 'I Walk the Line' so many years earlier, it sounded like a voice calling out, 'What are you doing there, boy?' I was trying to keep my eyes wide opened, too.

The task for the young artist was to discover how they had accomplished all of this, and to listen and learn, borrow and synthesize elements from each without copying any. Many of these records were hard to find and had to be zealously tracked down, borrowed, and stolen before they could be studied, as by an unusually diligent pupil.

> I copied [Robert] Johnson's words down on scraps of paper so I could more closely examine the lyrics and patterns, the construction of his old-style lines and the free association that he used, the sparkling allegories, big-ass truths wrapped in the hard shell of nonsensical abstraction—themes that flew through the air with the greatest of ease. I didn't have any of these dreams or thoughts but I was going to acquire them.[34]

All these influences came together with a variety of romantic, modernist, and Beat poets, nineteenth- and twentieth-century novelists, philosophers, and any other writer from whom he could learn some aspect of his art. "I had read a lot of poetry by the time I wrote a lot of those early songs. I was into the hard-core poets. I read them the way some people read Stephen King. I had also seen a lot of it growing up. Poe's stuff knocked me out in more ways than I could name. Byron and Keats and all those guys. John Donne." In "the Village" at the beginning of the 1960s he was encountering the Beat poets:

> The idea that poetry was spoken in the streets and spoken publicly, you couldn't help but be excited by that. There would always be a poet in the clubs and you'd hear the rhymes, and [Allen] Ginsberg and [Gregory] Corso—those guys were highly influential . . . . Someone gave me a book of François Villon poems and he was writing about hard-core street stuff and making it rhyme . . . . It was pretty staggering, and it made you wonder why you couldn't do the same thing in a song.[35]

The artist became well read and exposed to the world of art: Machiavelli, Milton, Locke, Montesquieu, Voltaire, Rousseau, Pushkin, Dostoevsky, Tolstoy, Nietzsche, biographies of historical figures, as well as a variety of contemporary artists were all studied with an eye to how any of it could be incorporated into his form of music. "Red Grooms . . . was the artist I checked out most. Red's stuff was extravagant, his work cut like it was done by acid . . . . It was bold, announced its presence in glaring details . . . . I loved the way Grooms used laughter as a diabolical weapon. Subconsciously, I was wondering if it was possible to write songs like that."[36] A major portion of *Chronicles* deals with influences, to the point of neglecting basic facts about the subject of this strange autobiography, memoir, or whatever one would call it. It is a book mostly about other people. In its pages, he never mentions even the names of his parents, his two former wives, or his several children; such is Dylan's way. By the end of the book, he emerges as a more mysterious figure than he was at the beginning, and the Dylanologists love him for it. What one does learn about this man is that he was, in his formative years, and remains to this day, as much of an aesthetic glutton as the faithful themselves. As noted, this man simply is his art, and the list of influences continues to grow. His latest record, for instance, *Shadows in the Night* of 2015, is an album of Frank Sinatra songs, completely rearranged, of course, and performed in a way that sounds nothing like Sinatra. No one could have anticipated a record like this one, any more than the several other departures this artist has taken for over half a century. "Instinct" is his invariable reply when asked for an explanation.

It is well known that artists—indeed anyone who does creative work for a living—have influences, yet what is striking in the case of this artist is the range and depth of these. The word "sponge" is often used by those who came into contact with him in his early years. So too is tradition, his sense of which is remarkably strong. His palette would become large and his knowledge of the American musical tradition vast. Dylan has repeatedly stated that his work was not written in an aesthetic vacuum but follows in the tradition into which he initiated himself in his early years. Nearly every facet of American music—blues, folk, rock and roll, country, gospel, swing—comes together in his work, and began doing so well before "reinventing oneself" became the thing to do. "Going electric" in 1965 was not the thing to do in folk music circles, and the condemnation that followed from folk hyper-traditionalists became part of the Dylan legend. Through fifty-some years and counting of following his instincts, Dylan has moved on from one unclassifiable non-genre to the next, confounding critics with some regularity while also, he insists, working within the rules of his tradition.

When speaking of inspiration, Dylan consistently emphasizes two themes which, at first glance, appear to conflict: mystery and appropriation. In 2012, an interviewer asked him, "Can you talk a little about your songwriting method these days?" His reply: "I can write a song in a crowded room. Inspiration can hit you anywhere. It's magical. It's really beyond me."[37] He also had this to say about his early songs in a speech for MusiCares in 2015:

> These songs didn't come out of thin air. I didn't just make them up out of whole cloth . . . . It all came out of traditional music: traditional folk music, traditional rock and roll, and traditional big-band swing orchestra music. I learned lyrics and how to write them from listening to folk songs. And I played them, and I met other people that played them, back when nobody was doing it. Sang nothing but these folk songs, and they gave me the code for everything that's fair game, that everything belongs to everyone. For three or four years, all I listened to were folk standards. I went to sleep singing folk songs . . . . I could learn one song and sing it next in an hour if I'd heard it just once.

What Mitscherling calls a "form" and an "energic intention," Dylan here speaks of as a code that he was learning to follow and take further: "I thought I was just extending the line."[38]

One can only extend what one has first apprehended. Traditional folk music is an aesthetic form which, like any other, one may appreciatively grasp or not. To write in this form is to take up an intentional structure that is found in the tradition and to follow where it leads. Dylan describes it as follows:

> What happens is, I'll take a song I know and simply start playing it in my head. That's the way I meditate . . . . I meditate on a song. I'll be playing Bob Nolan's 'Tumbling Tumbleweeds,' for instance, in my head constantly—while I'm driving a car or talking to a person or sitting around or whatever. People will think they are talking to me and I'm talking back, but I'm not. I'm listening to the song in my head. At a certain point, some of the words will change and I'll start writing a song.[39]

He provides several examples of this in his MusiCares speech, including the following:

> If you had listened to Robert Johnson singing, 'Better come in my kitchen, 'cause it's gonna be raining out doors' as many times as I listened to it, sometime later you might just write 'A Hard Rain's A-Gonna Fall.' I sang a lot of 'come all you' songs. There's plenty of them. There's way too many to be counted. 'Come along boys and listen to my tale / Tell you of my troubles on the old Chisholm Trail.' Or, 'Come all ye good people, listen while I tell / the fate of Floyd Collins, a lad we all know well.' . . . If you sung all these 'come all you' songs all the time like I did, you'd be writing 'Come gather 'round people wherever you roam.'[40]

This, according to the artist, was what Hammond was able to discern in him: "he saw me as someone in the long line of a tradition," not "some newfangled wunderkind on the cutting edge." This performer "knew the inner substance of the thing," whatever it was he was listening to and endeavoring to make his own.[41] This is not a casual mode of listening—a simple matter of being entertained—but listening with an inventor's ear. What can be done with this, "what does that phrase mean," what follows from it and how can it be modified—are the kinds of question that are asked.[42] It neither comes out of thin air nor merely echoes what comes before. In a word, artistic creation is derivative, from the best to the worst and from the most innovative to the most hackneyed. Invention is an appropriation of the tradition in which one stands. One does not sit around waiting for lightning to strike, but listens attentively, meditatively, and habitually, follows songs where they lead, appropriates, borrows, and extends at will. This is explicit to the self-understanding of folk music in particular. As Pete Seeger expressed it,

> The moment I became acquainted with old songs I realized people were always changing them. Think of it as an age-old process, it's been going on for thousands of years. People take old songs and change them a little, add to them, adopt them for new people. It happens in every other field. Lawyers change old laws to fit new citizens. So I'm one in this long chain and so are millions of other musicians. [43]

This is an observation that Seeger likely learned from his father, musicologist Charles Seeger, who had written, "conscious and unconscious appropriation, borrowing, adapting, plagiarising, and plain stealing are variously, and always have been, part and parcel of the process of artistic creation . . . . The folk song is, by definition and, as far as we can tell, by reality, entirely a product of plagiarism." [44] Implicit in the word itself, folk music, like all folk art, belongs to everyone and no one. Who owns the duck decoy form, the antique weathervane, the child's sampler, or the quilt? Can one plagiarize works of plagiarism? Every form and element is handed down and varied in ways the artist need not even be aware of, and Dylan's peers in the Greenwich Village scene saw nothing wrong in this. Even the arrangement on Dylan's version of "House of the Risin' Sun"—a song of uncertain origin—on his debut album was taken from Dave Van Ronk, and shortly thereafter it was taken from Dylan by Eric Burdon and the Animals, who made it into a number one hit. The examples are endless. There is an anonymity to folk music that is fundamental to how it has long been conceived, by the performers themselves and by the authoritarians who police it. An entity that calls itself the International Council for Traditional Music decreed in 1954 that folk is nothing more or less than

> the product of a musical tradition that has been evolved through the process of oral transmission. The factors that shape the tradition are: 1) continuity which links the present with the past; 2) variation which springs from the creative impulse of the individual or the group; and 3) selection by the community which determines the form or forms in which the music survives.

There is more than a little politics involved in this, as anyone familiar with the early chapter of the Dylan legend knows, some of it involving the vexed question of whether sound caused by vibrating guitar strings may be converted into electrical impulses without incurring the wrath of the gods. For the orthodox upon whom the wayward youth was said to be turning his back, proper practice is to revere the old over the new, to revive and adapt received songs rather than compose new ones—although some allowance of the latter was permitted—to preserve the anonymity of traditional forms, and above all else to keep it acoustic and to have nothing to do with popular music and especially rock and roll. Romanticism and left politics held sway in the minds of the hyper-traditionalists, but for Dylan the point was and is to find what is alive in the old forms and to inhabit them in a style that is invariably the artist's own. One helps oneself to any and all received elements, both lyrical and melodic, not for conservation's sake but to make the work speak. Art speaks in the voice of the artist, whose work is less to repeat than to modify according to what the work of art itself requires. The point that the hyper-traditionalist misses is that art and tradition itself live in a condition of constant variation. They are not museum pieces frozen in time, but an active presence to be taken further and improved by the lights of some particular human being.

The artist, like the philosopher, participates in a tradition by appropriating it. It speaks through one if it speaks at all, and is modified in the same process that keeps it alive. The process is dialectical: an artist who neither knows nor stands in a tradition has nothing to say, and tradition without invention is a fossil. In the case of the artist of whom I have been speaking, it is not difficult to see that this performer who so knows his tradition is also no slave to it, and it is precisely this that makes his art work. He makes the tradition of American music his own, not only by knowing it and following in kind, but by selectively synthesizing this element with that, repeating here and reversing there, in accordance with the artist's acquired habits and instincts. Despite the unparalleled influence that he has had on songwriters for half a century, there is an inimitability about Dylan. No one else sounds like that; the combination of poetic art, melody, voice and phrasing is utterly singular, even as each of the elements is borrowed. The lyrics resist description, but combine verse with elements of prose and vernacular speech, often resulting in a poetic hodgepodge, where one element does not follow another in any tidy sequence, even as the piece as a whole manages to hang together. The language is typically fast and loose; the rhymes are often out of left field; a long and seemingly unsingable line may be inserted in the middle of a verse. The poet also has a penchant for sudden reversals and a fierce wit. (I would quote examples here but cannot for copyright reasons.) Ginsberg described Dylan's early lyrical poetry as "chains of flashing images," where one picture follows another for no discernible reason but that it works.[45] Why it is not gibberish is sometimes difficult to say, nor is it obvious that this matters. As Bell writes, Dylan learned from modernist and Beat poets that "images need not form an orderly queue on their way to a conclusion . . . . One typical summary of modernism's arrival in America speaks of poets investigating 'fragmentation, ellipsis, allusion, juxtaposition, ironic and shifting personae, and mythic parallelism.' The description fits the Dylan of the mid-1960s like a mitten. It became the Beat template, after all."[46] Dylan would not turn it into a formula, however, and what he was writing in the

1960s—the period that biographers and commentators on this artist so often fasten upon, sometimes inexplicably ignoring everything he has produced since then—changed considerably and often in the decades that followed. Part of the logic behind the chain of images consists in its performance quality. The poetry is invariably part of the music and does not work on the page in the same way as when it is sung, and sung by this artist. Dylan's voice and phrasing are part of his art, and while many of his songs have been covered and re-covered by other recording artists, the meaning varies with the artist and indeed with the performance by Dylan himself, who has long made it a habit to vary the arrangement of his songs in concert in ways that his audiences sometimes must work to recognize.

There is something perplexing in Dylan's music—shifts in genre and sound, wild visions, moral urgency, and weird mythology lumped together with absolute conviction, even when it does not work (and it does not always). The listener's experience is of a persistent ambiguity, elusiveness, and difficulty that reflects both how this artist appears to see the world ("you're talking to a person that feels like he's walking around in the ruins of Pompeii all the time") and quite possibly himself.[47] Behold the art and behold the man; the sense of life appears the same (insofar, of course, as one ever knows the latter, and his several biographers have had a difficult task of it). "[T]he stuff I write does come from an autobiographical place," he points out. The music follows in a tradition, but the tradition "was a counterpart of myself . . . . It was my place in the universe, always felt like it was in my blood."[48] Personal, autobiographical writing was a departure from folk orthodoxy, for which the ideal was communal and anonymous composition, yet what Dylan was demonstrating in his earlier days is that tradition does not speak for itself and that to give a convincing performance of even a traditional song, one must bring precisely oneself to the performance. Great art is soulful, and whose soul but the artist's comes to bear in performing (which means interpreting, appropriating) a song? One makes the song one's own; its energic intention is allowed to reverberate in that internal echo chamber that is the artist's soul (we must use metaphors here), where it meets an intention of the artist's own. The "wellspring of creativity" has the structure of a dialectic, where tradition and invention are the poles, and creativity is the work of running back and forth between them. What comes out of this bears the traces of what is passed down and what lies within in about equal measure, and, when it works, there is a matching of aesthetic elements that is more felt than understood. In music that is sung, the words must match the sound. If a folk singer in 1965 decided to write the verses that became "Subterranean Homesick Blues," an acoustic guitar and harmonica will not do. The torrent of words requires a band, and it was a band (The Band) that he began to hear behind several of the songs on his first (half) "electric" album, *Bringing It All Back Home*. As a biographer writes, "If you choose electricity, you have to think differently. You have to think of a musical instrument as a gesture. For the singer of songs it becomes something more than the folk notion of 'accompaniment.' . . . Some of the things he was writing in 1965 were unimaginable—could not have been imagined—without amplified sound."[49] The wordplay on "Subterranean Homesick Blues" was only served by electric instruments and drums played at a fast tempo, while the verses of "It's Alright, Ma (I'm Only Bleeding)" and "Mr. Tambourine Man" still worked well acoustically. The wildness of the words matched the wildness of the band, just as his band of today matches in a very different way the kind of old-style blues (if that is what one would call it) that he currently prefers. It is a question of fit: words and melody, instrument X and instrument Y (drums, for instance, require that other instruments be amplified to be heard), singer and band, theme and tempo, arrangement and production, and so on. The artist, as Mitscherling states, *"is a perceptual matchmaker."*[50] The perplexing quality in Dylan's art is partly owing to the performer's inveterate habit of matching elements in ways that music listeners had not heard before and the surprising ways in which it all typically works. The music is not what one expects, nor is the artist himself. Who expected the follow-up to *Blonde On Blonde* (1966) to be *John Wesley Harding* (1967), or *Time Out Of Mind* (1997) to follow *World Gone Wrong* (1993)?

Matchmaking is instinctive. If it is over-thought or translated into propositional language, it does not work. "I don't give too much thought to individual lines. If I thought about them in any kind of deep way, maybe I wouldn't use them because I'd always be second-guessing myself. I learned a long time ago to trust my intuition."[51] Speaking of his most recent album of original songs, *Tempest* of 2012, Dylan stated: "*Tempest* was like all the rest of them: the songs just fall together. It's not the album I wanted to make, though. I had another one in mind. I wanted to make something more religious. That takes a lot more concentration—to pull that off ten times with the same thread—than it does with a record like I ended up with, where anything goes and you just gotta believe it will make sense."[52] In this case, it is not the artist's intention in that other, more common, sense of the word—something like a state of mind, an emotion, or a purpose—but an energic intention or *logos*, something that is in the songs themselves and resistant to conceptual articulation, that is the album's connecting thread. In artistic creation, one does what feels right, and intellection can be an obstacle. When it works, it can happen quickly and seemingly without effort ("I felt like I was just putting words down that were coming from somewhere else, and I just stuck it out"), and when the instincts become blocked, they can remain blocked for years, a phenomenon of which Dylan has also experienced his share.[53] Through all the changes in musical direction, which have seldom been of immediate commercial benefit, the artist follows his instincts without seeming to care in the least what anyone thinks about it. "Most striking of all," Bell writes of the "going electric" episode, "is the absence, yet again, of self-doubt"; "[y]et again, the impervious self-belief, the absence of doubt, *the gall*, is startling. Dylan knew he was right; the world would have to catch up . . . . Whoever 'Bob Dylan' happened to be, he believed utterly in the art of Dylan."[54]

Whether it is exactly oneself that the artist believes in or something else—one's work, aesthetic judgment, instincts, or whatever it might be—is difficult to specify, yet the artist in question has long spoken in this connection of truth. There is truth in art, and it is not only hermeneutical philosophers who maintain this. To cite the MusiCares speech again, "Sam Cooke said this when told he had a beautiful voice. He said, 'Well, that's very kind of you, but voices ought not to be measured by how pretty they are. Instead they matter only if they convince you that they are telling the truth.' Think about that the next time you are listening to a singer."[55] No one has ever described Dylan's voice as pretty. If the singing works at all, it is because it says what is true. "I've got to know that I'm singing something with truth to it. My songs are different than anybody else's songs. Other artists can get by on their voices and their style, but my songs speak volumes, and all I have to do is lay them down correctly, lyrically, and they'll do what they need to do."[56] Dylan, of course, does not have a theory of truth, but when he uses the word in this connection, as he has long done, he appears to mean "disclosure" or "insight" into what something means. An artist, he writes in *Chronicles*, is "someone who could see into things, the truth of things—not metaphorically, either—but really see, like seeing into metal and making it melt, see it for what it was and reveal it for what it was with hard words and vicious insight."[57] When he speaks with admiration of other artists, it is for the truth that their music contains, far more than its beauty: "To Woody Guthrie, see, the airwaves were sacred. And when he'd hear something false, it was on airwaves that were sacred to him. His songs weren't false."[58] It is truth that makes a song come alive and speak, and it is the performer's task to make this possible. The artist is a believer, and not only in the words, but in the larger and properly musical intention of the song.

There is a longstanding tendency of those who write about art to analyze and schematize in ways that if successful (and they never are) would effectively pin down the thing itself, and it is to Mitscherling's credit that his phenomenological account of artistic creation manages to shed some light into this dark corner of experience without falling into this trap. Dylan himself has always mocked efforts by music critics to theorize and compartmentalize what it is that he does, insisting that what makes art speak is its ability to tell the truth and that the process by which it is created is an inventive appropriation even while remaining to a large degree mysterious. "I'm working," the artist says, "within my art form. It's that simple. I work within the rules and limitations of it . . . . It's called songwriting. It has to do with melody and rhythm, and then after that, anything goes. You make everything yours. We all do it."[59] One borrows and is borrowed from and originates nothing in a vacuum. One follows the *logos*, tracks intentional structures found in the tradition in which one stands, and synthesizes, reinterprets, and enhances what one finds. Creation is inventive appropriation.

NOTES

1. Jeff Mitscherling, *Aesthetic Genesis: The Origin of Consciousness in the Intentional Being of Nature* (Lanham: University Press of America, 2010), 2. Hereafter cited as AG.

2. AG, 2.

3. AG, 1, 4.

4. AG, 128.

5. Jeff Mitscherling, Tanya DiTommaso, and Aref Nayed, *The Author's Intention* (Lanham: Lexington Books, 2004), 119.

6. AG, 47.

7. AG, 53.

8. Martin Heidegger, *The Basic Problems of Phenomenology*, trans. A Hofstadter (Bloomington: Indiana University Press, 1988), 61.

9. AG, 29.

10. AG, 28, 121, 52.

11. AG, 113, 86.

12. Plato, *Ion*, trans. L. Cooper, in *The Collected Dialogues of Plato*, eds. Edith Hamilton and Huntington Cairns (Princeton: Princeton University Press, 1987), 533d, 533e–534a, 534d.

13. Heidegger, "On the Origin of the Work of Art" in *Basic Writings*, ed. David Farrell Krell (London: Harper Perennial, 2008), 166.

14. Mitscherling et. al., *The Author's Intention*, 27, 110.

15. AG, 56.

16. Mitscherling et. al., *The Author's Intention*, 114.

17. AG, 56.

18. AG, 60.

19. Mitscherling et. al., *The Author's Intention*, 106.

20. Interview with Paul Zollo, in *Bob Dylan: The Essential Interviews*, ed. Jonathon Cott (New York: Wenner Books, 2006), 380.

21. AG, 72.

22. Friedrich Nietzsche, *Twilight of the Idols*, trans. R. J. Hollingdale (New York: Penguin, 2003), Maxims and Arrows, sec. 33, p. 36.

23. AG, 2, 3.

24. Mitscherling et. al., *The Author's Intention*, 109. Mitscherling and his coauthors are quoting Mark Twain, "Those Extraordinary Twins" in *Pudd'nhead Wilson* (New York: Penguin, 1987), 229.

25. Heidegger, *Poetry, Language, Thought*, trans. A. Hofstadter (New York: Harper Perennial, 2001), 6; Heidegger, *Discourse on Thinking*, trans. J. M. Anderson and E. H. Freund (New York: Harper Perennial, 1969), 44.

26. Bob Dylan, *Chronicles*, volume one (New York: Simon and Schuster, 2004), front pages.

27. Ian Bell, *Once Upon a Time: The Lives of Bob Dylan*, volume one (London: Mainstream Publishing, 2012), 325. See also Bell, *Time Out Of Mind: The Lives of Bob Dylan*, volume two (London: Mainstream Publishing, 2014).

28. Robert Shelton, *No Direction Home: The Life and Music of Bob Dylan* (Montclair: Backbeat Books, 2011), 228.

29. Dylan, *Chronicles*, 279.

30. Bell, *Once Upon a Time*, 28.
31. Interview with Jonathon Cott, in *Bob Dylan: The Essential Interviews*, 265.
32. Interview with Robert Hilburn, in *Bob Dylan: The Essential Interviews*, 432.
33. Dylan, *Chronicles*, 244, 245.
34. Ibid., 216–7, 285.
35. Interview with Robert Hilburn, in *Bob Dylan: The Essential Interviews*, 434.
36. Dylan, *Chronicles*, 269–70.
37. Interview with Mikal Gilmore, *Rolling Stone*, 2012.
38. Dylan, MusiCares Speech, 2015.
39. Interview with Robert Hilburn, in *Bob Dylan: The Essential Interviews*, 437–8.
40. Dylan, MusiCares Speech, 2015.
41. Dylan, *Chronicles*, 5, 18.
42. Interview with Jon Pareles, in *Bob Dylan: The Essential Interviews*, 394.
43. Pete Seeger, Interview in *No Direction Home: Bob Dylan*, Directed by Martin Scorsese (Spitfire Pictures, Grey Water Park Productions, 2005).
44. Charles Seeger, "Who Owns Folklore? A Rejoinder" in *Western Folklore*, April 1962.
45. See Ralph Gleason, "The Children's Crusade" in *Ramparts*, March 1966.
46. Bell, *Once Upon a Time*, 554.
47. Interview with Mikal Gilmore, in *Bob Dylan: The Essential Interviews*, 425.
48. Dylan, *Chronicles*, 199, 240–1.
49. Bell, *Once Upon a Time*, 415.
50. AG, 2.
51. Interview with Robert Hilburn, in *Bob Dylan: The Essential Interviews*, 400.
52. Interview with Mikal Gilmore, *Rolling Stone*, 2012.
53. Dylan, booklet included in *Biograph* box set.
54. Bell, *Once Upon a Time*, 379, 431.
55. Dylan, MusiCares Speech, 2015.
56. Interview with Jon Pareles, in *Bob Dylan: The Essential Interviews*, 393.
57. Dylan, *Chronicles*, 219.
58. Interview with Paul Zollo, in *Bob Dylan: The Essential Interviews*, 379.
59. Interview with Mikal Gilmore, *Rolling Stone*, 2012.

Chapter Nine

Our Connection to Nature

Siby George

Two prominent philosophical responses to the contemporary ecological crisis are in vogue. The first is, broadly stated, a pursuit of knowledge and truth perceived to be currently absent but urgent and necessary: knowledge of the intrinsic value of nature and non-human life. This debate is centered on the question of whether such knowledge can be claimed to be true in a robust sense. Much of environmental ethics and philosophy is entangled in the project of generating robust reasons for the rational subject to represent or mirror objective nature to its mind as intrinsically valuable. This debate leaves you with the sense that inaccurate reasons have compelled humanity into an avaricious exploitation of the environment, while accurate reasons that await articulation can salvage the situation. An undoubtedly productionist metaphysics underlies such a claim.

The second philosophical response to the ecological crisis, mainly inspired by Edmund Husserl's phenomenological philosophy, rather than engaging with the production of reasons, examines how our primal concepts and ideas, including our reasons, emerge out of our unthought involvement with the world. These primal concepts and ideas often articulate the generic as well as specific human interests and projects underlying the dominant formations of what we historically consider reasonable approaches to phenomena—especially the predominantly exploitative attitude towards nature. This strand of phenomenological philosophy came to be referred to as ecophenomenology. Its dominant affiliations are with Martin Heidegger's criticalhermeneutical exposition of western metaphysics as doomed to be set on a world-dominating trail of technological understanding of reality and his alternative proposal of dwelling caringly in the world amidst the things with which humans can get meaningfully involved, and it is also affiliated with Maurice Merleau-Ponty's phenomenology of the body.[1]

In this essay, I want to suggest that the realist strand of phenomenology of *Aesthetic Genesis*[2] has the potential to bring together the above two philo-sophical responses to the ecological crisis by way of its proposal of under-standing intentionality (usually taken to be the directedness of consciousness, in phenomenological literature) as the directedness of reality as such. Wheth-er for undercutting the predilection for human consciousness in order to thus come to revalue the intrinsic worth of all beings, or for evoking fresh ways of looking at the world, I shall argue, the understanding of intentionality as directedness of reality as such is a credible manner of procedure.

THE MODERNIST PREDILECTION FOR CONSCIOUSNESS

Western philosophy has for long tended to consider consciousness as the unique differentiating marker of human beings.[3] Of this venerable tradition, the most conspicuous name is that of Descartes, who at the dawn of the modern period in mid-seventeenth century found what is indubitable to the human searcher to be consciousness or mind: "A thinking thing . . . I mean a thing that doubts, that understands, that affirms, that denies, that wishes to do this and does not wish to do that, and also that imagines and perceives by the senses."[4] He enunciates two markers for differentiating "real human beings" from machines and especially from "irrational animals." These are language and consciousness. "The first is that they would never be able to use words or other signs by composing them as we do to declare our thoughts to others."[5] The second is "they have no mental powers whatsoever, and that it is nature which acts in them, according to the disposition of their organs."[6] The conse-quence that Descartes draws from these two differentiating traits of humans is that the consciousness-animated human soul is of "a nature entirely inde-pendent of the body."[7] He concludes, therefore, that the human soul would survive the body's death, a feat that merely animal bodies cannot achieve.

The predilection for consciousness, and the derivative predilection for human beings, who alone are thought to be appropriately conscious, is deep-ly rooted in the Hellenistic-Hebraic trajectories of the western intellectual tradition, which took a uniquely articulated ethical form in Immanuel Kant's deontological musings. Conjecturing on the beginning of human history in 1786, Kant wrote that the human being might have come to reject her/his natural urges by "becoming conscious of one's reason as a faculty that can extend itself beyond the boundaries to which all animals are confined," and discovered in her/himself "a capacity to choose a way of life for himself and not, as other animals, to be bound to a single one."[8] While answering the question, "What is Enlightenment?" in 1784,[9] Kant saw this natural progres-sion of rational consciousness in human beings as fulfilling itself in the Enlightenment and its representative motto *"Sapere aude!"* or "Have the courage to make use of your own intellect!" (without the direction of another). He takes rational consciousness to be the distinguishing mark of the human species that vests all moral value upon itself. In *Groundwork of the Metaphysics of Morals* (1785), Kant writes that natural beings like animals, without rational consciousness, "have only a relative worth, as means, and are therefore called *things*, whereas rational beings are called *persons* because their nature already marks them out as an end in itself, that is, as something that may not be used merely as a means, and hence so far limits all choice (and is an object of respect)."[10]

In the 1797 treatise *The Metaphysics of Morals*, Kant specifically observes that human duty towards nature and animals is indirect and not moral in itself. Since animals can feel pain, the human being must refrain from causing them uncalled-for harm, stipulates Kant, but only because "it dulls his shared feeling of their suffering and so weakens and gradually uproots a natural predisposition that is very serviceable to morality in one's relations with other people . . . considered as a *direct* duty, however, it is always a duty of the human being *to* himself."[11]

Much has been written about the modernist (Cartesian-Kantian) construction of the autonomous rational individual and the role of modern thinking and culture in the active production of the global ecological crisis. In his critical study of international environmental politics, Hakan Seckinelgin observes that modern international politics is immunized beforehand from the ecological question, because what is considered political involves only autonomous human subjects, nation states, and their ends. The discursive terrain of political processes is already sealed off to non-human beings as interested parties in the discourse. "It is clear from the Kantian genesis that in order to be able to bring nature into the political debate and thus move into an ethics of ecology, a new constitution of human subject must be devised."[12] Seckinelgin's suggestion amounts to an ontological rethinking of the human being that could undergird a politics of "ecological relationality," which is ultimately able to challenge "the abstracted autonomous human subject" by virtue of "the relational ethics of belonging to the same space." What Seckinelgin has in mind here is the Heideggerian notion of dwelling. I shall argue below that the realist phenomenology of *Aesthetic Genesis* can also contribute to the project of undercutting the Cartesian-Kantian picture of the autonomous rational subject, in a different but significant way.

THE PREDILECTION FOR INTENTIONALITY

Put in a single straightforward statement, the Copernican hypothesis proposed by Jeff Mitscherling in *Aesthetic Genesis* means that intentionality is not about the directionality of human consciousness as such; rather, the de-

veloped form of intentionality as found in human beings is itself a variant of
the intentionality of nature, even if of the highest degree.[13] Consciousness
does not exhaust intentionality, which is not a thing but "a feature of the
natural world" that "serves to join" human mind with object.[14] Intentionality
involves the relational character of the universe as a whole and of its separate
elements; it unites all beings. To exist means to "intend" towards some object
or other. In reflective thinking, acts of intending or relating with objects
relate with further acts of intending or relations. "This is also how things
grow. Relations get together, intentions intertwine."[15]

The mode of being of bodies is said to be material; ideas are said to be
ideal; and intentional relations are said to be subsisting. The work of art is
said to subsist as a relation between the author or admirer, and the work
itself. Similarly, organisms that do not simply exist but live, grow, and die,
subsist towards their intentional *telos*.[16] The Aristotelian conception of final
causality is acknowledged as the conceptual basis of the predilection for
intentionality as such, over and above intentional consciousness. According
to this conception, there are no permanent essences; rather, "essences subsist
in the relation of the form and the matter of entities . . . More precisely stated:
An essence subsists in the particular manner in which the matter of an entity
is informed."[17]

The subsistence of intentional relations in consciousness and in sentience
is differentiated in the following manner:

> On this view, neither consciousness nor intentionality is unique to humans.
> The behavior of dogs, cats, insects, plants, and even single-celled organisms
> must be described as intentional. But does this indicate consciousness, or mere
> sentience? It seems that a rather high degree of bodily complexity (many
> tendings, or tensions) is a condition for the emergence of what we recognize as
> consciousness. But there must certainly be a spectrum, or graduated scale,
> here, so it would perhaps be more precise to regard and locate what we call
> consciousness as at the 'higher' end of the spectrum of complexity of sen-
> tience. It might seem odd to say that a paramecium is 'conscious,' or that the
> behavior of a slug or an African Violet is 'intentional,' but this language usage
> is entirely in keeping with the concept of intentionality and consciousness that
> I am here suggesting. For example, it may or may not be the case that human
> consciousness is different from other sorts of consciousness in that it's guided
> by some quite peculiar sort of intelligence, but the presence of some sort of
> guiding force does seem to be necessary to account for my experience. There
> is certainly 'willing' going on here, maybe even at the 'level' of brute sensa-
> tion.[18]

That is, consciousness is a natural but complex development out of the directional *telos* inherent in nature and its many organisms. This concept of intentionality is suggested to be a new way of overcoming subject-object dichotomy, because here intentionality is not a feature of consciousness, but con-

sciousness is a more complex development of intentionality. "As directed-ness characterizes all of creation, from the simplest and most basic constitu-ents of what we call 'inorganic matter' to the most complex organic systems of nature, some degree of intentionality is to be acknowledged at every level of creation."[19] This view of intentionality finds the lost Cartesian connecting link between matter and mind in their shared formal identity in intentional structure. Their ontological identity is natural and, thus, not unbridgeable. Intentionality in this sense is the Aristotelian purposiveness hidden in nature. But in the realist phenomenological avatar of this Aristotelian notion,

> purposiveness belongs to the very nature of matter (most clearly in the case of organisms, but a similar account may be given of 'inorganic' nature), and when we regard natural entities or nature as a whole as 'acting with some purpose,' it is not only unnecessary but indeed illegitimate to infer that this purpose must have been bestowed by some separate intelligence.[20]

Thus, intentionality is considered as the natural purposiveness of the whole of nature and its various elements, and consciousness and intelligence as the more complex development "of features that are to be found at every level of nature."[21]

In this sense, the realist phenomenology of intentionality of all beings in *Aesthetic Genesis* is naturalistic. It accords a specific predilection for inten-tionality which is natural to reality as such. This, however, is not a naturalism in the sense of materialism. *Aesthetic Genesis* considers substances not as stuff (*hyle*), but as ontologically distinct kinds of activities or ways of being. There are three substances in this sense, each with its own kind of being: material bodies with material being, ideal entities with ideal being, and inten-tional activities with intentional being. The stuff (*hyle*) is that upon which a physical shape (*morphe*) or a formal idea (*eidos*) can incarnate, which can mean material existence in the world, the spatio-temporally bound existence of a particular entity in the mind or consciousness, and the formal existence of an idea. Form is, rather, something like the universal idea of a thing, expressible in language. This is how *Aesthetic Genesis* distinguishes between *morphe* and *eidos*. Hence, "physical" does not necessarily mean "material." "Physical" could be material or immaterial shapes of the spatio-temporally bound world.[22]

Hence, the Aristotelian naturalism of *Aesthetic Genesis* is not material-ism. Material body is a necessary condition for the possibility of embodied cognition or mind, but this claim of necessary condition is not a claim about identity. That is, mind or embodied awareness is not body. "I do not reduce nature, or that which is natural—and this includes the mind and the soul—to matter, or that which is material. To render something 'natural' is to render it 'physical,' which means (again following Aristotle), 'comprehending both the material and the immaterial.'"[23] In this conception, therefore, the soul is natural but not material; the soul, mind, and body are "thoroughly *natural* modes of being of living organisms."[24] Erazim Kohák, treading a similarly realist phenomenological line, defines naturalism in the following way:

> [A]ny philosophy which recognizes the being of humans as integrally linked to the being of nature, however conceived, treating humans as distinctive only as much as any distinct species is that, but as fundamentally *at home* in the cosmos, not 'contingently thrown' into it as into an alien context and 'ek-sisting' from it in an act of Promethean defiance.[25]

Hence, the naturalism of *Aesthetic Genesis* does not reduce consciousness to matter but considers it as integrally linked to the immanent intentional being of nature and at home with it as all beings are.

THE PREDILECTION FOR THE REAL

The realist phenomenology of *Aesthetic Genesis* is committed to a real world that exists independently of human consciousness and the independent subsistence within the world of intentional entities with intentional being such as forms.[26] But the intentional being of consciousness is considered neither unique, nor something higher than that of the world or of other intentional entities. Consciousness is one of the many forms of intentional entities. Realism in this sense is uncompromising. In the composition of the meaning of an object, the whole of the object is neither intentional nor ideal, although some aspects of it are. It has also a material element. Even in such a thing as a work of art, a work of fiction to be precise, which is usually considered to be purely intentional, the material element is present: "whereas the material book possesses *material being*, and the concepts and word-meanings possess *ideal being*, the literary work of art possesses *intentional being*."[27] This should not, however, lead us to think that "the real" is purely material; rather, the being of the real is a mixture of ideal, intentional, and material being. Rejecting the later Husserlian idealistic language of the constitution of the object in the consciousness of the subject, *Aesthetic Genesis* maintains that "[t]he subject 'is' in a certain way by means of the object, and the object and the subject are in a sense ontologically identical: they are as one in the intentional activity, engagement, or behavior that gives to each of them their 'activated' form as poles of an organic relation."[28] The term "aesthetic genesis," thus, invokes the similarity between our creative activities of art and our everyday activities of aesthetic/perceptual apprehension of the world. We are generating the sensory world each moment, as we always "inform" the aesthetic data that swarm our senses. Art is intensification, acceleration, and enhancement of aesthetic genesis. Just as there cannot be an artist without forms of art, there cannot be a subject without objects and the world of objects. The sensory intensification of art in material objects like paper, canvass or stage is foreshadowed in the sensory apprehension of the object outside consciousness in consciousness. In this sense, experiential production and artistic production are similar. In this sense, experience of the world is "the aesthetic genesis of *this* artworld that all of us artists, we insatiable aesthetic metaphysical gluttons, are living in."[29]

For the phenomenological tradition inaugurated by Husserl, Franz Brentano's idea that the cognitive act is something internal to the mind was something cardinal. The challenge to this aspect of phenomenology, raised by the realist phenomenology of *Aesthetic Genesis*, however, does not lead to a simple claim about the experience of the independent existence of subject or object. The subject and the object of the act of consciousness, as far as phenomenology is concerned, whether realist or idealist, arise only within the act of consciousness. But in *Aesthetic Genesis*, the subject does not constitute the object; both of these poles of consciousness arise in consciousness, and consciousness does not exist in a realist sense without the *subsistence of the relation* between the subject and the object. Consciousness is not a thing upon which is superimposed the subject and the object; it is not a kind of river upon which floats a paper boat. Independent of its objects, there is not consciousness or any form of intentionality.[30] "Both mind and world exist, and they exist independently of each other—but they do not exist independently of the subsisting relation that gives rise to and (dialectically) maintains each of them. This subsisting relation is intentionality at work, and we find intentionality at work everywhere."[31]

Intentionality is, therefore, the relation that makes both the world and the subject who perceives the world possible. The subject and the object do not exist outside the subsisting relation that maintains both of these. Isn't that an idealistic position? It is not, because *Aesthetic Genesis* is buttressed with the Copernican hypothesis that considers the intentional relation of subsistence not as human consciousness *per se* but as an aspect of the natural world; consciousness is one of the many differing shapes of intentionality.[32] Intentionality is thus, "found to reside in the structures of the natural world itself, and . . . the human consciousness that we have long privileged as the origin of intentionality appears now to find its own origin in the intentional being of nature."[33] The world is real and objective, because the manifold elements of the world, in utterly varying degrees of perfection, tend towards objects, and nature as a whole towards its own teleological perfection. The world really exists, not because consciousness perceives or constitutes it, but because intentional relations subsist everywhere in nature, objectifying the various elements of the world and the world as a whole.

Now, ecophenomenology is by and large realist. In his response to the volume, *Eco-Phenomenology: Back to the Earth Itself* (2003), Iain Thomson describes the two broad strands of ecophenomenology in the following way: the Nietzschean-Husserlian strand of naturalistic ethical realism, wherein ethical values are matters of fact in the world, and the Heideggerian-Levinasian strand of transcendental ethical realism, wherein our openness to the environment helps us discover not matters of fact or value or any entity as such, but a transcendental source of meaning or Being.[34] From this description, we must be forced to take the realist position of *Aesthetic Genesis* as the Nietzschean-Husserlian naturalistic ethical realism as opposed to the Heideggerian-Levinasian strand of transcendental ethical realism. I shall make a decision on this in what remains of this chapter, after summarizing Thomson's argument.

According to Thomson, in naturalistic ethical realism, ethical value is non-subjective and, thus, an aspect of the real world. One common agreement among naturalistic ethical realists, points out Thomson, seems to be that "the very notion of something's being 'good' is ultimately rooted in the objective conditions required to sustain and enhance the life of an organism, while the 'bad' comes from those conditions which diminish or eradicate such life."[35] Thomson is worried that such general principles are in fact useless in resolving actual ecological disputes. He is worried that a rigorous observance of the principle of sustaining the conditions of life in general could undermine "what human beings prize most highly." He believes that the Heideggerian-Levinasian transcendental ethical realism, according to which humans indirectly participate in making their world intelligible, can be a more helpful approach in ecological ethics. We are able to see what truly matters when we are open towards the environment, but the meaning we thus perceive in the environment is not reducible to facts, values or entities in any way, because it is that general horizon on the basis of which facts, values and entities become intelligible. The world or horizon thus opened up, contends Thomson, can help us make distinctions between anti-humanistic eco-fascism and totally speciesist anti-environmentalism. However, it is questionable whether Thomson's conclusions take us any further in our grappling with the environmental crisis and the questions it has thrown up. While affirming that the environmental crisis is ultimately a crisis of meaning, Thomson notes that what counts for transcendental ethical realism "is not life *per se*, but rather a life that has a temporally-enduring world that matters to it explicitly."[36] However, the speciesist preference for human Dasein and its world-forming ability as opposed to the worldlessness of inanimate things and the world-poverty of non-human animals[37] is unavoidable in such a characterization of the value of the environment. Would anything environmental ever become preferable in a culture of humanistic speciesism, as modernity is? Can world-formation-capacity be the basis for environmental decision making? Isn't something other than world-formation, like the intentionality of nature, required to distinguish between a "constellation of intelligibility" that is totally destructive of the environment like modernity is, and the one that is permeated with a sense of respect for non-human beings?

Is ethical value an objective given in *Aesthetic Genesis*, as in naturalistic ethical realism? There is surely a declared position against subjectivism and relativism.[38] But this position is not in any way a claim about the objectively independent existence of ethical values out there in the world, as is the case with Thomson's naturalistic ethical realism. To be sure, such a claim is made by Erazim Kohák when he argues that the objective world is arrived at by abstracting from "the value-laden world I actually experience. Nor is the value and meaning structure that makes my world intelligible one I invent. It is one I find, constituted by the presence of purposive life, including my own, prior to my reflecting upon it."[39] This is, however, a position that *Aesthetic Genesis* rejects. The formal aspects of ethical behavior are natural and universal, in the sense that they can be found wherever there are human beings, but are not aspects of the objects of the world. "Most philosophers who have argued for the objectivity of moral value have assumed that moral values lie somewhere beyond and outside of the realm of human action, and that our intellect has the task of 'seeing' and conceptually formulating these transcendent values in such a way that they might inform moral behavior."[40] The assumption that such values are self-evident is challenged by *Aesthetic Genesis*, for if they were, pre-modern communities would not have failed to grasp them. If they are evidently present somewhere (as in a Platonic heaven) for our diligent analytic intelligence to discover/ uncover, it would appear that we are better and clearer thinkers than Kant and other philosophers, able to have clarity over their "subjectivistic presupposition." *Aesthetic Genesis* considers such a view of grasping the evidential nature of moral values as a corollary of the problematic idea of progress.

In *Aesthetic Genesis*, moral values become evident when they are conceptually and rationally formulated. In that sense, "they are human constructs that come after moral behavior, not before it."[41] Something virtuous already animates and "informs" human action, before it is conceptually formulated and articulated. Virtues and vices inform human behavior, just as matter is informed by forms like table or pen. The intentional relation between action and its form as grasped by consciousness is moral value. Hence, moral value is not an objective property of the world, but an intentional being or form assumed by the relation between humans and their world. But there can be goodness in the world as, for example, in flourishing nature or the gurgling river. This is its intentional *telos* towards its perfect form. However, even a positive human disposition of understanding the "goodness" of the river and preserving it for that sake has to take a form of human behavior, which can become a conscious value only when it is represented by the human mind as such.[42] At the same time, moral value is not subjective.

> The virtues are no more subjective than is the form of a tree. The tree can't be
> a tree without its form, and courageous behavior cannot be courageous without
> its form. But just as the form of a tree is embodied differently in different sorts
> of trees, so is courage embodied differently in different sorts of behavior. This
> difference in behaviors is apparent between individuals in the same culture,
> but it is perhaps more evident between diverse cultures, separated by space
> and/or time . . . The determinate 'location' of the behavior determines also the
> manner in which it comes to be conceptually formulated as a particular 'vir-
> tue.'[43]

According to *Aesthetic Genesis*, metaphysical questions like whether these forms exist independently of human behavior are a matter for the gods, not for scientists or philosophers or theologians.

This view is certainly realist, but not in the sense of realism attributed by Thomson to naturalistic ethical realism. Value is not an object hidden in the thing, awaiting discovery by a human mind. It is the form of human action. At the same time, representing the meaning of the form of human action differently by different individuals and communities in different cultural contexts is accepted as different ways of interpreting the real "informing" of human action by virtues/values. Virtues are forms of human behavior, which become values when they are consciously represented as such. Neither a radical relativism of meaning of ethical rules nor a radical absolutism is a plausible position in this narrative. This conception is realistic, because differences are due to changes in the meanings of words (ideal being), and not due to the intentional or material being of the thing or its form. Such changes in meaning occur gradually in the process of historical evolution. The meanings of words like "courage" or "fidelity" are "intersubjectively constituted, sometimes with reference to the etymology of the words, and always with reference to the more comprehensive intentionality guiding the word usage of those speaking the language."[44] Even with regard to something like a literary work of art, the *logos* that guides the creator and the interpreter/reader of the work is the form that allows both the creator and the re-creator to participate differently in that which is the same. Hence, the two are able to say that they are participating in and understanding the same intentional object and its intentional being. The difference is animated by the re-creator's history, situatedness, and all that is unique about her/him and the sameness is animated by the form or *logos* of the work—its intentional being.[45]

The realism of *Aesthetic Genesis* resists the privileged place granted to language in hermeneutic philosophies, whether Heideggerian-Gadamerian or Derridian-post-structuralist. While it acknowledges the role played by language (ideal being) in the re-creation of our world, it considers the interpretive role of language as secondary to the perceptive process of our engagement with the external world, although language is still definitive. Accordingly, "pre-linguistic experience is already 'understandable'" and "sensation and other non-linguistic types of experience inform such 'higher' types of experience as discursive thought, or intellection."[46] At the same time, the process of "informing" is not one-way. The world and consciousness mutually inform each other. While *Aesthetic Genesis* accepts the role of prejudice in our grappling with the external world and the mutual informing of the world and consciousness (the "hermeneutic circle" in other words), its realist thesis underlines that (i) we can suspend prejudices sometimes or reflectively, and that (ii) pre-linguistic experience has its own understanding. Whether "understanding" in this sense is still linguistic or proto-linguistic is a question that is left open in *Aesthetic Genesis*.

Therefore, Thomson's distinction between naturalistic and transcendental ethical realism does not strictly apply in the case of *Aesthetic Genesis*. It is neither "naturalistic," in the sense that ethical value is an objective property of the world we are dealing with, nor "transcendental," in the sense that, when we are appropriately open to nature, what we receive is Being or the source of meaning rather than meaning *per se*. Ethics, in this sense, is realist, because it is the real form of human behavior that we consciously come to call "good"; it is not transcendental, in the sense that there is no separate, transcendental condition for meaning other than meaning itself. Intentional consciousness does not discover objective values in nature or world. Virtues are intentional beings that give form to human behavior towards the world. The world is real; words and ideas in our minds about the world are real; and the form of our relation with the world is real. They are different sorts of being. While the value-laden form of human behavior, whether it is towards nature or towards other humans, is real across cultures, the realizations and meanings of these forms are cultural, contextual, and linguistically specified. What we, thus, can glean from *Aesthetic Genesis* is a realist-interpretive thesis, which is neither naturalistic ethical realism nor transcendental ethical realism. Just as the meaning of the literary text is not totally different between the author and the reader, and possibly not totally the same, the meaning of our experience is neither absolutely irreducible and unique, nor totally reducible to a single, universal given. This explanatory strategy of *Aesthetic Genesis* has interesting bearings on environmental ethics.

OUR REAL AND MORAL CONNECTION TO NATURE

Aesthetic Genesis rejects both transcendentalism (Heideggerian total understanding of Being that determines every being as being) and idealism (Husserlian ideal constitution of the world within consciousness).[47] In the genesis of our meaningful relationships with the world, material being of things, ideal meaning of words, and subsisting meaning of intentional relations play equally vital roles. Heidegger's fundamental ontology, a purported critique of Husserl's idealistic turn, is, thus, seen as equally anthropocentric and subjectivistic as the idealist phenomenology of the later Husserl, because the intentionality of Dasein is thoroughly anthropocentric in effect, although Dasein as such is not reducible to the human.[48]

The doctrine of *Aesthetic Genesis* is an extension of Husserl's intentionality thesis. Intentionality or directedness is attributed specifically to organisms, even of the most rudimentary variety.[49]

> An entity that possesses organic unity is dynamic and energic: It is constantly actualizing its various potentials throughout its life. This sort of unity is to be distinguished from that which may belong to artificial entities such as tables and chairs, and inanimate natural entities such as rocks; whatever unity such entities may exhibit remains static and lifeless.[50]

While discussing the intentionality of literary works and their continuous reinterpretation and retranslation, *Aesthetic Genesis* agrees that a permanently fixed interpretation or translation is impossible, because any living language is constantly changing, and the interpretive flux is a reflection of this dynamism inherent to language. The immediate appendage is that "the changing nature of language is but a reflection of the changing nature of being itself, and that the ever-changing, ever-evolving nature of God's creation renders necessary its constant re-interpretation and re-translation."[51] That is, although intentional meaning does have a form to base upon, what it captures in language and culture does keep changing, not simply because language and culture are dynamic, but because reality itself is so. The Aristotelian teleological and evolutionist imports of *Aesthetic Genesis* are undeniable. The suggestion, therefore, is this: "Perhaps this ongoing creation, from its very essence as 'ongoing,' supplies us with the direction for its re-interpretation, and for the perpetual intersubjective re-constitution of its individual intentional objectivities . . . Perhaps all of creation is intentional in this sense."[52] While in *Aesthetic Genesis* the intentional being of nature is constantly alluded to (as evident in the book's subtitle), what is definitively stated there as self-evident is the intentionality of organisms. This ambiguity is settled in Mitscherling's most recent publication. Accordingly, "realist phenomenology, adopting many of the insights of Aristotelian metaphysics and the Aristotelian account of cognition, regards all of creation as informed and purposive, and human consciousness and intelligence as simply more complex developments of features that are to be found at every level of nature."[53] The conclusion to the analysis in this context is that it is not necessary to consider the first cause as superseding nature, but as natural; that is, the first and final cause of nature as "informed matter ordered purposively."

That which allows the predilection for rational consciousness in the analyses of Descartes and Kant as shown in the first section of this chapter is the unique difference of consciousness from matter. If there are two unmixable categories in the world, it appears in their analysis that they are matter and mind. The realist phenomenological argument of *Aesthetic Genesis*, that consciousness is a form of intentionality, which is central to nature as such but is more clearly manifest in living organisms and even more so in human consciousness, is certainly a plausible and productive way of undercutting the predilection accorded to human consciousness in our modern global culture and of looking at environmental ethics as such. From this point of view, what allows a defense of the unique privilege of consciousness is merely the already assumed speciesist privileging of its intentional being, a ready case of begging the question. The intrinsic worth of consciousness as the only intentional or meaning-invested "thing" in the world is, therefore, a red herring re-appearing again and again in our moral discourses on nature. This strand of *Aesthetic Genesis* pulls it away from the Heidegger-inspired phenomenological response to the ecological crisis, which, as Iain Thomson describes it, is humanistic and to that extent anthropocentric. According to Thomson, the naturalistic strand of phenomenological eco-philosophy tends "to generate anti-human consequences that render their widespread acceptance extremely unlikely, leading to a practical dead-end" that suggests eco-fascist, anti-democratic solutions.[54] I want to suggest that this is where the realist phenomenology of *Aesthetic Genesis* can turn out to be helpful. It can show, on the one hand, that intentionality is central to nature as such and hence not a prerogative of human consciousness, but it can also help us to see that our moral culture and judgments, though potentially and formally universal, are fraught with radical differences, which we can, nevertheless, overcome gradually through the dialogical arrival at objectivity in our ever-growing and wider intersubjective global community. A kind of Gadamerian fusion of horizons that helps human groups to be concerned about radical prejudices, to suspend them, to move towards agreeable ethical strategies in contentious matters like the ecological crisis, and to be discerningly aware of irreconcilable differences, should never be caricatured as mere utopia.

Hence, the moral strand of the argument of *Aesthetic Genesis* that moral value is a real intentional form of human behavior, which is grasped in various cultural-linguistic traditions of the world—a strand that does not take *Aesthetic Genesis* too far away from the contemporary interpretive revolution in the human sciences—is valuable as far as environmental philosophy and ethics are concerned. How do we understand and appreciate the sheer variety of responses to the ecological crisis available in the world today? First of all, we can foster worldviews and cultures that in some way are attuned to the intentionality prevalent in nature, unlike the Judeo-Christian-Western mainstream global cultures. In the Indic (Hindu-Buddhistic-Jain), animistic, tribal, pagan, native American and such other cultures, one might still find a ready acceptance of the intentionality of nature, which is simply not available in the dominant Western tradition which is now unmistakably in its global trail. [55] And second, we can attune our global culture to the human connection to and our intentional solidarity with nature. A change in our global discourses about nature and a self-conscious destabilizing of the privilege we ourselves have granted to our species alone can destine our common history differently and in a more eco-friendly direction. This insight of the realist phenomenology of *Aesthetic Genesis* is invaluable, in the sense that this argument has the demonstrative angle regarding intentionality as central to nature as a whole, and the cultural angle that sees the necessity of bringing about changes to our common discourses in order to intersubjectively objectify what is argumentatively demonstrable.

In this sense, it is not the merely naturalistic and rational assertion that there is intentionality in nature that seems to move *Aesthetic Genesis*, but the non-naturalistic and yet realist assertion that the intentionality of nature has become hidden in the dominant cultural history of the West in the past four hundred years. Such an insinuation, for instance, is clear in the discussion on the soul: "the ancient Greeks and the medieval thinkers regarded the soul as something entirely natural, and as an integral part of natural creation." [56] It is the mechanistic modern worldview that gave rise to a different understanding of the soul. Descartes discarded the Greek distinction between the animating or life-giving soul and rational mind, and located the supposedly non-extended soul in the pineal gland. The contemporary understanding of the mind as a thing attached to the brain or the neural network is still not distant from the Cartesian tradition. The difficulty such a view has in explaining the location of motor skills or memory or any faculty is still considered irresolvable: "if memory were indeed something 'stored' materially in the flesh of the brain, then to 'recall it' in one way at one moment and in another way at another moment would entail that alteration of the material flesh of the brain is responsible for the alteration of memory." [57] Similarly, *Aesthetic Genesis* would agree that the disappearance of our sense of the ensoulment or intentional being of nature is a part of the particular historical development of our global intellectual culture, modeled after the European scientist culture of the last four hundred years. Its own thesis of the intentionality of nature, which I have laid bare above, thus calls for the re-attunement of our intellectual-cultural sensibilities towards the lost sense of the intentionality of nature. Such is, I believe, the final statement of *Aesthetic Genesis*:

> The re-thinking of the concept-terms that I have been suggesting in *Aesthetic Genesis* enables us to formulate a more comprehensive view of nature itself, and to regard it not as a machine constructed out of dead matter but as a vast

organism the life and workings of which cannot be satisfactorily explained by the paradigms of modern thought.[58]

Avoiding the purely materialist or purely spiritualist thesis, for example, what we can say about the thesis of embodied cognition in contemporary philosophy of mind, according to *Aesthetic Genesis*, is merely that the cognizing human being is "an incarnated soul, a natural soul that is an integral part of the organism of the natural world," which of course is itself animated, ensouled, or intentional.

Another possible and important strand of *Aesthetic Genesis* is the link one can see in its thesis of nature's intentionality with the Gaia hypothesis of the biologist James Lovelock. The Gaia hypothesis, taking scientific and philosophical cues, considers the earth as "a single self-sustaining unit, even a living being, possibly a conscious one."[59] The figure of Gaia is the Greek goddess of the Earth, living, feeling, sensing, knowing, responding, reacting and self-regulating. Lovelock personifies the earth as "a single living entity, capable of manipulating the Earth's atmosphere to suit its overall needs and endowed with faculties and powers far beyond those of its constituent parts."[60] The theory is scientific and philosophical. Lovelock took care to detail the scientific side of the theory in *The Ages of Gaia* (1988).[61]

The alliance between Gaia theory and phenomenology is occasionally acknowledged, as by David Abram in his much admired (and Merleau-Ponty-inspired) *The Spell of the Sensuous* (1996):

> The similarity between such animistic worldviews and the emerging perspective of contemporary ecology is not trivial. Atmospheric geochemist James Lovelock, elucidating the well-known Gaia hypothesis—a theory stressing the major role played by organic life in the ceaseless modulation of the earth's atmospheric and climatic conditions—insists that the geological environment is itself constituted by organic life, and by the products of organic metabolism. In his words, we inhabit "a world that is the breath and bones of our ancestors."[62]

Similarly, Gaia theorist Stephen Harding acknowledges Abram's insights as helpful:

> Abram takes up Merleau-Ponty's notion of the collective 'flesh of the world' to speak of this vast, planetary tissue of sensations and interdependent perceptions in which our own lives (like those of the trees, the crows, and the spiders) are embedded. The term 'flesh' provides Abram with a way of speaking of reality as a fabric woven of experience—and hence of the material world as thoroughly animate and alive.[63]

Gaia theory is beginning to recognize "the teleological character inherent in the notion of cognition" and "a residual form of teleology within the notion of intentionality, as inherent to life, but which does not, however, 'require an extra, transcendental source, as in Kant.'"[64] The philosophical proposals of *Aesthetic Genesis* can contribute to our understanding of the intentional being of the earth as a whole, of Gaia.[65]

Aesthetic Genesis, thus, can be seen as a useful way of relooking at the question of our connection to nature in the present era of our historical disconnect with nature, in an attempt to rediscover the historically lost sensibility of interconnectedness with nature. This connection was real and vital for premodern peoples and tribal communities still untouched by the globally permeating modern metaphysics. In the language of *Aesthetic Genesis*, we have inherited today a differentiated understanding of the "form" of the living planet, although the form as such or the intentional being of nature as the living organism has not changed. The modern project of disenchanting the magical powers of the living earth and the dynamic natural phenomena, and objectifying them either as inanimate matter or as non-intentional animal beings, summarizes the intellectual history behind our contemporary incredulity towards the intentionality of nature. There are strands in current ecological philosophy and ethics, which are not only busy listing reasons to attribute intrinsic value to nature, but which are also busy reimagining and re-attuning humanity into a culture of connection with nature. As I have argued in this chapter, the line of thinking in *Aesthetic Genesis* can make important contributions in this regard. Indeed, the phenomenology in *Aesthetic Genesis* is an ecophenomenology, as it denies the predilection for consciousness as the solely intentional being, and posits the origin of consciousness in the intentional being of nature.

NOTES

1. See: Charles S. Brown and Ted Toadvine (eds.), *Eco-phenomenology: Back to the Earth Itself.* (Albany: State University of New York Press, 2003).
2. Jeff Mitscherling, *Aesthetic Genesis: The Origin of Consciousness in the Intentional Being of Nature.* (Lanham: University Press of America, 2010). Henceforth cited as AG.
3. In the major Indian philosophical traditions, for example, this differentiation between human and non-human reality in terms of consciousness is not taken for granted. In Upaniṣadic thinking, there is of course the absolute privileging of consciousness, understood as the substratum of all object-awareness. Consciousness itself is not defined by intentionality or object-directedness, although intentional awareness is said to be its empirical nature. Getting rid of the intentional condition of empirical consciousness is said to be the ultimate *telos* of consciousness, considered as reality in its final characterization. Consciousness in this form is considered as permeating all empirical reality in degrees of variation, and the fascinating aspects of human consciousness are only symbolic of the ultimate nature of reality (consciousness) underlying every being. In this sense, pure consciousness is "prapañcopaśamam, śāntam, śivam, advaitam" (destructive of the phenomenal world, quiet, blissful, and non-dual without a second) according to the seventh verse of the Māṇḍūkya Upaniṣad (See: Bina Gupta, "Advaita Vedānta and Husserl's Phenomenology." *Husserl Studies* 20:2 (2004): 119-134).
4. René Descartes, *Meditations on First Philosophy with Selections from the Objections and Replies,* trans. Michael Moriarty (Oxford: Oxford University Press, 2008), 20.

5. René Descartes, *A Discourse on the Method of Correctly Conducting One's Reason and Seeking Truth in the Sciences*, trans. Ian Maclean (Oxford: Oxford University Press, 2006), 46.

6. Ibid., 48.

7. Ibid., 48.

8. Immanuel Kant, *Toward Perpetual Peace and Other Writings on Politics, Peace, and History*, ed. Pauline Kleingeld and trans. David L. Colclasure. (New Haven: Yale University Press, 2006), 26–27.

9. Ibid., 17.

10. Immanuel Kant, *Practical Philosophy*, trans. & ed. Mary J. Gregor. (Cambridge: Cambridge University Press, 1996), 79.

11. Ibid., 564. Kant argues in one of his lectures, according to the notes of Georg Ludwig Collins, a student: "So if a man has his dog shot, because it can no longer earn a living for him, he is by no means in breach of any duty to the dog, since the latter is incapable of judgement, but he thereby damages the kindly and humane qualities in himself, which he ought to exercise in virtue of his duties to mankind." Immanuel Kant, *Lectures on Ethics*, ed. Peter Heath and B. Schneewind, trans. Peter Heath. (Cambridge: Cambridge University Press, 1997), 212.

12. Hakan Seckinelgin, *The Environment and International Politics: International Fisheries, Heidegger and Social Method* (Abingdon: Routledge, 2006), 107.

13. AG, 5.

14. AG, 26.

15. AG, 115.

16. AG, 126.

17. AG, 76.

18. AG, 51.

19. Jeff Mitscherling, "A Phenomenological Analysis of Basic Concepts Shared by Evolutionary Theory and Intelligent Design" in *Irreconcilable Differences?: Fostering Dialogue among Philosophy, Theology, and Science*, eds. Jason C. Robinson and David A. Peck, 61–74. (Eugene: Pickwick Publications, 2015), 71.

20. Ibid., 73.

21. Ibid.

22. AG, 30–31.

23. AG, 32.

24. AG, 32.

25. Erazim Kohák, *The Embers and the Stars: A Philosophical Inquiry into the Moral Sense of Nature*. (Chicago: The University of Chicago Press, 1984), 8.

26. AG, 19.

27. AG, 18.

28. AG, 116.

29. AG, 4.

30. AG, 52.

31. AG, 53.

32. AG, 19.

33. AG, 128.

34. Iain Thomson, "Ontology and Ethics at the Intersection of Phenomenology and Environmental Philosophy" *Inquiry* 47:4 (2004: 380–412), 380.

35. Ibid., 390.

36. Ibid., 402.

37. See: Martin Heidegger, *The Fundamental Concepts of Metaphysics: World, Finitude, Solitude*, trans. William McNeill and Nicholas Walker. (Bloomington: Indiana University Press, 2001).

38. AG, 61.

39. Erazim Kohák, "An Understanding Heart: Reason, Value, and Transcendental Phenomenology" in Charles S. Brown and Ted Toadvine (Eds.), *Eco-Phenomenology: Back to the Earth Itself*, 19–35. (Albany: State University of New York Press, 2003), 25.

40. AG, 61.

41. AG, 62.

42. Heidegger has consistently criticized the modern notion of "value" as representational. He writes with reference to Nietzsche's concept of value: "In characterizing value as a viewpoint, the one essential thing for Nietzsche's concept of value follows: as a viewpoint, value is always posited by a seeing and for a seeing. This seeing is of such a kind that it sees in that it has seen, and that it has seen by re-presenting to itself as a particular thing that which was sighted, thereby positing it. It is only through this setting within representation that . . . this seeing becomes a point of sight, that is, becomes what matters in seeing and in all activity directed by vision. Before this, therefore, values are not something in themselves, so that they could be taken when necessary as points of sight." Martin Heidegger, "Nietzsche's Word: 'God is Dead'" (1943) in *Off the Beaten Track*, trans. Julian Young and Kenneth Haynes,157-199. (Cambridge: Cambridge University Press, 2002), 170.

43. AG, 62.

44. AG, 57.

45. AG, 129–30.

46. AG, 10–11.

47. AG, 16.

48. AG, 15.

49. *Aesthetic Genesis* argues that an extremely simple organic substance like a paramecium is seen to be intentionally directed under the microscope. It explores every direction, responding vigorously to impediments placed on its path. "Both its motility and its responsiveness indicate *intentional* behavior: the organism is tending towards and tending away from elements in its environment, and this is precisely what 'intentional being' most fundamentally is" (AG, 70). With the complexity of the organism, the complexity of its intentionality increases. Humans have the capacity of using words in language which have ideal being or significata. The ideal being of words can themselves get more complex with figures of speech and metaphors.

50. AG, 13.

51. AG, 57.

52. AG, 57.

53. See Mitscherling, "A Phenomenological Analysis of Basic Concepts Shared by Evolutionary Theory and Intelligent Design," 73.

54. Thomson, "Ontology and Ethics at the Intersection of Phenomenology and Environmental Philosophy," 401.

55. I have argued the case of the tribal worldviews in the face of the global ecological crisis in the following articles: (i) "The Interconnectedness Sensibility: Tribal Ethos and Environmental Ethics" in *Beyond Humanism: Philosophical Essays on Environmental Ethics*, ed. Saji Varghese, 127-165 (New Delhi: Concept Publishing, 2014); (ii) "Earth's the Limit: The Sense of Finiteness among the Hill Tribes of Northeast India" in *Environmental Values Emerging from Cultures & Religions of the ASEAN Region*, ed. Roman Meinhold, 91-122. (Bangkok: Assumption University, 2015).

56. AG, 101.

57. AG, 104.

58. AG, 142.

59. Derek Wall, *Green History: A Reader in Environmental Literature, Philosophy and Politics* (London: Routledge, 1994), 74.

60. James Lovelock, *Gaia: A New Look at Life on Earth* (Oxford: Oxford University Press, 2000) (first edition in 1979), 9.

61. James Lovelock, *The Ages of Gaia: A Biography of Our Living Earth*, Second Edition (New York: Norton, 1995).

62. David Abram, *The Spell of the Sensuous: Perception and Language in a More-than-human World* (New York: Vintage, 1996), 19 n.4.

63. Stephen Harding, *Animate Earth: Science, Intuition and Gaia*, Second Edition. (Devon: Green Books, 2010), 73.

64. Luciano Onori and Guido Visconti, "The GAIA Theory: From Lovelock to Margulis; From a Homeostatic to a Cognitive Autopoietic Worldview" *Rendiconti Lincei*, 23:4 (2012: 375-386), 382.

65. Of course, the hypothesis of the intentionality of Gaia itself is beset with paradoxes, as Bruno Latour argued in his 2013 lectures in the University of Edinburgh titled "Facing Gaia: A New Enquiry into Natural Religion." While agreeing that the concept of Gaia allows us to see the intentionality of all agents in the network of nature (consistent with his actor-network theory), who are modifying their environment to suit their purposes better as evolutionary understanding teaches us, Latour disagrees with Gaia theory that this view would help us to understand the intentionality of nature as a whole or Gaia. The persistence of inanimism or the non-intentionality of nature is inexplicable for Latour. But the understanding that every being is intentionally directed toward its own purposes, he argues, leads to the conclusion that there cannot be an overall intentionality of the whole or Gaia in that case, but merely an overall chaos, because the intentionality of each being is intersected and impeded by the intentional directions of other beings (see Peter D. Burdon, *Earth Jurisprudence: Private Property and the Environment*. [Abingdon: Routledge, 2015], 64-65). However, we cannot consider at this point the nature of the overall intentionality of Gaia as a settled issue.

Chapter Ten

Intentionality and the New Copernican Revolution

Realist Phenomenology and the Extended Mind Hypothesis

Aaron Massecar

This essay shows how Mitscherling's *Aesthetic Genesis* provides a framework wherein realist phenomenology and classical pragmatism can work together towards describing intentional structures. This account can then be used to describe an ontology that makes sense of some of the claims of contemporary cognitive science.

A brief note should be made at the beginning about the current scene in phenomenology. One might wonder why we should be referring to phenomenologists from over a hundred years ago when there are plenty of exceptional phenomenologists today. The problem is the kind of phenomenology that is dominant today. Most contemporary phenomenology is inherited from the later Husserl and, as such, is too nominalistic. This contemporary form of phenomenology might give an account of the appearance of objects, but it does not provide an ontology of objects. If phenomenology is to be grounded in anything other than phantasy, then it needs an ontology. Realist phenomenology can provide just such an ontology.

INTRODUCTION

Recent work in cognitive science is challenging the distinction between the inside and the outside of the mind. Many have pointed to Andy Clark and David Chalmers' 1998 essay "The Extended Mind" as inaugurating this particular form of debate. In that article, Clark and Chalmers argue that features of our environment play an active role in our cognitive processing. The active process of the environment has been characterized by others, like J.J. Gibson, as "affordances"; Jay Schulkin uses the term "visceral appraisal mechanisms"; and Mark Johnson and George Lakoff conceive of an "organism-environment coupling." Each of these thinkers is pushing for an active externalism that seeks to explain how we offload cognitive functioning onto our environment and how that offloaded cognitive functioning influences future experience. Although this debate is relatively recent within cognitive science, it parallels a similar debate that took place one hundred years ago with Edmund Husserl and his students, a debate that Jeff Mitscherling highlights in his work, *Aesthetic Genesis: The Origin of Consciousness in the Intentional Being of Nature.*

Many of Husserl's students were displeased with his insistence that objects of experience were constituted solely by acts of consciousness. His students, in particular Roman Ingarden, Max Scheler, and Adolph Reinach, were deeply concerned that Husserl's position led directly to an idealism that neglected the role of the external world in constituting objects of consciousness. Each of these thinkers, in his own way, articulated a form of realism that could have supplemented Husserl's studies. Ingarden focused on aesthetic experience, Scheler on ethical experience, and Reinach on laws. Ingarden, Scheler, and Reinach were representatives of a movement within phenomenology called "realist phenomenology" that was working to demonstrate the role that the external environment plays in our cognitive processing. This is precisely the work of the *New Copernican Hypothesis* that Mitscherling characterises in his book.

The main concept that hangs in the balance between Husserlean idealism and his students' realism is the notion of intentionality. Husserl appropriated the medieval notion of intentionality through Franz Brentano's nominalist reading of medieval thinkers like Duns Scotus, in particular Scotus' work on universals. Had Husserl read the medievalists more directly, then he might have derived a different notion of intentionality with a more realist bent.

This is precisely the way that C.S. Peirce read the scholastics, and thus he ended up with precisely this form of realism, a realism he referred to as "extreme scholastic realism" (Collected Papers 8.208).[1] His reading of first and second intentions led him to argue for a view of experience that sees our feeling, acting, and thinking as mediated by signs that are themselves determined by objects that play an essential role in determining different forms of interpretation. In other words, signs interpret intentional structures.

Mitscherling's work seeks to reappropriate this realist move by reexamining the nature of consciousness as arising from intentional structures found in experience. This essay will demonstrate how Mitscherling's work performs this reappropriation and the consequences that this will have for extending the extended mind hypothesis. I will do this by showing how Husserl's position could be supplemented with the realist tradition and also show how a likeminded thinker, Charles Sanders Peirce, was working through these same problems. Peirce's work, like that of most of Husserl's students, has largely been passed over in the tradition. Bringing Peirce together with the realist phenomenologists based on the framework that Mitscherling provides will then help to provide some direction for contemporary cognitive science.

REALIST PHENOMENOLOGY

In *Ideas: General Introduction to Pure Phenomenology* (1913), Husserl articulates the different reductions that are necessary in order to grasp the essences of objects. In bracketing and suspending the natural attitude, Husserl thought that he was able to simultaneously grasp the essences of objects as constituted by consciousness and leave aside any questions about the relationship between objects of consciousness and their existence external to consciousness. The essences were important, not their existence apart from any possible experience. This is an echo of Hegel's move against Kant's *ding an sich*. Instead of claiming that we don't have access to the thing in itself, as Kant ambiguously does, Hegel claims that the object as it is grasped by consciousness is in fact more than a mere shadow of the thing in itself, but is instead the real object, as it is in itself. Husserl takes this seriously and says that we have access to the real essence, because it is constituted by noetic acts of consciousness. But because of the *epoché* that brackets the natural attitude, the connection between the object and the external world is lost. This approach is problematic, because it generates an idealism that is necessarily disconnected from the external world. As such, on Husserl's account, the intentional object and intentionality itself are necessarily constituted by the mind. The point, from the realist phenomenologists' rejoinder, is that the intentional structures are at least partly found in experience rather than constituted by acts of consciousness. This, I believe, is what Gibson is offering and what Clark and Chalmers are pointing towards. More on that later.

There are numerous phenomenologists who identify themselves with the Realist Phenomenological movement, such as Adolf Reinach (1883–1917), Edith Stein (1841–1942), Roman Ingarden (1893–1970), and Maurice Merleau-Ponty (1908–1961). This section will highlight two of those thinkers' works, those of Roman Ingarden and Adolph Reinach. Part of Ingarden's work was to critique the metaphysical idealism apparent in Husserl's transcendental philosophy of the *Logical Investigations* and *Ideas*.[2] Ingarden attempted to convince his teacher, Husserl, that the intentional objects that he was describing were not entirely dependent on an individual for their constitution, that there was something real and external that corresponded to those intentional objects that Husserl thought could only be constituted by acts of consciousness. In order to make this general claim, Ingarden attempted to demonstrate the existence of at least one intentional object that was not dependent on consciousness for its continued existence.

Ingarden chose the literary work of art to demonstrate that "not all of the objects of consciousness were constituted solely through the intentionality of consciousness—in other words, that non-ideal, or 'real,' elements were also involved in the constitution of (at least some of) the objects of consciousness."[3] If it could be shown that the literary work of art had intentional being that depended on a schematic structure that, once created, did not depend on the material existence of that object, then it could be shown that the intentional being or the essence of the work had a real existence independent from both the material existence and from the sustained existence of that essence in consciousness. Ingarden's work, *Controversy over the Existence of the World,* was a further development of his program of realist phenomenology. Ingarden demonstrated that at least the literary work of art has an essence that is neither dependent on material existence nor on acts of consciousness for the sustained existence of that object, once the object has been created. If this is the case for the literary work of art, then it should be the case for other intentional objects.

Reinach took a slightly different approach, one that has been mistreated by some contemporary thinkers. There was an article published not too long ago by Kimberly Baltzer-Jaray that brings to light some of the difficulties that have arisen in the secondary literature with respect to understanding Reinach's work.[4] In particular, Barry Smith and Artur Rojszczak have argued that Reinach is a Platonist. Baltzer-Jaray shows, step-by-step, how this interpretation has gone wrong. Her conclusion serves as a good starting point for our discussion.

Reinach is not a Platonist. He does not hold that essences are entities existing in some other world. Instead, Reinach states that essences are grasped by beginning with words and signification. Words and their significations point to objects. Certainly those words and their significations could point to material objects, but it is not the material objects with which we are concerned: "If by contrast we aim to grasp the essence of red or of color, then, in the last analysis, we need only to fix upon some perceived, imagined, or represented color, and, in what is so presented, lift the essence (So-Sein), the 'whatness,' of the color away from that which, as singular or actual, is of no interest to us."[5] It is not the particular entity that we are concerned with in the particular moment, but what the essence of that object is.

There are others who were not happy with Husserl's work. Max Scheler, through his critiques of Kantian formalism, attempted to show that values are direct objects of perception, thus showing that ethical objects are not dependent on sustaining acts of the mind. Unfortunately, partly because of the war, these students were not able to fully develop the kind of thinking that might have moved contemporary phenomenology away from idealism towards realism.

THE PEIRCE CONNECTION

This move, the move towards a realist phenomenology, is precisely how I read Charles Sanders Peirce's work. It is interesting to note that Peirce and Husserl both started using the word "phenomenology" most prominently around 1901.[6] Just a couple of years later, Peirce abandoned the term "phenomenology" in favor of the term "phaneroscopy." Spiegelberg suggests that this move towards phaneroscopy allowed for a discussion of the *phaneron*, or the real object, which for Peirce was important because of his intention to develop a foundation for the sciences. In Peirce's terms:

> The word [*phaneron*] is next to the simplest expression in Greek for manifest. Etymologically, evident is nearer to it. . . . There can be no question that [*phaneros*] means primarily brought to light, open to public inspection throughout. The manifest is that which a person who does not willfully shut his eyes to has no choice but to believe in. We find ourselves rather forced to accept the cognition than persuaded by any ulterior reason to do so. . . . the source of the affection is not within us,—when it might be a too narrow association or other defection of experience or faulty disposition,—but lies without us in the very object we wish to know, a circumstance which insures its involving genuine knowledge . . . . Upon that recognition we submit ourselves to it gladly for experience has taught us that our inward inclinations to belief are often our enemies, the majesty of reality our best friend. No mere typical instance of the manifest can be cited than one in which I look at [as] object and form the judgment, It seems red. If anybody were to ask me how I could be so sure that it truly seems red, I should probably answer instinctively, 'Do I not see it? Seeing is believing, here.' For I certainly do not see that it seems red; for what I see is an image, but what I say is a judgment, an object which has not a feature in common with an image. But I have a sense that the judgment is determined by the action of the perceptual image upon it, somewhat as the latter is determined by the real external object.
>
> Such being the implications of the Greek word [*phaneron*], in the interests of that exactitude of terminology without which no study can become scientific, I desire to have the privilege of creating an English word, phaneron, to denote whatever is throughout its entirety open to assured observation. No external object is throughout its entirety open to observation. (MS 337: 4–8, 1904)

It is clear by this rather long quote that Peirce is not interested in describing something that may or may not have a connection to the object that caused the image. Rather, he is using the word "phaneron" to describe that which is open to public inspection, because it is an image that is determined by the external object. The most important sentence that can be used to back this up comes at the end of the first full paragraph: the judgment is determined by the image, and the image is determined by the real external object. One would be right to read a form of Kantian transcendentalism in this model, if for no other reason than simply because Peirce read so much Kant in his early years. Peirce's image and judgment match up well with Kant's intuition and concept. The difference between the two comes when we see that Peirce isn't making a transcendental argument about the reality of noumena, but is rather claiming that the real external object determines the image which determines the object. This claim is unjustified from an epistemological perspective, since the grounds for making this claim would require the individual to be both the experiencer and the experienced simultaneously, a position that might not be justified from an epistemological point of view—but this position is not unjustified from an ontological standpoint. I believe that the ontological claim is substantially more important for Peirce than the epistemological. This is especially the case if we understand the late articulation of Peirce's notion of philosophy as being grounded in phenomenology, up through the normative sciences, and to metaphysics. It is clear from this framework that epistemology is not one of Peirce's main areas of focus. The pursuit of phenomenology itself isn't important for Peirce, but what phenomenology pursues is important. The object of that pursuit is the phaneron.

The adoption of the term "phaneron" might have actually been an improvement over the term "phenomenon" because, according to Spiegelberg, "[T]he literal meaning of the Greek term [phaneron] suggests more than a mere 'phenomenon' (which merely appears), namely something that reveals itself in its real nature . . . ."[7] This simple move, no doubt inspired by Peirce's recognition that the lack of connection between the object and the image would lead to nominalism, ensures that there is public access to the real external object through its effect on the image. He repeats the point again in 1905:

> Phaneroscopy is the description of the phaneron; and by the phaneron I mean the collective total of all that is in any way or in any sense present to the mind, quite regardless of whether it corresponds to any real thing or not. If you ask present when, and to whose mind, I reply that I leave these questions unanswered, never having entertained a doubt that those features of the phaneron that I have found in my mind are present at all times and to all minds. So far as I have developed this science of phaneroscopy, it is occupied with the formal elements of the phaneron. (CP 1.284, 1905)

Here is a major point of divergence between Husserl and Peirce: the idea that the real object is given in the appearance of the thing.

In any real object, that is, any permanent appearance, we may distinguish two elements, the permanence and the appearance. The permanence, the reality, is called by Mr. [William] James the being; the appearance or emergence into the world of phenomena is called the existence. This distinction is no mere logical convenience or necessity, but is a real partition, for it lies in the very esse of a thing. The reality is that on which the appearance is founded, and, therefore, the 'being' of a thing is its creator, while the 'existence' is the creature in himself. But the creature, because he does not contain within his own self the essence of his being, is, in himself, a mere phantom and no reality. (W2: 433)

There is a section in Peirce where he seems to be saying that the real object is what is immediately before the mind:

[T]he reader of this page directly perceives the very page itself some ten inches from his eye, and that another person, looking over his shoulder, will see the very same object, although under a different angle, and although each sees the real object, not in its entirety, but only as it is related to his own viewpoint, literal and tropical. (CP 8.186)

The problem here relates to the idea of what exactly is just before the mind; what is the nature of the real object that is being viewed here? It would seem to be the physical object itself, but this is not entirely correct. In viewing an object, there isn't a clear line of distinction between the image of the perceptual judgment and the perceptual judging itself.

(3) The third cotary proposition is that abductive inference shades into perceptual judgment without any sharp line of demarcation between them; or, in other words, our first premisses, the perceptual judgments, are to be regarded as an extreme case of abductive inferences, from which they differ in being absolutely beyond criticism. The abductive suggestion comes to us like a flash. It is an act of insight, although of extremely fallible insight. (CP 5.181)

Peirce mentions this with respect to abductive inference, but there appears to be no reason why it can't be applied to all forms of perceptual judgment. When we reflect on the activities of consciousness and step away from the moment of experience, then we might be able to form the abstractions and distinctions that are required in order to describe the different components of experience. But in the moment, these distinctions are not perceived. What this means is that there is something present in the moment of experience that includes the real external object, the image, and the judgment.

Though in the moment of experience we are not capable of making a distinction between the external object, the image, and the judgment, if we reflected on the activities of consciousness and wanted to make these distinctions regarding the object, image, and judgment, we can. Peirce provides an early description in 1865:

[there is a] distinction between thing, image, and form established in the lecture upon the definition of logic. A representation is anything which may be regarded as standing for something else. Matter or thing is that for which a representation might stand prescinded from all that could constitute a relation with any representation. A form is the relation between a representation and thing prescinded from both representation and thing. An image is a representation prescinded from thing and form.

Derived directly from this abstractest triad was another less abstract. This is Object—Equivalent Representation—Logos. The object is a thing corresponding to a representation regarded as actual. The equivalent representation is a representation in any language equivalent to a representation regarded as actual. A Logos is a form constituting the relation between an object and a representation regarded as actual.

Every symbol may be said in three different senses to be determined by its object, its equivalent representation, and its logos. It stands for its object, it translates its equivalent representation, it realizes its logos. (W 1:274, MS 106, 1865)

This quote complicates matters slightly, insofar as it introduces some new terminology, but that terminology will be helpful for us later on. The main thing to begin paying attention to is the role of the *logos*. This is a very early account, but already we can see the workings of a move that is going to complicate the picture for Husserl. A *logos* "is a form constituting the relation between an object and a representation regarded as actual." It is the relation here that is important. The symbol is the realization of the *logos*. The symbol is the realization of the relation between the object and a representation. Peirce doesn't spell it out here, but the very definition of a symbol is such that it carries with it some sort of behavioural modification. That behavioural modification on the part of the interpreter is in the form of an emotional, energetic, or logical interpretant. We will return to this point below.

There is another quote that needs to be mentioned here, and so I beg the reader to bear with me as we work through this.

When the connection with things is eliminated from qualities, we have Pure Forms. When the material and mental element is eliminated from representations we have Concepts or, as I prefer to say in order to avoid the apparent connection with the mind, Logoi. The three prescinded elements are fictions. The embodiment of a pure form in noumenal matter makes a thing with qualities. The realization of a pure form in the mind makes a mental representation. The embodiment of a pure form in a logos united with noumenal matter gives an outward representation. The use of these phrases is to formulate the analysis of a thing, a thought, and a representation into three several elements on the one side and one common element on the other.

The relevancy of this analysis consists in this, that if logic deals with the form of thought, it can be studied just as well in external as in internal representations, while by so doing we shall avoid all possible entanglement in the meshes of psychological controversy. Logic then deals with representations. But not with all kinds of representations. Representations are of three sorts.

1st Marks, by which I mean such representations as denote without connoting. If the applicability of a representation to a thing depends upon a convention which established precisely what it should denote, it would be a mark. A proper name is an instance.

2nd Analogues, by which I mean such representations as connote without denoting. A picture for instance which is a representation (whether intentional or not) of whatever it looks like, really resembles everything more or less, and so denotes nothing; although we may infer what was intended.

3rd Symbols, by which I mean such representations as denote by connoting. Of these three kinds of representations logic evidently refers only to the last, taking account of signs and analogues only when their laws happen to coincide with those of symbols or when combinations of symbols produce non-denotative or non-connotative representations. (An Unpsychological View of Logic to which are appended some applications of the theory of Psychology and other subjects, W 1:307-308 MS 109, May 1865)

The connections here with Kant are more obvious than before. The main distinguishing characteristic is that Peirce does not make of the noumena the unknowable ground of the representation; rather, the material that is then is combined with the pure form yields the object.

Peirce is clear here that he wants to use the language of "logos" in order to avoid the psychological connections that are normally associated with the internalization of the form. By making this move and internalizing the form of necessity, Kant was able to overcome Hume's challenge and state that necessity was something that we bring to experience, but in doing so, he radically subjectivized any discussion of the forms of judgment. Peirce is using the language of the *logos* as something independent of the individual acts of consciousness in order to avoid the subjectivity of Kant. Peirce's point is that this distinction can only be made as a fiction and is not something that can be distinguished in the moment of experience.

The next move that Peirce makes is to say that the study of the *logos* is logic. Logic isn't simply the structure of our thought, but logic is the structure of thought itself. This is what allows Peirce to say that thought is not in the mind, but mind is in thought. This seems a bizarre claim, until the background of that claim is made clear.

One more piece needs to be added to this. Logic is the structure, the form, and the content is the sign. Thus signs are the material that is structured by logic. For Peirce, there are 10^{66} different kinds of signs, but the main signs that are usually associated with Peirce are the icon, the index, and the symbol on the object side, and the emotional, energetic, and logical interpretant on the side of the subject (a trichotomy that matches up with aesthetics, ethics, and logic).

Now the problem of what the 'meaning' of an intellectual concept is can only be solved by the study of the interpretants, or proper significate effects, of signs. These we find to be of three general classes, with some important subdivisions. The first proper significate effect of a sign is a feeling produced by it. There is almost always a feeling which we come to interpret as evidence that we comprehend the proper effect of the sign, although the foundation of truth in this is frequently very slight. This 'emotional interpretant,' as I call it, may amount to much more than that feeling of recognition; and, in some cases, it is the only proper significate effect that the sign produces. Thus, the performance of a piece of concert music is a sign. It conveys, and is intended to convey, the composer's musical ideas; but these usually consist merely in a series of feelings. If a sign produces any further proper significate effect, it will do so through the mediation of the emotional interpretant, and such further effect will always involve an effort. I call it the 'energetic interpretant.' The effort may be a muscular one, as it is in the case of the command to ground arms; but it is much more usually an exertion upon the Inner World, a mental effort. It never can be the meaning of an intellectual concept, since it is a single act, [while] such a concept is of a general nature. But what further kind of effect can there be? (CP 5.475)

It is the emotional that will become the focus of the latter portion of this section on Peirce. As a preparatory note, it should be stated that the emotional should not be understood as belonging to emotions, but rather that the emotional interpretant is the feeling that is elicited by the qualities of the object. Aesthetics is the study of feeling, so, in this sense, we can see that the emotional/feeling interpretant is the site of aesthetics. Aesthetics is the study of feeling. Ethics is the study of the energetic interpretant or action. Logic is the study of the logoi which take the form of mental representations. These mental representations are not merely things that exist in the head, but are rather representations of the *logos* itself. The *logos* is the form of relations between objects and representations, but there is no reason to think that the form of relation between objects and representations only holds between objects and relations; these relations should equally hold between one object and another, especially independent of a perceiving consciousness. There is no reason to think that humans have some sort of privileged access to reality that is not open to non-human forms of perception. In this sense, anything that perceives and acts on that perception is acting on an understanding of the *logos*.

FEELING

This section will provide a general description of feelings. It starts with a distinction between feelings and emotions and then focuses on the relationship between feelings and qualities, parts and wholes, and then on the interpretation of feelings. The point of this section is to demonstrate the importance of feelings in all of the actions that we perform.

It should be noted at the outset that feelings are not identical with emotions. A feeling is a quality of immediate consciousness, and an emotion is the feeling itself that can only be understood insofar as it is mediated through the attribution of a word such as "green" or "soft." In Peirce's words, "any emotion is a predication concerning some thing" that is external to the individual. (W 2:172, 1868) Peirce's point here is that emotions, such as anger, are predicated of objects external to the individual; emotions are what we use to describe our feelings towards an object that we believe has caused that emotional state.

Every feeling "has its own positive quality which consists in nothing else, and which is of itself all that it is." (CP 1.306, 1907) Every feeling is characterized by a quality that pervades that feeling. In order to explain this, Peirce asks the reader to think about anything by itself and "drop the parts out of attention." (CP 1.318, 1910) For example, think about a sunset. The sunset is composed of numerous components—the sun, the landscape, the clouds, etc. —but the sunset itself is characterized by a quality that is itself without parts. Think also about driving a car, the grip of the steering wheel, the yellow light, the cyclist ahead. At each moment, there is one single quality, one single feeling that pervades consciousness, despite the fact that there are a plurality of things happening simultaneously. Of course, this does not rule out the possibility that, at any given moment, the feeling can be interrupted by a chilly breeze or your passenger telling you to slow down. Each moment is characterized by a single quality that pervades that moment.

We can analyze those feelings, break them apart and examine the component qualities that give rise to the feeling experienced as a whole, but it is important to note that our experience is always of wholes first and parts second. Every object of experience is experienced in terms of the whole object, which imparts a quality that is felt by consciousness. Peirce is, again, arguing against Kant here:

> Kant gives the erroneous view that ideas are presented separated and then thought together by the mind. This is his doctrine that a mental synthesis precedes every analysis. What really happens is that something is presented which in itself has no parts, but which nevertheless is analyzed by the mind, that is to say, its having parts consists in this that the mind afterward recognizes those parts in it. Those partial ideas are really not in the first idea, in itself, though they are separated out from it. It is a case of destructive distillation. When having thus separated them, we think over them, we are carried in spite of ourselves from one thought to another, and therein lies the first real synthesis. An earlier synthesis than that is a fiction. (W 6:449, CP 1.384, 1887–88)

Wholes are presented to the mind prior to parts. The objects before consciousness are wholes that are only later broken down into their component qualities through carving up that experience into parts. This carving up of experience happens through destructive distillation, through analyzing that experience and paying attention to its component qualities. Concepts and ideas are the tools we use in order to perform this destructive distillation. Imagine, for example, walking into a waiting room. First there is the experience of the room as a whole, then the awareness of the chairs for sitting, the magazines for reading, the reception window for checking in, the other people as potential conversationalists, etc. The room is experienced as a whole first, and then those parts are separated out from the whole. Bringing our initial expectations to bear on the situation as it currently presents itself and relating all those parts back together, we can confirm that this is, in fact, a waiting room.

There is another point to make here. The experience of the parts within that waiting room can then be further analyzed, thus making what was previously a part, now a whole with its own parts, e.g., legs, shoes, jacket, hat, etc. The whole imparts a particular feeling to the observer, but the experience of each one of those parts also has a particular feeling associated with it that then influences the way that the whole will be felt. In this sense, parts can become wholes when analyzed separately from the whole to which they belong.

In brief, a feeling is a sensation that is not attributed to any particular object: "for by feeling I mean nothing but sensation minus the attribution of it to any particular subject." (CP 1.332, c.1905) A feeling on its own contains no attribution to any subject because there is no separation between the subject and the object. To attribute a feeling to something, the feeling must be held in retention and then mediated through signs and predicated of a particular subject. The feeling then loses its immediacy and individuality and gains generality through being mediated by a representation. At this point, the feeling has been succeeded by a representation of it. This is what allows Peirce to say that "the feeling is simply a quality of immediate consciousness." (CP 1.307, 1907) Feelings on their own are not attributed to any subject and are the qualities of immediate consciousness.

Once a feeling is mediated through a representation, the representation calls for interpretation—once we know what the feeling is, we respond to that feeling. The important point here is that every act of interpretation or response has feeling at its foundation. (EP 2.409, 1907) There are three main modes of interpretation that we have towards feelings: emotional, energetic, and logical. The emotional interpretant is the emotional response produced by a given sign. The energetic interpretant is either the muscular or mental effort produced by a sign, and the logical interpretant is the thought produced by the sign.

Thought, therefore, is but one kind of interpretation, and it is ultimately grounded in feeling. We can act, and often do act, without the necessity of thought.

FEELINGS AS SIGNS

Aesthetics is the proper domain for the explanation of feelings. It should be clear that the majority of our activities are guided by feeling and not by thought. This section will focus on a description of feeling in terms of Peirce's semiotics.

Up until now, the focus has been on explaining feelings as they are experienced, that is, from the perspective of the one having the feeling. At this point, it is worthwhile to spend a moment on the structure that makes those feelings possible.

The role of feeling in the structure of symbols becomes clearer when considered in relation to Peirce's triad of icons, indices and symbols. However, it is worth briefly focusing on this triad to bring to light the role of feeling in the structure of symbols. Peirce is very clear that symbols are "attached to" indices and icons: "Now every symbol must have, organically attached to it, its Indices of Reactions and its Icons of Qualities . . . " (EP 2:193–194, 1903) Icons, as representations of feeling-qualities of objects, are contained within symbols. The symbols determine the way in which the icons will be interpreted. That interpretation can take the form of the emotional, energetic, or logical, but each interpretation is prefigured in advance by the way in which the symbol is to be understood. Take, for example, certain expectations that we might have about an old friend that we haven't seen in quite a while. We will likely use all of the symbols through which we interpreted that friend's behavior in the past in order to explain his or her behavior today, thus not allowing our friend to fully exhibit how he or she might have changed. A friend who was previously spontaneous because of a desire to be perceived as "fun," and thus liked by others, might today really enjoy change and thus constantly seek out new environments in order to change with those environments. In both situations, the individual behavior as an icon is spontaneity, but the way in which that icon is interpreted depends on which symbols we employ in interpreting that behavior: in one way, it appears as a desire to be liked and in another, it appears as a desire for change. Or, as another example, we might have heard a lot about the architectural splendors of a particular city before visiting that city. Upon arrival, we notice all of the awe-inspiring architecture that the city has to offer. There might not be any more or less impressive architecture in this city than in previous cities that we have visited, but because of the expectation to experience this architecture, we are primed to look for and confirm our expectations. There might be exactly the same number of icons of baroque architecture in two cities, but because we have primed ourselves to look for these icons in one city, we will think that there are more examples of baroque architecture in one city than another. We look to confirm pre-existing biases that we acquire through prior experiences. In this way, symbols can condition in advance how certain icons should be interpreted. A certain amount of novelty or misinterpretation is possible, but this is not the norm; the norm is that the majority of the interpretations of icons are determined in advance by the governing symbol. Every symbolic interaction with the world, which is to say, every active moment of our lives, involves iconic representations.

It could be argued that we use only those representations that permit a successful navigation of our environment, that permit the perpetuation of a calm and stable belief set. We interpret our environment in a particular way, we behave in a particular way, because that behavior provides for the fulfillment of our aims. Now, the iconic representation of any given object is not a complete representation of that object, because there is an infinite series of adumbrations that are equally possible ways of interpreting the object, but the incomplete representation that we employ involves the background set of beliefs that condition that object to be experienced in a particular way. This background set of beliefs conditions the feeling that one is to have relative to a particular object, and it is against this background set that we must struggle if we are serious about changing our beliefs. The difficult thing, and this is something that Peirce points to, is that there is something about the object and the environment that allows for the object to be interpreted in a particular way.

There are two things at play here: one is the fact that the symbol is historically conditioned to result in specific interpretations of a particular object, and the second is the fact that the object lends itself to be interpreted in specific ways.

The thing about the object that allows it to be interpreted in a particular way might just be how it fits with the background set of beliefs, i.e., its historical conditioning; and this interpretation has very little to do with the object itself, except insofar as the object has some quality that allows for that discrimination to take place, however slight that quality might be. One could imagine mundane examples like a stapler having the quality of hardness, which makes it different than my fist and permits it to be used as a hammer, but one can also imagine more insidious examples, such as the color of someone's skin, which permits a discrimination that sets that person apart from others. We can see here that there is a certain quality that the stapler has that allows for a discrimination between it and other objects around it, but the way in which the object is understood is heavily conditioned by the way that the agent interprets the object for a particular use. This is not to say that anything that goes along with the difference in quality, the historical conditioning, is in any way correct, but it does explain how the background set of beliefs conditions something to be represented in an icon based on a certain quality. (In fact, we can go further, to say that there is no distinction in itself but only historical conditioning that forces the recognition of a distinction that does not otherwise exist, but this would take us further afield from our present study.) The role that this different quality plays within the symbolic interpretation of that object depends on a background set of beliefs that are, for the most part, not part of the conscious process of the interpretation of that object.

What needs to be understood from the previous is that Peirce makes room in his philosophy for the discussion of a third realm of reality. This realm should be understood as the same realm that Husserl opens up through his phenomenological research. The main difference between these two thinkers is that Peirce sees the object of phenomenological/phaneroscopic research to be the real object itself, as mediated through images, and not something that solely exists for the individual consciousness; it is the object as it would exist for any consciousness, human or not.

But what we mean by "the object" is ambiguous here. It is important to remember that the object can be divided up into the material, the formal, and its relations, but this is not a distinction that is made in the moment of experience. As such, any attempt to talk about the ideal object as separate from the material object is already an abstraction that needs to be justified. The movement towards the formal/relational object that Husserl makes is therefore a move that must be justified in advance. If this move is starting from the Kantian paradigm of finding universality in the constitution of objects by sustaining acts of the mind, then we can see that there is going to be a problem accessing the real object as it exists independently from sustaining acts of consciousness from the very beginning. This is precisely the situation that the students of Husserl are left with.

Unfortunately, the word "image" carries with it connotations of a static object, such as a picture. But this is not what Peirce intends. There isn't room to explore the topic in this paper, but suffice it to say that an image is a representation of the future behaviour of an object that is derived from past experiences. An image is a condensed version of our prior experiences that we attribute to an external object. The image is a representation of how an object will relate to its environment when certain conditions are present. It is this *esse in futuro* of facts about how objects behave that is important. (CP 2:148) For the purposes of this paper, though, the key point is that images are determined by real external objects, which predicts a move that Husserl's students will also make beyond the epoché.

Husserl was famous for his epoché, his bracketing off of assumptions about the existence of the external world. He claimed that this was necessary for knowledge of the essences of objects. Because of this bracketing, we have access only to the appearances of things. For Peirce, a move like this could lead us only into nominalism and wouldn't account for the shared public access to those objects. Instead of this movement inwards, Peirce would argue that the image before consciousness, the image about which judgments are formed, is determined by the real external object.

To sum up, Peirce's description of the nature of philosophy begins with phenomenology/phaneroscopy, then moves up through the normative sciences, and then to metaphysics. That is, from the basic description of the way in which experience presents itself, through aesthetics, ethics, and logic, we are able to grasp the ontological principles that underlie the appearance of phenomena. It is worth noting that the normative sciences of aesthetics, ethics, and logic/laws map onto the realist rejoinder (Ingarden, Scheler, and Reinach, respectively) against Husserl.

Peirce, building on the medieval conception of universals, sees objects in terms of their relational structures, in terms of the patterns of behaviour that they manifest when they come into contact with objects around them. These relational structures are not static and transcendent, as some critiques of universals would have it, but are in fact constantly in the process of development and are immanent to experience, constantly conditioning objects of experience in a lawlike and general manner. Laws describe relations among relations. Peirce will develop this description of laws into semiotics. "Semiosis" is the movement of patterns of behaviour that individual objects manifest when they interact with one another. Semiotics, then, is the formal description of patterns of behaviour.

PEIRCE AND THE REALISTS

The following section will identify some of the areas of discordance between Peirce and Husserl, and how Peirce overlaps with the Realists, in particular with regard to the forms of behavior that manifest signs.

Peirce's classification of the forms of behaviour, or semiotics, develops into 10^{66} different classes of signs. Peirce's characterization here is different than what we would find with Husserl, insofar as Husserl wrote about intentionality and Peirce wrote about semiotics, but they both went back to the medieval tradition of first and second intentions. The point that really distinguishes Peirce from Husserl is Peirce's insistence that thought is not in the mind, but that the mind is in thought. The mind develops out of a more primitive semiotic process.[8] The structure of thinking is certainly something in which the mind is heavily implicated, but the content of thought is the relational structures that one finds immediately present in experience. The relational structures are given in experience and are not constituted by activities of consciousness. These structures play a constitutive role, an active role in cognition. Without these structures, there would be no cognition. One should be able to see, then, that Peirce is better aligned with the realists like Reinach than the idealists.

Reinach and Peirce make a similar move: once we have abstracted from the particularity of a given object and have come to understand the type to which an object belongs, then we are operating at the level of the essence of that object. Understanding the type or the essence is more than merely understanding the general categories within which the material object can be placed; understanding the essence involves understanding the way in which the object responds to and is affected by its environment. In short, it means understanding the relations between that object and its environment. These relations exhibit patterns of regularity sufficient for Reinach to call them laws, but for Peirce, not all patterns of regularity should be considered laws. For those that do not exhibit sufficient patterns of regularity that is necessitated by law, those patterns should be understood as habits. Thus, we can see that Peirce's work on habits opens up a broader category than that of Reinach and, in doing so, allows for a description of vagueness that is not permitted within Reinach's description of laws. Vagueness is important for understanding that the periphery of signs is not distinct but is rather imprecise. Semiosis works in the absence of definite boundaries.

For Peirce, vagueness is characterized by a sign that lacks complete determinateness but is sufficiently determinate to be distinguished from other signs and sufficiently determinate to convey meaning to an interpreter. (EP 2:351, 1905, Issues of Pragmaticism) For example, "that apple was sweet" is a meaningful statement that does not necessitate the existence of a particular apple in front of both myself and the interpreter. In like fashion, I could say "apples are sweet" and thereby establish a relationship between apples and sweetness in the mind of the interpreter that doesn't require the existence of any apple now or in the future. This is a vague statement insofar as it is not completely determined, but that in no way takes away from the ability of the statement to convey meaning. Vagueness is important, because it allows for generality in a way that laws do not. The way in which signs function, and the way in which signs are interpreted, is vague. They constantly require further determination, further activities of the mind for their clarification. This determination should be understood by first looking at how the mind is related to the world by signs. We will look at how this relationship plays out in contemporary cognitive science discourse, in order to show how an appropriation of the realist tradition will help to avoid some of the problems associated with cognitive science.

THE CURRENT LANDSCAPE

In Clark and Chalmers' 1998 essay, "The Extended Mind," the authors use a hypothetical case of Inga and Otto, who both want to go to the Museum of Modern Art. Inga remembers where the museum is; therefore, she consults her memory *in* her head. Otto suffers from Alzheimer's, but he is aware enough to be able to use a notebook; he consults his notebook in order to determine that the Museum of Modern Art is on 53rd St. The only difference between the two is the location of what they consult. Inga consults her beliefs in the form of memories, and Otto consults his belief in the form of his notebook. The point here is that the action-forming properties of the belief are essential, not where the belief is located. In this sense, we can say that the environment plays an active role in the formation of our activities.

This is the same kind of organism-environment coupling that one can find in the works of Johnson and Lakoff. In Johnson's solo book, *The Meaning of the Body*, the discussion is more about meaning, as opposed to simply cognition. "The key to my entire argument is that meaning is not just what is consciously entertained in acts of feeling and thought; instead, meaning reaches deep down into our corporeal encounter with our environment."[9] Meaning is constituted in our encounter with the world. The meaning that we experience is not based on some purely subjective feelings; meaning results from organism-environment coupling. "They are qualities in the world as much as they are in us. They are the qualities of different experiences that involve both the structure of the organism and the structure of its environments inextricably woven together, and even attuned to one another." The environment affords certain opportunities for engagement, and it is in this engagement that meaning is constituted. Within every situation, we find ourselves permitted to perform or not to perform certain activities, certain "possibilities for interaction and engagement."[10]

According to more contemporary work, these ideas are about affordances in our environment. Mark Johnson, reacting to the representationalist model of human experience in *The Meaning of the Body*, writes:

> We must resist the strong temptation to think of these structures in the traditional representational way, as though they were internal mental representations. . . . this temptation arises from the fact that scientists can stand back and reflect on a certain pattern of neural activation in the organism and then compare this with what they think the organism is encountering "in the world." This reproduces the inner/outer dichotomy and misleads us into thinking of a neural activation pattern as being some internalized quasi-entity that stands in an intentional relation to some independent pattern in the world. Instead, the correct way of describing an activation pattern is to say, first, that it constitutes some part of our experience of an "affordance" (Gibson 1979) of the world for us; and, second, that the pattern is both a model of and a model for possible

experience and action. It is a model of structures of recurring organism-environment coupling, and it is a model for possible perceptions and actions that one might experience. Once again, however, it is not a model in the sense of a conceptual or propositional construct that we are reflectively entertain in some inner mental theater. Rather, neural activation patterns are merely recurring structures of experiences actual and possible, retain in the organism as synaptic weights (i.e., as the tendency of certain neurons to fire when stimulated by inputs from other neurons).[11]

In this quote, Johnson is arguing against the traditional representational model of perception that holds that there is a representation somehow being played on some internal screen, as though ideas themselves are somehow "in" the mind. It would seem to be the case that ideas are in the mind based on an external perspective, but if we are to be faithful to experience, we do not experience ideas in the mind any more than we think that the trees outside the windows are in the mind. What we need to do, following Peirce and also Johnson here, is to say that thoughts are not in the mind, but the mind is in thought. There is a pattern of regularity to our experience such that the regular objects of our experience are predictable in a myriad of ways.

Johnson makes another important move here. He says that there is an activation pattern that constitutes some part of our experience of an affordance of the world *for us*. This pattern is directly tied to action. He then ties the experience of patterns of our experience to neural activation patterns and describes this in terms of neural firing. I think that Johnson falls prey to his own critique here: he criticizes the scientists for observing brain activity and positing what they think the organism is encountering in the world, but then he flips the equation and says that our experience of patterns is manifested in our neural firing. Though it might be the case that there is a connection there, he can't criticize the scientists against the experiencers and then use the experiencers to justify the biology.

What we seem to get when we walk away from Johnson's work is a picture that, whether intentionally or not, is heavily reductionist: it implies that experience can be reduced to brain activity. I don't think we should be operating with this model. And this is where things get weird, if they haven't already gotten there.

The embodiment of meaning to which Johnson refers is precisely the kind of embodied cognition that Jay Schulkin is referring to when he discusses a "visceral appraisal mechanism." Much of Schulkin's empirical research has focused on the extent to which the body is actively engaged in appraising the environment long before cephalic processes are involved. Schulkin:

At each level of the neural axis there are visceral appraisal systems that are integral in the organization of action. Cognition is not one side of a divide and viscera the other, with action merely a reflexive outcome. Research over the past fifty years, especially since the 1970s, has demonstrated that the brain is not carved up into structures functioning in isolation. Appraisal systems reside at every level of the nervous system. [12]

Information processing is not limited to cephalic or cortex-based processing; rather, information processing, appraisal mechanisms, are found all throughout the nervous system. Certainly, my knuckle skin cannot simply decide which pair of gloves it wants to keep it warm, but my skin will respond to environmental stimuli before any of my conscious processes are involved. The point that I am driving at here is simply that there is empirical evidence to demonstrate that information processing, which is the heart of cognitive behaviour, is not reliant on the cortex.

When we place Schulkin's work alongside Johnson, we get the idea that visceral appraisal mechanisms are reflecting qualities of the environment; the body is the recipient of the activity of the environment. The kinds of structural conditions that are required for this kind of active externalism can be found earlier, in the work of J.J. Gibson's *The Ecological Approach to Visual Perception.* [13]

Clark and Chalmers, and Johnson and Lakoff, amongst others, make constant reference to J.J. Gibson's affordances as the kind of active externalism that allows us to make sense of the positive contribution of the environment for cognition.

Affordances are features of our environment that permit certain forms of activity, forms of behavior. The door handle affords an opportunity for opening the door, the coffee for elevating my mood. According to Gibson, these affordances are directly perceived in the environment.

When Gibson provides a brief historical account of the idea of affordances, he refers back to gestalt psychology. Within gestalt psychology, the whole object is perceived; colours are seen right along with values. Christian von Ehrenfels, who was a member of the school of Brentano, was one of the first to popularize the term *Gestalt*. So, digging a little deeper into the term that Clark and Chalmers use, "affordances," we have come back to the School of Brentano. Arguably, the most influential member of that school was Edmund Husserl. Gibson used what was available to him in order to understand the effect of the world on our cognition. Unfortunately, he didn't have the realists available to him, and as such did not have the capacity to see that his notion of affordances as playing a strong constitutive role in cognition had allies in the realist rejoinder. If he would have had access to these works, then perhaps Johnson, Lakoff, Schulkin, Clark, and Chalmers would have less of an uphill battle.

If we take a little bit of a closer look at this notion of affordances, then we have to admit that there are certain patterns of regularity that exist in our environment. These patterns of regularity are not themselves material objects, nor are they simply the way in which we conceptualize them. If this were the case, then we would be able to conceptualize them in whichever way we want. We must think of these affordances as some form of existence that is neither material nor ideal, but intentional.

This is what the scholastics, in particular Scotus, had in mind when they discussed intentional being. Intentional being can be divided up into first intentions and second intentions, and second intentions concern us here. The second intention is the species-form of an object. More specifically, the species that an object belongs to is most adequately characterized based on the patterns of behaviour (habits) that a being manifests. These intentions are not based on the ideal existence in the mind of the interpreter; they are also not reducible to the material manifestation of the object. Rather, we need to think of these intentional structures as operating in a third form of existence.

These intentional structures are not free-floating around the universe; they are tied to the material manifestation of the object. But what is important to note is that they are not dependent on the material manifestation of an object.

This third form of being is what the realist phenomenologists are after in their criticism of Husserl. Take, for example, as Roman Ingarden does, the literary work of art. The evocation of the story of Holden Caulfield sitting at his window, wearing his *people shooting* hat, "I shoot people in this hat," evokes, to the right audience, an entire narrative structure that belongs to Salinger's *The Catcher in the Rye*. The mode of existence of Holden Caulfield is neither strictly ideal, nor is it strictly material. There is something about the way in which the character relates to the narrative structure, and is embedded within that narrative structure, that reveals a mode of existence that then relates to us in a particular way.

Johnson would likely reduce this form of relation to neural firing, but the potency of the form of relation must be accorded its own status, independent of the neural firing—where is it when the neurons are not firing? If we ask this simple question, then there is going to be a problem with Johnson's model. If the form of relation is the neural firing, then where is the form when the neurons are not firing?

There is some really interesting work done by Jay Schulkin that brings this material together. In particular, Schulkin examines the nature of the emotions in order to show how the rational/emotional divide is problematic at best. What I want to get at with Schulkin is to demonstrate that he is moving cognition out of the mind and into the body. I think we need to take it a step further and show that cognition is actually happening in the environment of which the individual is a part. Realist phenomenology allows for this sort of explanation. Again, the mind is in thought rather than thought being in the mind.

Once we move cognition out of the mind and into the body, we can then take the further step and move cognition out of the body, into the environment. This is called "offloading," and Johnson describes it like this:

> Like social insects, we tend to offload much of our cognition onto the environments we create. We tend to accomplish this in two ways: first, we make cognitive artifacts to help us engage in complex cognitive actions (Clark 1998); and, second, we distribute cognition among members of a social organization.[14]

Here we can see the specific move that Aristotle would have loved: once the basic needs are addressed and the problems are solved, then we are free to design our environment in such a way that it houses the cognitive processes. This process is specifically the process of informing our environment, or as Hegel might say: "Work . . . is desire held in check, fleetingness staved off; in other words, work forms and shapes the thing. The negative relation to the object becomes its form and something permanent, because it is precisely for the worker that the object has independence."[15] What we should pull out of this is a view that the human is an adaptive organism. This organism adapts to its environment by offloading cognitive processes onto the surrounding objects. By thereby informing objects, placing forms in objects, the cognitive operations of the organism are thereby lessened. These cultural artifacts prefigure how individuals will engage with and respond to the environment.

For some reason, we have a tendency to be resistant to the idea that our environment contains cognition, and perhaps this comes from thinking of cognition as this highly evolved, infinitely nuanced process; but once we see that our environment contains within it cognitive processes, and we see that cognitive processes are not unique to the cerebral cortex, then we can readily say that we have infused our environment with forms.

These forms are modes of relating to the essences of objects. These essences are the habitual patterns of behaviour that the mind comes to recognize and expect. This recognition and expectation takes the form of anticipation that manifests itself on a corporeal level and not primarily on the cerebral level. This is not something radically new, but is in fact something that early phenomenologists were talking about over a century ago. Max Scheler was talking about it with respect to values—they manifest themselves in the activity of relating to the objects that we use in our environment.

It is cognition already.

We must think that there is a mode of existence that is relational. This is to rethink what an essence is. An essence is not an eternal, immaterial entity, but is simply the way in which something tends to behave. The way we experience these essences are in terms of predictions—expectations of the behavior of some thing. This is not a purely cognitive activity, but is a felt perceptual awareness that manifests itself in the body. There are numerous studies that demonstrate the affective response that we have towards the expectation of particular result. What this does is to break down the mind-body dualism inherent in so many discussions today. A discussion of predictions demonstrates that the strict hierarchy that exists between the affective and the cognitive is not as simple a distinction as one might like.

There is one last point that I would like to make: bodily movements effect thought patterns. There have been more than a few studies that have demonstrated that something as simple as sitting with a confident posture increases the likelihood that someone will demonstrate confident behaviour.[16] There is not enough room to pursue it here, but it could be said that the form is one and the same in both the movement of the body and the movement of thought.

RELATION TO CONTEMPORARY COGNITIVE SCIENCE AND THE FUTURE

This analysis forms the basis on which I believe it is possible to move past the nebulous concept of affordances and to begin to show a deeper characterization, a more nuanced characterization of affordances as semiotics. In a way, it is meant to shatter the general category of affordances into different kinds and to show that these affordances are not in isolation but always belonging to a network of relations.

In terms of what Peircean semiotics can offer to help explain this, we can turn to the immediate and dynamic object, and the immediate and dynamic interpretant. For Peirce, semiotics always involves a triadic relation between a sign, an object, and an interpretant. A sign is anything that conveys meaning or information to someone about some thing. The point is that it puts us in connection with something beyond itself. This means that each sign belongs to a network of relations that points beyond. The nodes in the network are the individual objects. These individual objects do not demonstrate the entirety of their relations all at once, of course, but do so over an extension of time.

Where do we go from here? That depends. If we're interested in empirical verification, then we already have it through laws and through measurement of visceral appraisal mechanisms. If we're interested in developing the theory, then we really should look more closely at Peircean semiotics in order to show how intentional structures directly influence our thinking. A stronger claim, and I believe that this is Mitscherling's claim, is that consciousness arises out of our particular brain's interaction with intentional structures.

NOTES

1. I am using the standard practice of referring to Peirce's Collected Papers by volume and paragraph number, e.g., "CP 7.417" refers to volume seven, paragraph 417. Citations of the Writings of Charles S. Peirce and of the Essential Peirce are by volume and page number, e.g., "W 2:233" refers to Writings volume 2, page 233, and "EP 2:202" refers to Essential Peirce volume 2, page 202. Unpublished manuscripts are indicated by "MS" and the manuscript number with the page number following. Thus, "R 400:12" refers to manuscript 400, page 12.

2. See Jeffrey Mitscherling, *Aesthetic Genesis: The Origin of Consciousness in the Intentional Being of Nature*. (Lanham: University Press of America, 2010), 17–19.

3. AG, 17.

4. Baltzer-Jaray, Kimberly, "Adolf Reinach is not a Platonist." *Symposium* 12:1 (2009) 100-112.

5. Willard., David *Concerning Phenomenology*, trans. of Adolf Reinach's *Ueber Phaenomenologie*. N.d. Accessed July 31, 2015. http://dwillard.org/articles/artview.asp?artID=21.

6. It is also very interesting to note that one of Peirce's students, Christine Ladd-Franklin was travelling back and forth between Peirce and Husserl, but was unable to bring the two to read each other.

7. Spiegelberg, Herbert, *The Phenomenological Movement.* (Dordrecht: Kluwer Academic Publishers, 1994), 180.

8. Short, T.L., *Peirce's Theory of Signs.* (New York: Cambridge University Press, 2009), 53.

9. Johnson, Mark, *The Meaning of the Body.* (Chicago: The University of Chicago Press, 2007), 25.

10. Johnson, *The Meaning of the Body*, 90.

11. Johnson, *The Meaning of the Body*, 159.

12. Schulkin, Jay, "Cognitive Functions, Bodily Sensibility, and the Brain" *Phenomenology and the Cognitive Sciences* 5:3 (2006) 341–349, 342.

13. Gibson, J.J., *The Ecological Approach to Visual Perception*, (New York: Taylor and Francis, 1979).

14. Johnson, *The Meaning of the Body*, 150.

15. Hegel, G.W.F., *The Phenomenology of Spirit*, tr. A.V. Miller. (Oxford: Oxford University Press, 1979), section 195.

16. Cuddy, Amy J.C., Caroline A. Wilmuth, and Dana R. Carney. "The Benefit of Power Posing Before a High-Stakes Social Evaluation." Harvard Business School Working Paper, No. 13-027, September 2012.

Chapter Eleven

Perfect Empiricism

*Mitscherling's Aristotelian Phenomenology,
the* Logos, *and The Problem of Ideal Objects*

Conrad Hamilton

"Being that can be understood is language."[1] This phrase—from Hans-Georg Gadamer's magnum opus *Truth and Method*—is one we've heard time and time again, albeit in different permutations, with nothing but the words changed, for the past century.[2] We find it in Russell's attempts to create a logical basis for mathematics; in Heidegger's conception of *Dasein* and his disambiguation of common words; in structuralism's channelling of Saussurean linguistics; in Derrida's notion of *différance*.

Far from being a compulsion unique to the twentieth century, this fascination—with the representative power of linguistic signifiers—is only the apotheosis of Kant's conception of representations (thoughts or ideas) as belonging to a special epistemic realm—that of transcendental subjectivity. Once the Cartesian idea of the "ontological reality" of representations had collapsed—the notion that all you have to do to grasp the thing signified is to know the abstract structure of the signifier—it was only a matter of time before language itself, its constitutive power, became the subject of interrogation.[3] It is entirely understandable, then, that language-based philosophy—and of particular importance to its development was Friedrich Schleiermacher's founding of the modern hermeneutic tradition—grew up in the wake of the Kant's "Copernican Revolution."

It would be impossible, given the confines of this essay, to engage in a protracted discussion as to the merits of the centrality of language—and, consequently, the primacy of epistemology—to contemporary philosophy.[4] But it is worth posing the question, as the new materialists have, of whether there may be another way available to us—one which rejects the primacy of epistemology. Fortunately, in probing into this, we are aided by the sagacious philosophical achievements of Jeff Mitscherling—and in particular, the third volume of the trilogy of books which comprise his original project, *Aesthetic Genesis*.

A word on Mitscherling's importance: if one surveys the work of the school of thought which was first described as "speculative realist," and later as "new materialist," it can be said that many of these works forego a thorough effort to address the question of the constitution of objects. In other words, how is it—either epistemologically or ontologically—that objects come to be formed and endure over time, obtaining and maintaining their identities? As Steven Shaviro has observed,[5] the process philosophy of Alfred North Whitehead[6] (as well as other thinkers who Shaviro understands as being indebted to him, including Deleuze and Gilbert Simondon) represents a substantial attempt to resolve this problem—one that is largely absent in the work of thinkers such as Graham Harman, who tend to simply presuppose the existence of objects (a claim that is, in effect, metaphysical).

We find a similar approach in Mitscherling's work. In his efforts to erect an ontology of "things" not encumbered by the typical constraints of post-Kantian philosophy, he does not merely presuppose the objects in question, but rather demonstrates *how* they come to be understood. And while Mitscherling's primary influences are Aristotle and the realist phenomenology of the Munich-Göttingen school, it can also be said that his philosophical project responds to Hans-George Gadamer's *Truth and Method*, definitively surveying the limitations of philosophy which takes language as the horizon of thought.

To understand Mitscheling's project, it is necessary to understand the philosophic conundrum to which he is responding. This is the problem of the presupposition of objects—not only a defect of many of the new materialists, but also one shared with phenomenology. Early phenomenologists such as Edmund Husserl—while tremendously insightful in terms of their descriptions of how objects are perceived—lacked a sufficient philosophical basis for their positing of "essences" (*to ti ên einai*[7]).

> In view of these explanations, we may be justified in saying that Husserl's argument about the relation between evidence and truth is involved in a peculiar circularity: it refers to evidence in order to establish the thesis that there exist ideal objects such as pure meanings. This justification can refer to evidence only if evidence guarantees truth. That again is established by Husserl by means of the proposition that evidence itself already includes the perception of ideal states of affairs and objects. In order to justify the belief in such a region of ideal essences, Husserl must already presuppose them. In any case, Husserl's peculiar manner of establishing the existence of ideal objects already presupposes their existence. His proof, upon examination, is seen to be merely a closer elaboration of his thesis.[8]

Husserl's failure to resolve this problem—of the constitutive basis of eidetic reduction—is part of the reason why, in his later works, he eventually lapsed into idealism, foregoing the original mantra of phenomenology: to get "back to the 'things themselves." And while the Munich and Göttingen phenomenological circles—which included many of Husserl's former students such as Ingarden, Stein, and Reinach—came to reject his increasingly idealist bent in the aftermath of the *Logical Investigations*, much of their work also possessed the same underlying flaw.

To begin with ontology is not altogether the wrong approach. Aristotle did it with the *Categories*—enumerating everything that could be expressed without composition or structure, as a preliminary for subsequent inquiries. And Hegel, in the preface to the *Phenomenology of Spirit*, criticizes the idea that philosophy should "deliberately hold [itself] back from conceptual thinking"[9] (in Hegel's system, unlike Kant's,[10] Spirit initially adopts a stridently ontological pose—with self-certainty—before eventually engaging in a process of self-scrutiny; it can therefore be said to begin with ontology). Yet both these thinkers are nevertheless thoroughly historical in their sensibility. This is obviously the case with Hegel, whose system portrays the constant upending of the epistemological conditions whereby objects are perceived. But it is also—albeit more subtly—true of Aristotle; a fact observed by Hegel in his *Lectures on the History of Philosophy*:

> Aristotle has the patience to go through all conceptions and questions, and from the investigation of the individual determinations, we have the fixed, and once more restored determination of every object. Aristotle thus forms the Notion, and is in the highest degree really philosophic, while he appears to be only empiric. For Aristotle's empiricism is a totality because he always leads it back again immediately to speculation; he may thus be said to be a perfect empiricist, yet at the same time a thinking one. If, for example, we take away from space all its empirical determinations, the result will be in the highest degree speculative, for the empirical, comprehended in its synthesis, is the speculative Notion.[11]

Aristotle, as Hegel points out, does not simply posit arbitrary determinations—on the contrary, his specifications arise from an extensive (and openly acknowledged) engagement with the history of Greek thought. Far from being presented as the incontrovertible truth, much of Aristotle's philosophy—having arisen from firsthand observation, or the consideration of existing texts—also, implicitly, lends itself to emendation.[12]

This is also, of course, true of Hegel—albeit more systemically. For contra the view of Hegel as some kind of unabashed idealist—the "strong correlationist" caricatured by Meillassoux in *After Finitude*—it is in fact the case that, for Hegel, the ontological clearing house of the *Phenomenology of Spirit* is a springboard for the subsequent *Science of Logic* and *Encyclopedia*, in which thought entrances externality via the syllogistic structure, culminating in the "disjunctive syllogism." What it returns with is a grasp of what Robert Stern has described as "ontologically primary wholes"[13] —those unshakable substances which resist predication. It is for this reason that Hegel—far from being viewed as an exponent of idealism—was described in his own time as "The German Aristotle."[14]

Mitscherling's debt to Aristotle does not need to be stressed—indeed, his entire system can be seen as a skilful blending of Brentano's Aristotelian-inspired concept of "intentionality" with realist phenomenological influences. But less apparent is his relationship to Hegel,[15] whose system permits both ontology *and* epistemology, without trivializing either. Significant in this respect is that Mitscherling's interpretation of Aristotle's concept of "habit" [*hexis*] has much in common with Hegel's reading. This quote from *De Anima* is crucial to Mitscherling's work:

> Generally, about all perception, we can say that a sense is what has the power of receiving into itself the sensible forms of things without the matter, in the way in which a piece of wax takes on the impress of a signet-ring without the iron or gold; what produces the impression is a signet of bronze or gold, but not qua bronze or gold: in a similar way the sense is affected by what is coloured or flavoured or sounding not insofar as each is what it is, but insofar as it is of such and such a sort and according to its form.[16]

But Mitscherling relies on a certain interpretation of it. As Catherine Malabou has observed in her landmark work, *L'Avenir de Hegel*, Hegel posits a reading of Aristotle in which the form taken on by the mental apparatus in *De Anima* changes that apparatus itself (a formulation comparable to Malabou's own conception of "plasticity"[17]). In fact, in the *Lectures on the Philosophy of History*, Hegel cites this passage by Aristotle —where the "piece of wax takes on the impress of a signet-ring"—in support of his reading:

> That is to say, the wax does not, indeed, take in the form, for the impression remains on it as external figure and contour, without being a form of its real Being; if it were to become such, it would cease to be wax; therefore, because in the illustration there is lacking this reception of form into the Being, no thought is given to it. The soul, on the contrary, assimilates this form into its own substance, and for the very reason, that the soul is in itself, to a certain extent, the sum of all that is perceived by the senses: as it was said above, if the axe had its form in the determination of substance, this form would be the soul of the axe. The illustration of the wax has reference to nothing but the fact that only the form comes to the soul; and has nothing to do with the form being external to the wax and remaining so, or with the soul having, like wax, no independent form. The soul is by no means said to be passive wax and to receive its determinations from without; but Aristotle, as we shall soon see, really says that the spirit repels matter from itself, and maintains itself against

it, having relation only to form. In sense-perception the soul is certainly passive, but the manner in which it receives is not like that of the wax, being just as truly activity of the soul; for after the perceptive faculty has received the impression, it abrogates the passivity, and remains thenceforth free from it. The soul therefore changes the form of the external body into its own, and is identical with an abstract quality such as this, for the sole reason that it itself is this universal form.[18]

It is worth comparing Hegel's reading to Mitscherling's own account of habit formation:

As both Plato and Aristotle explained, it is through the repeated imitation of a certain sort of behaviour that the child comes eventually to participate in the same sort of being that informs that behaviour in the model imitated. Repeated imitation, in short, leads inevitably to participation. It is the same sort of habit-formation that is at work in our learning how to speak a language. And once learned, this language influences our behaviour most profoundly.[19]

By emphasizing the centrality of habit formation to human development, Mitscherling is able to—like Aristotle and Hegel—eschew the commonplace view of language as the starting-point of being, instead favouring the idea of a non-anthropocentric soul which can be found both in *De Anima* as well as in the *Anthropology* section of the *Philosophy of Spirit* (for Mitscherling—as well as for Aristotle and Hegel—plants and animals are both capable of "self-motion"; i.e., the self-initiated absorption of form).[20]

But this is only the start. By adhering to this "plastic" reading of Aristotle, Mitscherling is able to produce an even more novel conception: that the externalization of form—its alteration, through engaging with other "instance[s] of intentional being"—is aporetically connected to form's own self-actualization, or the realization of its potentiality. Expressed more succinctly, what this means is that—like in Hegel's system—for Mitscherling, intentional being is only capable of making the transition from potentiality to actuality via the intermediary of other beings.

The above claim requires elaboration. For Mitscherling, there are three kinds of being—"material being," "ideal being," and "intentional being." The first term—"material being"—describes the being of the material aspect of any matter-form composite. A rock, for instance, is constituted of minerals in the form of a rock. However, unlike plants, animals, or even aggregates of organic material (i.e. ecosystems),[21] they remain "static and lifeless."[22] The second term—"ideal being"—refers to concepts which "do not exist or subsist through time"[23] but are timeless, such as numbers. The third term— "intentional being"—refers to the form "of an organic unity": entities that are "dynamic and energic,"[24] and capable of change.

We can see from the above that intentional forms—e.g., the form of an organic unity—are not static. They can change. But they are nevertheless capable of subsistence: while it is hypothetically imaginable that humans in the future could evolve to learn how to fly, this is—within the temporal span of our lives—not possible.[25] What makes entities endowed with "intentional being" different than lifeless, static entities is that they can form habits: expediting the movement from A to B to C by actually suppressing the complexity of the intellectual calculation required to facilitate it (once I know how to set the alarm clock on my phone, for example, I can perform this exercise "habitually"—without expending the same mental energy as it required in the first place).

This brings us to an important point. For if humans—that is to say, the "form" of human—is only capable of realizing itself through the acquisition of habits, doesn't this necessarily mean that we can only realize ourselves through our encountering of other beings? Habit formation refers fundamentally to the process whereby we assimilate external beings into our own intellectual routine—but without other beings, there *is* no routine at all (the habit of making toast requires a toaster).

This dependency on external beings is not restricted to humans. Take Mitscherling's example of the "dynamic" and "energic" intention of an atomic bomb, supplied in Chapter 4 of *The Author's Intention*. The "dynamic" intention of an atomic bomb refers to what is conventionally described as its "potentiality"—that it *could* go off. The "energic" intention, by contrast, *is* the actualization of this potentiality—the fact of the bomb erupting. But for an atomic bomb to realize its energic intention, it has to encounter other beings: the intentional being of the humans tasked with discharging it, the material being that it collides with when it touches the ground, etc.

The necessity of the encountering of other beings for the realization of energic intention has, as mentioned above, ramifications for humans. This can be seen in Mitscherling's explanation of the formation of moral values in Chapter 3 of *Aesthetic Genesis*:

> Moral values as conceptually formulated are precisely that: they are conceptually formulated—that is, they are human constructs that come after moral behaviour, not before it. Yet what we come to regard as an identifiable virtue—say, for example, 'generosity'—informs human behaviour prior to its conceptual formulation. Moral virtues do not exist as individual, self-identical goals or targets that hover in some transcendent Platonic heaven of Ideas or Kantian kingdom of ends, like carrots held in front of a donkey. Such heavens and kingdoms are products of human intellectual intervention.[26]

What we see here is that Mitscherling, like Aristotle, holds that "moral behaviour" is in a sense inborn, or intrinsic to the "form" or "dynamic intention" of humans. But its articulation is nevertheless tremendously variegated—as

Mitscherling points out, the "Chile of 2007" differs considerably from the "Greece of 399 B.C."[27] in its particular conception of virtue (without citing the obvious example, we can further imagine societies in which the "form" of morality is entirely perverted). What is different about these societies is the kinds of *beings* that humans—who are, biologically, essentially the same—encounter. The unique and different circumstances of 2007 Chile and 399 B.C. Greece result in the formulation of decidedly different moral codes, though these are nevertheless anchored in the dynamic intention of the human form.

A consequence of this view is that Mitscherling—like Aristotle or Hegel (or, for that matter, Marx)—can be said to endorse a broadly "sociological" thesis: that societies play an instrumental role in furnishing the moral composition of their citizenry. For Aristotle, the highest form of the community is the *polis*, because it is only through public life that the inborn virtues of man can find their highest expression. But it is interesting to take into consideration that, far from being somehow "natural," the gap between the emergence of humans and the development of communities even remotely resembling the city-states of Ancient Greece is roughly 190,000 years—a gap Aristotle must've been at least vaguely aware of. The realization of form, then, or "energic intention," is not something merely *given* with "dynamic intention"—at least so far as complex beings such as humans are concerned. To free oneself from the trammels of ignorance vis-à-vis form can require centuries; it involves defeats and victories, the founding of communities and the scuttling of them.

A reading such as this may seem irresponsibly adventurous, given the relatively simplistic examples of dynamic and energic intention provided by Mitscherling. But it is not as eccentric as it seems. Take the role that he assigns to the *logos:*

> The 'logos' of the work of art is that which guides the artist and the audience alike in their respective cognitive activities of expression, communication and understanding in the creation of and re-creation of the work. In the light of what I have explained in the preceding chapters of *Aesthetic Genesis*, we can now identify the "logos" as the form of these cognitive activities. When we understand what is being said to us by another, we might say that our understanding is being guided by the same logos, or that our understanding and that of the speaker share in the same intention.[28]

The *logos*, for Mitscherling, refers to the directional thrust of intentionality—as he states elsewhere, an author also follows the *logos* when they compose a work of literary art. And for mutual understanding to arise, the same *logos* must be followed: when a reader is enraptured by a work; when they lose themselves in the world that it has created, they can be said to be following its *logos*.

The *logos* is not exclusively associated with literary works—all entities endowed with intentional being can be said to have a *logos*. It is worth, then, posing the question of what following the *logos* of different kinds of intentional beings would mean. An obvious condition of following the *logos* of a literary work of art, for instance, is that one understands the language of the work in question. But—as anyone who has tried to learn a language knows—this is far from a simple condition. To completely understand a language requires the mastery of a diverse array of semiotic features. Nor is the acquisition of a language a difficulty which solely concerns isolated individuals—to cite a famous example, the loss of Ancient Greek in Western Europe due to the collapse of the Roman Empire had a profound, adverse effect on the intellectual development of the region, and was only rectified through a sustained cultural effort.

Further extending this analysis of the conditions required to "follow" the *logos* of things other than a literary work of art has interesting implications. Isn't following the *logos* of an intentional being such as a plant, for instance, incumbent on the achievements of Theophrastus, and—later—the discoveries of modern botany? Isn't the *logos* of the sun better grasped due to the labours of Copernicus, Kepler, and Galileo? What we can see, here, is that grasping the ontological structure of objects—their directedness, or what Mitscherling refers to as "external teleology"[29] —is a necessarily *historical* process. Objects do not simply offer themselves up freely, in their totality.[30] But they *can* be understood, provided that they manifest themselves, and the proper epistemological conditions are met.

If the *logos* of beings endowed with intentionality can be understood, this is not to suggest that, in Mitscherling's work, there is a single, objective way of understanding them—it is rather the case that their potential, intentional relations are inexhaustible.[31] But even if they cannot be grasped *absolutely*, it is nevertheless true that their general features can be elucidated more or less accurately: to think that the sun is a foot in diameter is to grossly misunderstand its ontological structure. And it is similarly interesting to note that—following Mitscherling's distinction between "dynamic" and "energic" intention—it appears to be the case that intentional being, in Mitscherling's work, always exists *for an other*. A literary work of art can only actualize its energic intentionality when someone *reads* it, just as an atomic bomb can only do the same when it is detonated. The sun exists only in so far as it has intentional relations: to the planets which orbit around it, to the living beings on Earth, to the vast blackness of space.

All of this raises the problem of error. For if the actualization of the energic intention of an intentional being is dependent upon another entity's engagement with it—and that engagement is, in turn, conditional (if I cannot read a language, I cannot follow the *logos* of a literary work of art)—this means that Mitscherling, while a proponent of the view that intentionality resides in non-human entities, does not believe in an unadulterated form of object-causality, in which the reception of objects is wholly "realistic." Rather, like Hegel—who argues that the soul "assimilates this form into its own substance"—Mitscherling's system suggests that the reception of one intentional being by another is never 1:1: it is always determined, to a greater or lesser extent, by the substance which receives it. The mere existence of the Sun, to cite an example, does not guarantee that it will be understood as revolving around the Earth. Nor does the mere fact of an insecticide being set out guarantee that an insect which encounters it will not confuse it for food, provided it smells the same.

To understand the way that the theme of "error" relates to Mitscherling's work, it is helpful to consult the works of Aristotle, who addresses a similar problem in Book III of *De Anima*, invoking *phantasia*, or imagination, to elucidate it:

> That imagination is not sense is clear from the following considerations: Sense is either a faculty or an activity, e.g. sight or seeing: imagination takes place in the absence of both, as e.g. in dreams. Again, sense is always present, imagination not. If actual imagination and actual sensation were the same, imagination would be found in all the brutes: this is held not to be the case; e.g. it is not found in ants or bees or grubs. Again, sensations are always true, imaginations are for the most part false. Once more, even in ordinary speech, we do not, when sense functions precisely with regard to its object, say that we imagine it to be a man, but rather when there is some failure of accuracy in its exercise. And as we were saying before, visions appear to us even when our eyes are shut. Neither is imagination any of the things that are never in error: e.g. knowledge or intelligence; for imagination may be false. [32]

The way in which *phantasia* functions is illustrated in a graph employed by Victor Caston in his essay, "Aristotle and the Problem of Intentionality."[33] Note that *phantasma* here refers to a specific incident of *phantasia*, as shown in Figure 11.1.

In spite of a superficial similarity, it is crucial to mention here that Aristotle's conception of *phantasia* should not be likened to a conventional empiricist theory of knowledge. For while David Hume, to cite one example, argued for the relative clarity of "impressions," and spoke forcefully about

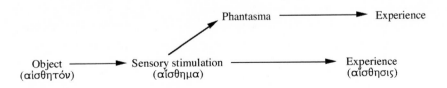

Figure 11.1.

the potentially deceptive nature of "ideas," for Aristotle intellectualization is crucial to the *dispelling* of *phantasmata*, a difference evidenced by their oppositional attitudes towards inductive reasoning[34] (for Aristotle, inductive reasoning is crucial to the enumeration of universal essences).

Understanding this about Aristotle also helps shed light on why he so meticulously described the views of Greek thinkers who preceded him, often parrying with their arguments—and why Hegel characterized his thought as in the "highest degree speculative": because Aristotle understood that in so far as objects do not freely offer themselves up to knowledge, the acquisition of knowledge is a historical and social process. And while Mitscherling does not explicitly refer to *phantasia* in either *The Author's Intention* or *Aesthetic Genesis*, one can infer it from his argument. For if it is possible to "follow" the *logos* of a work of art (or any being), then it must also be possible *not* to follow it, leading one to err.

Continuing this line of thought, it warrants mention that the risk of *phantasia* is not merely the misinterpretation of objects. Rather, it is only *through* the process of ascertaining the ontological structure of objects via their intentionality (including, following Mitscherling, "ideal" ones) that those same objects actually come to light. Columbus' goal was not to discover the Americas. He was searching for India, but only when Amerigo Vespucci began to suspect his error was the term "America" coined—a development which coincided with the acquisition of increased knowledge by Europeans of its geography, climate, ecology, etc. This is how knowledge of objects—beings—arises: language, or the designation of the object in and of itself,[35] is a consequence of the experiencing of its ontological structure.

Referring back to the problem cited with phenomenology—that it presupposes the objects which it investigates—one can see how Mitscherling's phenomenological adaptation of Aristotelianism potentially poses a solution. For in Mitscherling's work, it is implicitly the case that the grasping of the ontological structure of beings, the following of their *logoi*—or internal teleologies—epistemologically *founds* new beings[36] (and, consequently, linguistic structures). And in so far as this process of the constitution of objects is historical, it is possible to understand the breadth of Mitscherling's achievement: to have developed a system which amounts to nothing less than a radical, *historical* and *transitory*, refounding of phenomenology.

Viewing Mitscherling's project this way clarifies it considerably—it explains why, like Aristotle, he devotes so much energy to summarizing and countering of the views of the thinkers which preceded him.[37] It illustrates why the historical transmutation of language remains so important to his work, in spite of his avowed interest in ontology. And it also helps elucidate his relationship to Gadamer, as well as to Hegel:

> *Truth and Method* is a book that is very close in its strategy to Hegel's *Phenomenology of Spirit*, a fact that should not be surprising given Gadamer's admiration of Hegel and his supremacy in Hegel scholarship. Just as is the case with Hegel's *Phenomenology*, *Truth and Method* presents the account of a long journey undertaken by consciousness.[38]

If *Truth and Method* is analogous to the *Phenomenology of Spirit*, what, then, of *The Author's Intention*, which takes the former as its foundation? We should compare here Mitscherling's claim—about *Truth and Method*—that "Gadamer simply and mistakenly believes that all things having to do with author's intention necessarily have to do with the reenactment of the psychic experiences of another individual subjectivity"[39] —with Hegel's statement in the *Science of Logic* that "as the course of the *Phenomenology* brought out, it is only in absolute knowledge that the separation of the *subject matter* from the *certainty of itself* is completely resolved."[40] Mitscherling implicitly compares Gadamer's belief in the primacy of language—the "culminating point" of *Truth and Method*, where, in neoplatonic fashion, "Language turns out to be light"[41] —with the conclusion of the *Phenomenology*, in which Spirit has lost the "*certainty of itself.*"

This certainty is not lost permanently. On the contrary, in its traversal of Logic and Nature, Spirit succeeds in *recovering* its ability to posit ontological distinctions, albeit at a higher level of reflexivity. As Hegel states of "method" in the *Science of Logic*:

> In true cognition, on the contrary, method is not only an aggregate of certain determinations, but the determinateness in-and-for-itself of the concept, and the concept is the middle term only because it equally has the significance of the objective; in the conclusion, therefore, the objective does not attain only an external determinateness by virtue of the method, but is posited rather in its identity with the subjective concept.[42]

And this is the role Mitscherling's trilogy of works dealing with the subject of ontology play in relation to *Truth and Method*:[43] as a continuation that abandons Gadamer's ontological "metaphysics of light,"[44] showing how Gadamer's view of the intersubjectivity of language can in fact be applied to "all human activities."[45] We therefore don't have to stop at language, but can instead confront (and therefore change) the very way objects are brought to reality—and in doing so, reveal the "ontologically primary wholes," or universal essences, which previously informed our thoughts only abstractly.

There is, of course, much more work to be done in this vein. But to employ a distinction which Mitscherling is fond of, one can say that there are two ways to interpret his work—exoterically and esoterically. Exoterically, it presents realist phenomenology with an Aristotelian spin—a compelling reading, but nevertheless one overly dependent on the sort of arbitrary determinations decried by Hegel. Esoterically, it does something considerably greater. It explains, by appealing to the Aristotelian tradition, the way the objects of phenomenology are epistemologically constituted vis-à-vis intentional structures, thereby supplying eidetic reduction with an unprecedentedly robust foundation from which to commence with the realist investigation of essences.

There is a genesis here. But it is far more than aesthetic.

NOTES

1. Hans-George Gadamer, *Truth and Method*, trans. by Joel Weinsheimer and Donald G. Marshall (London: Bloomsbury, 2013), 490.

2. Thinkers such as Robert Sokolowski and Charles Taylor have argued that the reading of Gadamer as a linguistic constructivist is incorrect, that—for Gadamer—language only makes reality *more* intelligible to us. For more on Gadamer's concept of language, see Jason Robinson's essay in this volume as well as Jeff Mitscherling's Afterword.

3. My explanation here is partly indebted to Michel Foucault's description of the differing accounts of representation from the Renaissance to the present in *The Order of Things*.

4. Such an explanation would also risk redundancy, given the large audience of readers attracted by Quentin Meillassoux's *After Finitude* since its 2007 publication.

5. Steven Shaviro, "Processes and Powers," *The Pinocchio Theory* http://www.shaviro.com/Blog/?p=995 [accessed 15 August 2015].

6. In *Aesthetic Genesis*, Mitscherling cites Whitehead as a precursor, but claims that he never resolved the problem of "idealism/realism"—an assertion that could be extended to the list of Whitehead's successors supplied by Shaviro.

7. For Mitscherling, *to ti ên einai* refers not to "essence" in the sense that it is normally understood, but rather "that which was to be"—how the meanings which words refer to subsist regardless of whether the words themselves do. Jeff Mitscherling, *Aesthetic Genesis: The Origin of Consciousness in the Intentional Being of Nature* (Lanham: University Press of America, 2010), 123. Hereafter cited as AG.

8. Günther Patzig, "Husserl on Truth and Evidence," *Readings on Edmund Husserl's Logical Investigations*, ed. by J.N. Mohanty (The Hague: Martinus Nihjoff, 1977), 367.

9. G.W.F. Hegel, "The Phenomenology of Mind: Preface: On scientific knowledge – Φ 10," trans. by A.V. Miller https://www.marxists.org/reference/archive/hegel/works/ph/phprefac.htm [accessed 16 August 2015].

10. It should be mentioned that the last chapter of the *Critique of Pure Reason*, "The history of pure reason," Kant hints passingly at the historicization of epistemology that would later be so important for Hegel—even if Hegel's system is not historicist per se.

11. G.W.F. Hegel, "Hegel's Lectures on the History of Philosophy: Part One: Greek Philosophy – First Period, from Thales to Aristotle: Chapter III: First Period, Third Division B. The Philosophy of Aristotle," trans. by E.S. Haldane, Marxists Internet Archive https://www.marxists.org/reference/archive/hegel/works/hp/hparistotle.htm [accessed 20 August 2015].

12. It is widely speculated—and indeed, this view is held by Mitscherling—that much of what we refer to as Aristotle's "corpus" today was in fact authored by members of the Peripatetic school that followed in his wake. If this is true, it only reinforces the provisional—and by extension, collaborative—nature of Aristotle's philosophic output.

13. Robert Stern, *Hegel, Kant and the Structure of the Object* (New York: Routledge, 1990), 3.

14. Terry Pinkard, *Hegel: A Biography* (Cambridge: Cambridge University Press, 2001), 265.

15. Worth noting, here, is that Mitscherling frequently refers to Hegel—and, in particular, the role of intentional being in the *Philosophy of Nature*—in his lectures and course materials.

16. Aristotle, *The Complete Works of Aristotle*, ed. Jonathan Barnes (Princeton: Princeton University Press, 1984), 674, 424a18-424a23.

17. Thanks to Charlene Elsby for pointing out that, while there are similarities between Hegel and Mitscherling's readings of Aristotle, Hegel was by no means the *first* thinker to put forth this reading.

18. G.W.F. Hegel, "Hegel's Lectures on the History of Philosophy: Part One: Greek Philosophy – First Period, from Thales to Aristotle: Chapter III: First Period, Third Division B. The Philosophy of Aristotle," trans. by E.S. Haldane, Marxists Internet Archive https://www.marxists.org/reference/archive/hegel/works/hp/hparistotle.htm [accessed 23 December 2015].

19. AG, 38.

20. Unlike Mitscherling's arch-nemesis, Heidegger—who views the genesis of language as tantamount to the beginning of mankind—Aristotle and Hegel both assert the belief that "the power of setting itself in movement and arresting itself" is what distinguishes humans from inanimate natural things. However, this difference is merely quantitative: plants and animals, for instance, both are endowed with a relatively limited capacity for self-motion, and can therefore also be said to have souls. This is why, in *De Anima* and the *Philosophy of Nature* respectively, Aristotle and Hegel devote a great deal of attention to explicating the faculties of plants and animals, characterizing them as gradationally connected with humans. Aristotle, *The Complete Works of Aristotle*, ed. Jonathan Barnes (Princeton: Princeton University Press, 1984), 657, 412b1.

21. For Mitscherling, nature—not just entities such as plants or animals—are capable of habit formation. As thinkers such as Mikhail Bakhunin and James Lovelock have observed, the entirety of the Earth, for example, can be said to possess a kind of organic unity, functioning immunologically.

22. AG, 13.

23. AG, 41.

24. AG, 13.

25. Such a change would raise the question—in Aristotelian terms—of whether humans that could fly would still, essentially, be humans.

26. AG, 62.

27. Though it's not explicated in *Aesthetic Genesis*, Mitscherling appears to be referring to the August 29, 2007 protests against the economic policies of President Michelle Bachelet and the sentencing to death of Socrates, respectively.

28. AG, 130.

29. A similar distinction to the one made by Mitscherling—between "external" and "internal" teleology—is made by Hegel in the "Teleology" section of the *Science of Logic*. G.W.F. Hegel, *The Science of Logic*, trans. by George Di Giovanni (Cambridge: Cambridge University Press, 2010), 651–669.

30. In Timothy Morton's text *Hyperobjects*, he discusses how our modern scientific landscape has been transfigured by the arrival of "hyperobjects"—objects which can be scientifically ascertained to exist, but are not sensuously available to us, such as black holes. We might conclude, then, that today many of the objects of which we follow the *logoi* do not even exist to us, in their immediacy.

31. The same can be said of the status of objects in the work of Graham Harman, who states that "In every period of philosophy where Aristotle has had influence, specific entities have gained in stature and dignity." Graham Harman, The Quadruple Object (Zero Books, 2011), 17.

32. Aristotle, "On the Soul: Book III," trans. by J.A. Smith, The Internet Classics Archive http://classics.mit.edu/Aristotle/soul.3.iii.html [accessed 18 August 2015].

33. Victor Caston, "Aristotle and the Problem of Intentionality."*Philosophy and Phenomenological Research*, Vol. LVIII, No. 2, June 1998, 274. Diagram reproduced with permission from John Wiley & Sons Ltd.

34. Hume, to be fair, acknowledged the practical necessity of inductive reasoning.

35. This process of the identification of essences, of course, does not merely stop, as if existing geographical distinctions are somehow rationally unimpeachable. As David Harvey states, though "concepts of space and time" indeed "operate with the full force of objective

fact," they are nevertheless "socially constructed"—and thus, can easily be debunked or revised. David Harvey, *Annals of the Association of American Geographers*, Vol. 80, No. 3 (Sep., 1990), pp. 418-434

36. Mitscherling clearly rejects linguistic constructivism in the first chapter of *The Author's Intention*, where—*pace* Heidegger—he argues that, for Nietzsche, "From nerve impulse, to image, to word sound: in this manner does language arise, as the product of a series of metaphorical leaps." Mitscherling et al., *Author's Intention*, 12.

37. In *The Author's Intention*, in particular.

38. Mitscherling et al., *The Author's Intention*, 94–95.

39. Ibid., 97

40. G.W.F. Hegel, *The Science of Logic*, trans. by George Di Giovanni (Cambridge: Cambridge University Press, 2010), 29.

41. Mitscherling et al., *The Author's Intention*, 96.

42. G.W.F. Hegel, *The Science of Logic*, trans. by George Di Giovanni (Cambridge: Cambridge University Press, 2010), 738.

43. It is appropriate, given Mitscherling's disagreement with the notion of intentionality as a purely authorial construct, that the metaphorical re-enactment of the movement from the *Phenomenology* to the *Encyclopedia* he portrays is divided between two authors: Gadamer and himself.

44. Mitscherling et al., *The Author's Intention*, 97.

45. Ibid.

Chapter Twelve

A Relational Theory of Truth

Joshua Boyce

In empirical pursuits, "metaphysics" has, by and large, become a bad word, one that brings to mind debates as useless and contrived as the nature of angelic real estate on the heads of pins. This is, in some sense, understandable, if not deserved. Metaphysics can and has been taken to stand in for pure speculation, totally divorced from observable sense-data. This is unfair to the field of metaphysics, and to the field of philosophy more generally. Writing about the way that we ought to conceive about the metaphysical nature of sense-data, C. S. Peirce cautioned against a "wrong metaphysical prejudice": "Whether we have an anti-metaphysical metaphysics or a pro-metaphysical metaphysics, a metaphysics we are sure to have. And the less pains we take with it the more crudely metaphysical it will be."[1] The point is that, if we decide to reject all metaphysics on the grounds that it is too speculative, this is itself a metaphysical position. After all, the grounds on which it is rejected are necessarily prior to any empirical efforts. So the structure of our engagement with the universe must have some sort of theoretical basis, even if that theoretical basis is established after the practice of empirical science itself has begun.

In *Aesthetic Genesis*, Jeff Mitscherling lends a hand to just such an effort, proposing a paradigm shift—more precisely, what he calls a Copernican revolution—in the way that philosophers and cognitive scientists conceive of consciousness. Rather than characterizing the mind as a "thing," or "stuff" that is consciously directed toward the various phenomena of experience that surround it, Mitscherling describes a deeper relational structure—intentionality—from which consciousness originates. This intentional structure "subsists," and it is because of this that there can be something like consciousness:

Intentionality, that is to say, subsists independently of the human mind. The
operations of the mind, as operations of consciousness, are indeed characterized by intentionality, but this intentionality does not derive from the mind or
consciousness. Our mind becomes conscious when it operates intentionally,
and it does so by engaging with the intentional structures of the world of which
it is a part. To state it most simply, intentions—operations of intentionality and
structures of these operations—subsist 'objectively,' independently of the human mind. The mind operates, becoming 'conscious,' so to speak, when it
engages with and in these operations.[2]

Intentionality has hitherto been understood as something that takes place "in
the head"—that is, it is a process of a conscious mind, engaged in as an
activity of a conscious being, at whatever level that being is capable. Just as
Copernicus' efforts constituted a reversal of the dominant geocentric model
of the universe, so too does Mitscherling's proposed model of the mind (and
its relation to the world) constitute a reversal of the place of intentionality in
consciousness.

The purpose of this chapter is to assess the kind of metaphysical debate
that *Aesthetic Genesis* can promote (or perhaps instigate), and the extent to
which his conceptual terminology brings the usual advantage that philosophers bring to the table: the ability to make things clearer. Of particular
interest to me is the idea that intentional structures *subsist* through time,
grounding relations between material and/or ideal beings in this prior sense
of intentionality. Specifically, I will compare the concept of a being that
subsists to the concept of *emergence*, wherein complex relations between
smaller actors (say, neurons) gives rise to something that is not reducible to
the sum of its parts (say, mind, thoughts, or consciousness). After my com-
parison, I will assess whether the idea of subsistent relational structures
should supplant what I will call the anti-metaphysical (in the Peircean sense)
idea of emergent phenomenon, and, if we conceptualise our scientific
hypotheses and theories with this new metaphysical framework, what I think
it will mean for the truth-status of those hypotheses and theories.

I will also defend contemporary science, specifically against the charges
of materialism that Mitscherling lays out in *Aesthetic Genesis*. It is often
thought that contemporary scientists are both too dogmatic and too myopic to
see beyond the observable material immediately in front of them, but I will
make the case that this view of what scientists do (and the kinds of explanations they seek) is simplistic—that it paints a picture of science that is, to
paraphrase the passage from Peirce immediately above, more crudely materialistic than it actually is. However, it is also the case that philosophy can (and
often does) contribute to science by providing logical structure and criticism
of the principles underpinning scientific practice.

I will conclude that what Mitscherling has done is not properly understood as a revolution for cognitive science, although that label is entirely

appropriate with regard to realist phenomenology. However, whether or not Mitscherling's work is in fact a revolution or simply a terminological modification for the sake of clarity, his conceptual structure of subsistent (and thus changing) forms is an important contribution to both philosophy and contemporary science. It brings with it the conceptual apparatus necessary to settle an upheaval described by John Dewey in his lecture *The Influence of Darwin on Philosophy*. The upheaval that Dewey points to is that of the doctrine of evolution by natural selection exploding the long held position that the Aristotelian concept of species was "eternal" or "unchanging." Whether the then-dominant view was a correct reading of Aristotle or not is a secondary consideration: the view is displaced because what it says about the world is untenable. Dewey remarks that the "displacing of this wholesale type of philosophy will doubtless not arrive by sheer logical disproof, but rather by growing recognition of its futility."[3] That is, the reason that the then-dominant philosophy was displaced was not because some internal inconsistency was brought to light, but because of its complete failure to account for the facts of changing species. This new treatment of intentional being as something *relational*, and therefore as *subsisting* effectively evades the problem of explaining how species can change, with some coming into existence, while others become extinct. The problem simply disappears, because the concept does not require that one understand forms as eternal and static. It is a much more robust set of metaphysical tools.

Mitscherling tells us that contemporary scientists are best described as possessing a materialistic blind spot. Of Aristotle's four causes, they have discarded all but the efficient and material, as these are the only kinds of causality related to the kinds of explanations contemporary scientists like to seek: a reduction of the phenomenon in question to its material constituent parts. That is, the contemporary scientist only accepts this kind of material explanation (what, materially speaking, brings an object into existence) *as an explanation*—nothing else will do. As Mitscherling puts it: "[A] fundamental dogma of all current mainstream science remains that by 'causality' is meant 'efficient causality'—that is, the physically observable and quantifiably measurable effect exerted by one material body on another."[4] This is very likely true, but the fact that it is very likely true makes the particular phrasing of the accusation somewhat odd. To describe this as a "fundamental dogma" is strange, given that the aim of science as a practice is to take hypotheses and/or theoretical accounts for various objects of experience and go about settling which of these is best by appeal to empirical observation. The practice is, at its core, to dream up a way to subject an idea to a public standard of scrutiny. The very thing that Mitscherling criticizes about science is, in other words, what allows for it to be science to begin with—and what allows it to be as successful as it is when it comes to explaining the world in the most objective way possible.

Consider a criticism of philosophy along the following lines: "The problem with mainstream philosophy is that it is too concerned with the theoretical and logical underpinnings of practices, and does not concern itself with testing its propositions. It is therefore wedded to a dogma that metaphysics and logic come first." This is actually not an uncommon charge. The term *a priori*, for example, is itself used pejoratively in describing reasoning that is wholly detached from any worldly observation, and not only by contemporary scientists, but even other philosophers, such as Peirce. Now, this is obviously unfair: *a priori* reasoning is not invalid, and is entirely appropriate for its intended purpose. Mathematics is a field that is entirely *a priori*, and scientists do not typically have a problem with mathematics. I am certain that we could generate any number of similar criticisms, but the point is that it is odd to criticize a field of study for focusing on its subject. Scientists concern themselves with testable theories and hypotheses; philosophers tend to focus on logical and metaphysical consistency with regard to what current practices are. Hence, we have philosophies of a variety of fields ranging from economics, to history, to, in the present case, science—and more precisely, cognitive science.

Furthermore, to call the methodology of science a dogma is a bit too strong, since observations made by scientists have historically not only modified or overthrown particular hypotheses or theories, but have actually modified the entire methodological approach to testing and observational data in general. The example that I think illustrates this best is the peculiar case of *Clever Hans*, a horse that was supposedly able to do simple and even complex arithmetical feats after being trained by his master in the late 19th and early 20th century. The horse would answer questions posed to him by his master, or participants from the audience, by stamping his hoof the correct number of times. When the psychologist Oskar Pfungst decided to test the horse for himself in 1904, he realized that the horse could only answer correctly when someone (usually his trainer) knew the correct answer. Whenever "a questioner knew how Clever Hans should respond, the horse did well. When no one knew the correct response, the horse failed."[5] This discovery led to the implementation of blinding in studies of behaviour, as researchers realized that their desire for certain results, when mixed with full knowledge of the study, could skew and thus invalidate results.

However, it is not difficult to see how one might think that science is dogmatic, given the position that it has achieved in contemporary culture, and the somewhat cavalier attitude of many famous scientists regarding the position of science relative to other fields. Some, such as Richard Feynman, have been outright dismissive of the contribution that other fields, such as philosophy, can make to science. Feynman's infamous quip was that "philosophy of science is about as useful to science as ornithology is to birds."[6] I find this view wrongheaded, but the attitude behind it is a good foil for the introduction of what I see as the reason for a certain confusion in Mitscherling's description of science as having completely abandoned teleological explanations in favour of *purely* material explanations. There is, in fact, good reason to think that although the efficient cause is stressed, scientists still make appeals to both formal and final causes in their explanation of various phenomena—they just do it discreetly. The reason that this may not be immediately apparent is because of what comments like Feynman's illustrate: in science, the priority is practice; in philosophy, the priority is theory. By this I do not mean that science makes no use of theory, just that the theories it makes use of are developed through practice. That is, science and philosophy approach theory in different ways: science approaches it practically, subjecting theories to testing to see which theories get to stay; philosophy scrutinizes science itself in light of the motivations of scientists, their discoveries, and the development of scientific practices. This is the difference in my use of "theory" in each field: this sense of the word "theory" would, in science, be synonymous with "principles" rather than the particular theories scientists attempt to erect. All of this is to say that there is a difference between what scientists may promote in principle, and what kinds of assumptions might be invoked when it comes to providing a testable explanation (that is, a candidate hypothesis).

This also brings to light a problem of terminology. It is true that contemporary science has largely rejected Aristotle's account of causality, but not exactly in the way that Mitscherling presents. Or, put another way, the rejection of Aristotle's causality by contemporary science means that the terms are not used in the same way. The Aristotelian account of matter found in *Metaphysics* states that it is indeterminate, and what determines it is the formal cause; matter "does not exist in actuality, but exists in potency."[7] What "actualizes" the potential matter into the "thisness" or "thatness" that denotes an object of cognition is the combination of the formal and the material into an organic unity that can only be parsed apart upon reflection, after the act of cognition. That is, the form can be understood as a kind of principle of motion, acting through the movable (though, in itself, inert and indeterminate) matter: "[I]t is a mover because it is *active*; but it is on the movable that it is capable of acting, so that the actuality of both is one, just as there is the same interval from one to two as from two to one, and as the steep ascent and the steep descent are one, but the being of them is not one; the case of the mover and the moved is similar."[8]

Form and matter, ascending and descending in a sequence of numbers, and up and down are not the same things, but they are one in their being because there is never *actually* one without the other—they are necessarily relational with one another. We cannot have an elevator that goes up without the possibility that it can follow the same path back down (barring, of course, the possibility of its path being blocked; the point is that the possibility of its going up implies the possibility of its coming back down, as this is just a reversal of the path that already exists due to its having gone up). Form and matter are distinct in their being because we can think about them independently of one another, but in our experience they are never separate. I can think of trees *in general*, but I never perceive this. The object of my perception is always of *this* tree or *that* tree. The general is what informs my experience of the particular material instance. And what Aristotle describes as "moving," Mitscherling describes as "determining": "It seems, then, that the primary substance that 'confers' determinacy on the compounded individual substance is form. The form, in other words, is the cause of the determinacy of the individual substance."[9]

If cognition is the act of abstracting the form from the object of cognition, the form is that which determines what we recognise in the object. That is, it is what makes the indeterminate matter into an object, properly understood. And it is a condition of the possibility of our sensory experience of objects that demands the existence of what Mitscherling describes as an intentional structure that subsists independently of the subject and object of the act of cognition, whose existence is implied by the act of cognition being possible.

Mitscherling's criticism is that science (and in particular cognitive science), because of this rejection, cannot account for these relations that subsist and give rise to our cognition and/or recognition of the more general form in the particular instance:

> What I have been suggesting is that realist phenomenology's relocation of intentionality, putting it back into the natural world itself, enables us to account for behavior—and for the nature of the habits both of humans and the world—in a more satisfying manner than has so far been suggested by current cognitive science, which, while rightly stressing embodiment, still regards material being as exhaustively constituting the conditions of its behavior.[10]

The dogmatic position that only material accounts will suffice as legitimate explanatory inferences is indeed a hindrance. If matter is just that which is moved, and is indeterminate without the form that moves it, then by following the scientific route, what we do is render our accounts of all phenomena in the universe literally and figuratively inert. We have material entities whose interactions we cannot account for, that scientists appeal to, in attempting to explain the more and more complex phenomena of our experience. With the rejection of the formal and final cause of the Aristotelian framework, we are left with only the material and efficient, and thus we reduce what we see as determinate objects to indeterminate matter, completely lacking of the ingredients necessary for the experience to have occurred in the first place. In short, scientific analysis dismembers and kills the object (in roughly that order). The remedy, then, is to reintroduce the formal and final cause into scientific methodology through the acceptance of the intentional ontological structure that underpins all sensory (and so all conscious) experience. Hence, consciousness has an *aesthetic genesis*.

But there is one problem that presents itself with this treatment of science: suppose that when scientists say the word "matter" and philosophers say the word "matter," they do not mean the same thing. It is well established, by Mitscherling and others elsewhere, that science, as a practice, has rejected the Aristotelian causal model. Mitscherling expresses this as a rejection of formal causality (and, by extension, final causality, because we cannot explain the behaviour of the various objects and beings that constitute the universe), but if science in general has really rejected Aristotle's causal account, then it is very likely that scientists do not use Aristotle's terminology in the way that Aristotle does—the way that philosophers use the terms. This brings us to my earlier distinction between the practice of science and the principles scientists hold. In principle, scientists do not hold that the theories that they use to explain phenomenal experience exist in the sense that they are "true" in some absolute way. But this is not necessarily an unjustified position to hold when one considers the justification for holding that scientific theories are true. Because the justification for holding that a scientific theory is true is entirely contingent on the evidence at hand, and scientists are not blessed with a God's-eye view, they can never be certain that new evidence will not come to light that disconfirms it. So to hold that something is true in an unqualified sense when it is justified on scientific grounds is to claim the existence of potentially non-existent entities (it would also commit scientists to the untenable position that no future evidence will be forthcoming), and to hold such a position effectively undermines the logic behind the scientific method.

To illustrate why this approach to justification would undermine the scientific method, consider this example provided by Frank Ramsey: "Suppose the human race for no reason always supposed strawberries would give them stomach-ache and so never ate them; then all their beliefs, strictly so-called, e.g. that if I eat strawberries I shall have a pain, would be true; but would there not be something wrong? Is it not a fact that if they had eaten them they wouldn't have had a pain?"[11] Of course, those of us who have no pain when eating strawberries would likely contend that it is a fact that eating strawberries would not cause pain. But this statement speaks beyond the facts, because there are certainly those who will, for whatever reason, become ill after eating strawberries. Thus Ramsey denies that it is a fact, instead insisting that it is a consequence of the rule that the strawberry abstainers are wrong since, by and large, people do not become ill after eating strawberries.[12] This general rule is probabilistic, allowing for exceptions to the rule.

The scientific method is largely *abductive* logic (drawing an explanatory inference, or proposing a reasonable story, for a given phenomenon) exposed to empirical scrutiny through some means, which then allows for the accumulation of inductive support (or not, in the case that it is false). The whole point to the scientific method is to appeal to reality as a means of settling opinion.[13] As we will continually engage with reality, the logic behind the scientific method entails a probabilistic approach when using our rules to judge what will happen in any given case. So, if someone eats a strawberry, it is a certain fact whether or not she becomes ill, but this is only known *after the fact*. We cannot know that before the strawberry is ingested. We can only guess with varying degrees of certainty. Thus the scientific method employs abductive logic, which posits a hypothesis that is always open to disconfirmation, due to the nature of the justification it has; and inductive logic, which is entirely probabilistic, and the generalisations it makes shift along with the data from which it generalises. The logic and practice of science are necessarily future-oriented.

However, in practice, scientists can behave quite differently. Consider the famous remark made by J. B. S. Haldane, that teleology is a biologist's mistress: the biologist cannot go without her, but is embarrassed to be seen with her in public. The implication is that no scientist will hold that teleology (that is, final causality) is a principle of scientific inquiry, but regardless, the principle is smuggled in with the practice.

This seems plainly correct. Consider the following statement from Steven Pinker:

> If the mind is an organ for computation engineered by natural selection, our social motives should be strategies that are tailored to the tournaments we play in. People should have distinct kinds of thoughts and feelings about kin and non-kin, and about parents, children, siblings, dates, spouses, acquaintances, friends, rivals, allies, and enemies.[14]

This is a statement about the expectations one can have about human behaviour in light of the mind's being adapted for the survival and replication of the organism to which it belongs (or, for Mitscherling, which it inhabits). But how can a scientist speak of adaptation if they make no use of teleological concepts? There is also the concept of the recognition of distinct kinds of people. So it seems that there is something like a final and formal cause being put to use within the practice of science. It is simply the case that scientists do not want to commit themselves to what they perceive as *eternal* and/or *unchanging* forms, for the reasons that Dewey mentions: it is the "recognition of its futility" rather than "sheer logical disproof" that makes this view of form, or species untenable from the scientific perspective. The only reason to hold such a position is for reasons of dogmatism. Final causality has been interpreted as a directedness toward some ultimate aim that all of nature has—that is, the ultimate purpose of following God's divine will. It is not difficult to imagine why such a teleological view would be rejected by scientists: the idea that everything in nature is designed specifically to suit the purpose of a goal universally pursued by all of nature is an unjustified inference simply because it fails to line up with the facts. It also runs contrary to considerations of parsimony and is, in all likelihood, unfalsifiable. If this is what one gets with teleological metaphysics, one should indeed be embarrassed to be seen with it in public.

A description of the sort that Pinker provides is riddled with assumptions and descriptions of behaviour, functionality, directedness or a goal-oriented nature, and speciation. In other words, formal and final causality are already included, if not explicitly. The difference is that the forms (or species) are not static, and the *telos* is not some general aim that everything works toward, but rather operates in what we might call discrete final causes. What Mitscherling's efforts will likely allow is for scientists to take those "smuggled-in" concepts and make them fully explicit.

However, scientists might feel justified in asking what reason they have for bothering to make such assumptions fully explicit. After all, if the assumptions lead them to treat the objects of their inquiries as the Aristotelian might, what's the point in adding the metaphysical language and ensuring that they have the correct interpretation of final causality (that is, not the Christianised version appealing to the will of a transcendent guiding force). Different entities in nature, and nature itself, are recognised as behaving and having a variety of functions. Different species are recognised as distinct from one another.

The main difference here between the view Mitscherling advocates, and that which he describes contemporary scientists as holding, is that the explanation scientists provide is natural selection, "which has come to be interpreted as explaining the manner in which blind forces of a thoroughly material and mechanistic 'nature' give rise to precisely such complex emergent 'entities' as the human mind—and indeed, to 'life' itself."[15] In describing the concept of emergence further, Mitscherling says that it is essentially a reversal of the Aristotelian paradigm: it is the emergence of the non-material from the material. Or, as he puts it, "a machine constructed out of dead matter."[16]

By Mitscherling's description, contemporary scientists explain life by appealing to the theory of evolution via natural selection. Matter is inert, and only gains its non-material, formal elements by a process of interaction that is the result of forces acting more or less randomly on pieces of that matter. It is then this process that informs the matter in the way that it does. This is obviously contrary to Aristotle's view, which is that forms are only ever abstracted from particular instantiations. That is, the form is cognised, and then the matter can be intellectually separated from the form. So we could cognise a chair, and then after that cognition, consider that chair and the fact that it is made of wood, plastic or metal. But it is always that form that we cognise or recognise—it is thoroughly unnatural for me to look at a chair and not think "It's a chair," but instead something like "That wood is in the shape of a chair." The latter can only be done upon reflection after my initial cognition.

But the concept of emergence is not entirely without merit. Contemporary scientists no longer utilise Aristotelian metaphysics, and the reason for this is what Dewey describes above: there was deemed (perhaps erroneously) to be too much baggage with Aristotle, because forms were interpreted as eternal and/or unchanging. So new concepts were developed to meet explanatory demands. Complex phenomena that are resistant to a reductionist account need a different kind of origin story, and this is essentially all that the concept of emergence is—complex interactions between many different organisms and/or forces that cannot be parsed apart into a neat causal account, and so any phenomenon that resists such a causal account, such as consciousness, is said to *emerge* from those complex interactions. All of the factors in such a phenomenon influence the result, but an efficient cause cannot be singled out.

Duncan Watts says that "these influences pile up in unexpected ways, generating collective behavior that is 'emergent' in the sense that it cannot be understood solely in terms of its component parts."[17] This is also clearly not an arbitrary reduction, and there may indeed be some metaphysical work going on, even if it is not explicitly metaphysical. Sometimes scientists (or even groups of scientists forming historical movements, such as positivism or methodological individualism) seek to reduce the phenomenon in question to its component parts. But this is exactly the arbitrary move Peirce criticizes as "crudely metaphysical": those scientists have taken up the *a priori* position that to explain a thing, one must understand the smallest constituent parts of that thing, and, worse still, that the understanding of those smallest parts is what constitutes the only acceptable explanation of the greater subject of inquiry. Every object of study is thus treated in an excessively mechanistic fashion. But this cannot be the case with the concept of emergence. Notice that Watts' use of the term indicates that its purpose is to find out whether a reductive explanation will do or not. That is, the purpose of calling something "emergent" is to forbid explicitly its being explained in the sort of reductive terms a positivist might attempt. It is to work out what kinds of explanations are arbitrary and which are not.

Watts poses these questions to illustrate the drive behind the use of emergence as a concept:

> How is it, for example, that one can lump together a collection of atoms and somehow get a molecule? How is it that one can lump together a collection of molecules and somehow get amino acids? How is it that one can lump together a collection of amino acids and other chemicals and somehow get a living cell? How is it that one can lump together a collection of living cells and somehow

get complex organs like the brain? And how is it that one can lump together a collection of organs and somehow get a sentient being that wonders about its eternal self?[18]

These questions express what is sometimes called *the problem of scale*, i.e., the problem of how we can get from physics to chemistry; chemistry to biology, etc. How do we keep the natural laws we describe when moving from the scale of the individual atom to the chemical reaction consistent? This may not be too great a dilemma for the specialized scientist working solely in her particular field, as the concerns of those working in the field of cosmology are sufficiently separate from those working in the field of evolutionary biology that they need not necessarily overlap, but it does seem to be a pressing concern in cognitive science. The problem that cognitive scientists face is exactly the problem of scale, because they seek to explain how the mind works, exists, and interacts with its environment and other minds. The fact that the brain is examined through all the various means available to cognitive science shows that the physical correlate is sought in explaining both discrete mental acts and the total fact of consciousness, but this, at the same time, suggests that there is a major unresolved tension between the goals of the research, and the means pursued in the actual practice of science in the field. And this tension is actually crucial to the goals of science. If scientists want to understand reality, they must have a self-critical tool that is constantly open to revision, not just at the theoretical level, but at the methodological level as well. But this revision cannot be constant, or there would be no stable framework within which scientists could accumulate knowledge.

The focus of this chapter, however, is not the philosophy of science or cognitive science per se, but the debate, as I see it, between the contemporary scientific approach (broadly speaking) to consciousness, and Mitscherling's proposed alternative. As I see it, the crux of the matter rests in whether we ought to prefer the terminology of *subsistence*, or that of *emergence*. This is a debate between, as I have framed it, a "pro-metaphysical" and an "anti-metaphysical" metaphysics, and it is not immediately clear which should be preferred.

However, it is not clear that this issue is entirely disjunctive, either. Scientists engaged in inquiry may pay no mind to the "pro-metaphysical" side, despite any advantages its adoption might entail, simply because it may not be clear what is to be gained by changing the concepts one will use to describe the subjects that one studies. This, however, is why philosophers occupy this role, rather than scientists. Concerning consciousness, for example, a well thought-out and meticulously defined subject of study will do nothing but aid in the practical matter of its study. Consider Mitscherling's description of *mind*, set in opposition to the Cartesian *cogito*: "The ego is not presupposed by the activity—just the opposite: It is the activity that yields the ego. It is the intentional being of the entire organism that yields the existence of the self-reflective subject."[19] This is the Copernican revolution—the switch from the view that a mind is "thing" that every person has, and that engages intentionally with all of the various other things in its environment, to the view of the organism as an intentional being engaging in intentional structures yielding the mind as an activity. Yet this seems very similar to the description of emergence that Watts provides. The overlap can likely be attributed to the fact that, based on the description of intentional structures subsisting through time, any emergent phenomenon could also be described as subsisting.

But for my part, the decision does not come down to whether emergence or subsistent intentional structures make better conceptual sense of the human being, mind or soul. What I find most interesting is applying the idea of a subsistent entity to the concept of scientific truth. These entities subsist through time, and are not located in any particular place, or at any particular moment. Some of these entities can be altered and even destroyed due to the fact that they are relational. Consider Mitscherling's description of his relation with the chair:

> When I leave this city, the relation of my body to this chair will not subsist unaltered—that is, as identical, or self-identical—although one might want to say that some sort of spatial relation will continue to subsist for as long as both my body and this chair continue to exist. But as soon as either one of these relata ceases to exist, so too will any relation. The relation of my body to this chair, whatever sort of identities this relation may assume over the coming years, will simply cease to be—it will no longer subsist.[20]

So subsistent entities can exist, change and cease to be. What really intrigues me about this prospect is the idea that the change occurs by the relation between two entities. Mitscherling's relation with his chair changes as their relative positions change. Suppose that we take a different entity to be a hypothesis or theory. If we take a hypothesis or theory to be the result of a relation that human beings have with whatever phenomenon we take it to explain, then this view has a bearing on what we might be able to say the truth status of that hypothesis or theory might be. The real advantage that I see *Aesthetic Genesis* providing for science is that we now have the metaphysical concepts available to describe a currently accepted scientific fact as "true" without committing to its being true for all time. The reason this is the case is because we can describe the form of something—say, cancer—as a virus, and then later, with the advent of modern genetics, describe it as caused by what are essentially replication errors in the cells of the body. How can we describe each as true? Because the form changes as our knowledge deepens; and our knowledge deepens as we engage with that aspect of reality more, and perhaps differently. The two relata are *us* and the phenomenon studied—in this case, cancer. What I mean is that we can say that it is true that cancer has such and such a cause, because that is the form that cancer has at that point in time, if we conceive of it as a theoretical construct, and conceive of a theoretical construct as an entity that subsists. It is possible that with this understanding of formal structure, we no longer need to describe scientific truths with the hard qualification that by "true" we merely mean "not yet disconfirmed." Which definition of scientific truth is preferable is another paper (at least) on its own, but the metaphysical debate can be had, and this is due, in part, to the new approach in *Aesthetic Genesis*.

NOTES

1. C. S. Peirce, "On a New Class of Observations, Suggested by the Principles of Logic," in *The Essential Peirce, Vol. I*, Nathan Houser and Christian Kloesel, eds. (Bloomington, IN: Indiana University Press, 1992), 108.

2. Jeff Mitscherling, *Aesthetic Genesis: The Origin of Consciousness in the Intentional Being of Nature* (Lanham: University Press of America, 2010), 47. Hereafter cited as AG.

3. John Dewey, *The Influence of Darwin on Philosophy and Other Essays in Contemporary Thought* (New York: Henry Holt, 1910), 16.

4. AG, 90.

5. Richard Wiseman, *Paranormality: Why We See What Isn't There*, (London: MacMillan, 2011), 246.

6. Quoted in, Jerry A. Coyne, *Faith vs. Fact: Why Science and Religion are Incompatible* (New York: Viking, 2015), 189. Coyne disagrees with Feynman for reasons very similar to the ones that I will give, and his description of the relation of science and philosophy—that science is concerned with the accumulation of knowledge about the world, while philosophy is concerned with keeping the description of that knowledge logically consistent and with maintaining rigorous metaphysical structures for theoretical frameworks.

7. Aristotle, *The Basic Works of Aristotle*, Richard McKeon, ed. (New York: Modern Library, 2001); *Metaphysics* xi. 1. 1060a20.

8. Ibid., xi. 9. 1066a30–35.

9. AG, 78.

10. AG, 126–127.

11. F. P. Ramsey, *Philosophical Papers*, D. H. Mellor, ed. (Cambridge: Cambridge University Press, 1990), 161.

12. Ibid.

13. Or for Peirce, reliably fixing belief. See C. S. Peirce, *Writings of Charles S. Peirce: Vol. 3*, Christian J. W. Kloesel, ed. (Bloomington, IN: Indiana University Press, 1986), 254–256.

14. Steven Pinker, *How The Mind Works* (New York: W. W. Norton, 1999), 429.

15. AG, 141.

16. Ibid.

17. Duncan J. Watts, *Everything is Obvious Once You Know the Answer: How Common Sense Fails Us* (New York: Crown Business, 2011), 26.

18. Ibid., 62.

19. AG, 33.

20. AG, 127.

Afterword:
The Problem with Being
That Can Be Understood

Jeff Mitscherling

This afterword is not the proper place to discuss or respond at length to each individual paper collected in this volume. Such an exercise in repetition is rarely of much use or interest, and this would be especially true in the case of the present volume, given the exceptional quality and clarity of the contributions. The papers here collected do an excellent job of indicating central theses of my work. Some of the papers offer strong and helpful criticism, some illustrate how my work complements the work of other authors, and some describe directions in which my ideas might be further developed along lines that I had not previously considered. Simply stated: this is an excellent collection, and I am deeply honored and grateful that the authors here collected not only agreed to participate in the project, but that they put such a great deal of effort and care into their contributions. Still greater effort and care is required to compile and edit a collection such as this, and I owe special thanks to our editors, Charlene Elsby and Aaron Massecar, and not only for their editorial work and their own written contributions, but for having conceived of this project in the first place. I shall take the liberty of speaking for all of us contributors in thanking the two of you for having done such an outstanding job.

Although I just said that I can't name or respond to each of the authors individually, there is nevertheless one contribution to this collection that I really must address in some detail, for it could easily lead our readers to a fundamental misunderstanding not only of what I am attempting to achieve in *Aesthetic Genesis* (and indeed, in the entire project to which this book belongs, i.e., The Revision of Hermeneutic Ontology), but also of the problem I find in Gadamer's claim that "Being that can be understood is language." The author suggests that I have not properly understood and accurately represented Gadamer's position, and I would like to take this opportunity to discuss more fully my interpretation of that position and the problem that I see in Gadamer's concept of language. It could well be the case that my criticism of Gadamer is misdirected and that I have in fact misunderstood his concept of language; Robinson's treatment of Gadamer is certainly quite thorough and persuasive. If that is the case, the following discussion will serve nevertheless to clarify my motivations and basic intention in my project as a whole.

In his "Being that Can be Understood is (Not Just) Language: On Linguisticality and Intentionality," Jason Robinson writes:

> If we dismantle this element [of philosophy of language] in his hermeneutics, or substantially revise it in almost any manner, the risk to his entire project is nothing less than apocalyptic. In *Aesthetic Genesis*, Mitscherling proposes precisely such a revision. Mitscherling argues that there is something fundamentally wrong with Gadamer's claim regarding being and language; something that does not align with a closer examination of human experience and reality, and therefore, something that needs to be replaced if we wish to articulate a realist phenomenology.

I do indeed argue that there is something wrong with Gadamer's claim regarding being and language, but the revision I have suggested by no means suggests or was ever intended to constitute any "apocalyptic risk" to Gadamer's hermeneutics. Quite the contrary, in fact. My hope is that in providing for hermeneutic ontology a deeper and broader foundation—a foundation that may be constructed with the help of realist phenomenology—Gadamer's philosophical hermeneutics will be more firmly and convincingly established. Any criticism of Gadamer's work that I have ever offered has always been offered with this intention. I should explain this further.

My chief criticism of Gadamer's concept of language is that it always remained basically that which Heidegger proceeded to elaborate after *Being and Time*.[1] It is my opinion that this view of language severely restricts the scope of meaningful human experience and is incapable of providing Gadamer's hermeneutics with a sufficiently solid foundation. The most obvious problem with this view of language becomes evident when we see how Gadamer's own statements regarding the nature of language sometimes appear to be inconsistent and even self-contradictory. This is an indication not of error or confusion on Gadamer's part, but of his willingness to extend and broaden his hermeneutics over the years to take into account criticisms and suggestions from his readers, students and colleagues. Yet the problems that arise necessarily from the concept of language that he adopted from his teacher prove, I believe, to be simply unavoidable and intractable. The concept of language that Heidegger developed throughout his later works is as persuasive as it is poetic—its power might in fact derive precisely from this poetic character—but this concept, which always remained fundamental to Gadamer's hermeneutics, serves only to impede the analysis of the relation between language and cognition, the examination of the role that language plays in our encounter with the natural world (as distinct from our intersubjectively constituted lifeworld), and the investigation of human experience that is in principle ineffable. I speak at some length in *Aesthetic Genesis* of language and cognition, but very little about language, the world, and ineffable experience, so I'll discuss these briefly here. I'll begin with the Heideggerian-Gadamerian concept of "world".

Already in *Being and Time*, as well as in his subsequent writings—perhaps most definitively in "The Origin of the Work of Art" (1935–1936)—when Heidegger speaks of the "world" he is *not* talking about this physical world that we inhabit as embodied beings. That world is first brought to phenomenology by Husserl, Stein, and Merleau-Ponty—not Heidegger. The world of *Being and Time* is the world of interpreted meanings and significance, with meaning and significance both arising from the fundamentally temporal, and in a crucial sense *pre-spatial*, experience of *Dasein*. In short, it is an essentially epistemological construct. Whatever connection it may have to human embodiment is merely peripheral. [2]

I believe the first clear mention in *Being and Time* of *Dasein*'s "bodily nature" is at H108–109 (M&R, 143): [3]

> Out of this directionality arise the fixed directions of right and left. *Dasein* constantly takes these directions along with it, just as it does its de-severances. *Dasein*'s spatialization in its 'bodily nature' is likewise marked out in accordance with these directions. (This 'bodily nature' hides a whole problematic of its own, though we shall not treat it here.) Thus things that are ready-to-hand and used for the body—like gloves, for example, which are to move with the hands—must be given directionality towards right and left.

Dasein's directionality, according to Heidegger, is quite literally that which directs *Dasein*'s attention in such a way that entities may appear to *Dasein*. (In other words, *Dasein*'s directionality is the origin of intentionality.) Moreover, entities always appear, or are given, to *Dasein* as meaningful. The meaning of things, that is to say, is not the product of any sort of logically or chronologically prior act of meaning-constitution or meaning-bestowal on the part of a pure ego, as Husserl maintained. For Heidegger, such pure transcendental activity on the part of the ego is simply a fiction, as is the pure ego itself. We always find ourselves in the world, and this world is already meaningful for us at the very outset of our engagement with it. "Truth" happens in, and precisely *as*, *Dasein*'s "recognition" of this meaning: the truth of a thing "discloses" itself only through that thing's encounter with

Dasein, and this activity or process of disclosing is the mode of being of truth in the context of the meaningful nexus of significations that constitutes the "world". But this means that the meanings of things, while not bestowed upon them by an ego or transcendental subjectivity, are constituted intersubjectively as elements of the "totality of significations" in which we inhabitants of the lifeworld find ourselves. In other words, meaning is still bestowed on the object by an intentional consciousness operating within an intersubjectively constituted lifeworld.

Gadamer's indebtedness to Heidegger's thought is perhaps nowhere so evident than in his concepts of world and language. For Gadamer too, language is that whereby we humans first come to discover and live in a world, thereby "rising above our environment." As Gadamer writes (TM 444–445 [Language as horizon of a hermeneutic ontology]):[4]

> . . . unlike all other living creatures, man's relationship to the world is characterized by *freedom from environment*. This freedom implies the linguistic constitution of the world. Both belong together. To rise above the pressure of what impinges on us from the world means to have language and to have a 'world.' . . .
>
> To rise above the environment has from the outset a human—i.e., a verbal—significance. Animals can leave their environment and move over the whole earth without severing their environmental dependence. For man, however, rising above the environment means rising to 'world' itself, to true environment.

This distinction between world (*Welt*) and environment (*Umwelt*) will also be familiar to readers of Heidegger. Gadamer adopted it wholeheartedly, further elaborating the Heideggerian concept of world with special attention to the sorts of social and cultural practices and institutions that Dilthey treated at length, and further developing this concept through the examination of the intersubjective constitution of the values that identify a given culture or "world" and distinguish it from other cultures with their own distinctive values. It is important to recognize that the "world" that Heidegger and Gadamer speak of is not to be confused with the "natural world," or "nature". The world they are speaking of is an historically evolving realm of shared meanings and values, our cultural world. It is, in short, our *lifeworld*, not the natural world, and Gadamer's description of the essentially linguistic character of the lifeworld—including our encounters with other persons and with such cultural creations as works of art—simply does not apply to our everyday encounters with objects in the natural world. Language, for Gadamer, is a social and cultural achievement belonging exclusively to the lifeworld; it plays no role in what we might call our "brute encounter" with the physical reality of our environment.

My claim is that the ontological ground for philosophical hermeneutics must be able to deal with this "natural" dimension of human experience as well with the social and cultural, and that this ground is to be located in the realm of a non-linguistic experience that belongs by nature to all human beings (and to some extent all sentient beings) and that underlies and informs all human cognition. Robinson quotes one sentence from a passage of TM's Supplement II which, when quoted at more length, is particularly helpful in this regard (TM 547):

> . . . Now it is certainly the case that our experience of the world does not take place only in learning and using a language. There is a prelinguistic experience of the world, as Habermas, referring to Piaget's research, reminds us. The language of gesture, facial expression, and movement binds us to each other. There are laughter and tears (Helmut Plessner has worked out a hermeneutics of these).[5] There is the world of science within which the exact, specialized languages of symbolism and mathematics provide sure foundations for the elaboration of theory, languages which have brought with them a capacity for construction and manipulation which seems a kind of self-representation of homo faber, of man's technical ingenuity. But even these forms of self-representation must constantly be taken up in the interior dialogue of the soul with itself.
>
> I acknowledge that these phenomena demonstrate that behind all the relativities of language and convention there is something in common which is no longer language, but which looks to an ever-possible verbalization, and for which the well-tried word 'reason' is, perhaps, not the worst. Nevertheless, there remains something that characterizes language as such, and that is precisely the fact that language as language can be contrasted with every other act of communication. We call this difference writing and graphic transcription.

We have to note Gadamer's description of "language as language," in the second paragraph, as writing and graphic transcription. Gadamer always regarded language as, first and foremost, communicative speaking using conceptually meaningful linguistic formations that can be written down as words and sentences. *That* is what Gadamer initially, and always *primarily*, meant when he spoke of "language". By the time he wrote the passage just quoted,[6] probably in response to criticisms raised by readers (such as Habermas and Plessner), he had begun to modify his stance somewhat, and he was to modify his stance still further over the coming years, as he continued to develop his hermeneutics ever more fully. But as late as 1973, he still remained committed to the view of language as *Sprache* proper—as he remarks in this passage, "But even these forms of self-representation must constantly be taken up in the interior dialogue of the soul with itself" (i.e., they have to be linguistically expressed in thought)—and even in his latest works, it was spoken dialogue and the written word that remained "language as language."

In "Grenzen der Sprache" (1985)[7] Gadamer again speaks of a "broader" concept of language, but he again adds that his chief concern is with *Wortsprache*, i.e., the language of words that we employ in our social dealings with other people:

> There is no doubt that language must be seen not just as verbal language [*Wortsprache*] but as a form of communication. That means that a broader concept of language accompanies a more narrow one. In the broader sense language means all communication—including not just speech [*Rede*], but all gestures—that plays a part in the linguistic dealings of humans. Now there is the so-called animal language. But that is a separate theme. On the other hand, it is particularly important to me to take account of that in-between form, which without doubt is a separate type of form of communication; namely, the language that man speaks [*redet*] with animals and with certain domesticated animals is somehow understood. But of course verbal language [*Wortsprache*] stands at the center of my considerations.

In "Zur Phänomenologie von Ritual und Sprache" (1992), which Robinson also cites,[8] Gadamer again mentions this "broader sense" of language:

> Language, by the way, is not just verbal language [*Wortsprache*]. There's the language of the eyes, the language of the hands, pointing and naming, all of that is language, and that confirms that language exists always in our interaction with one another [stets im Miteinander ist]. Words are always answers, even when they're questions. . . . One has to ask oneself whether symbolic acts are not in the end earlier than the articulated verbal language. But can one speak here at all of earlier and later if everything is indeed conversation [*Gespräch*]?

The point I want to make in citing these passages is that, for Gadamer, even the non-verbal language of, for example, bodily gestures or art is always assimilated by, and in effect translated into, the verbal language through which alone, he claims, we are able to understand the meaning of our experience. Without being taken up in this way into the linguistic structures of our lifeworld, this non-verbal language could not be a form of communication at all. It could not, in other words, be "language as language," and it would remain without any meaning to us whatsoever. This view of language is dangerously similar to—if not in fact identical with—the intellectual operation of meaning-bestowal (*Sinngebung*) described by Husserl, and it is this "intellectualization" of all meaning that I wish to question. I shall return to this topic in a moment and explain that reference to Husserl. First, however, I have to discuss a further difficulty I find in Gadamer's account of language and human experience.

It is true that Gadamer never claimed that everything is language. As we read in the interview with Jean Grondin cited by Robinson: "No, no, I never meant and also have never said that everything is language. Being that can be understood is language. In this is hidden a limitation. So what cannot be understood can become an infinite task, the task of finding the right word that at least comes near to this 'thing,'—*Sache.*" Gadamer does say, however, that everything is conversation [*Gespräch*], as we read in the above-cited passage from 1992. There is an obvious difference between language and conversation, but my criticism holds for both, because in both cases the "thing" remains beyond our understanding, i.e., meaningless, as long as it remains excluded from the realm of our linguistic experience. To gain entry to this realm and thereby acquire meaning that can be understood, the "thing" must either be verbally identified (and we should note, by the way, Gadamer's reference in the interview with Grondin to "the right word") or it must somehow announce itself as a possible interlocutor waiting to be assimilated into the linguistic context of our lifeworld. The problem I see here is that the "thing" will always come to be and be understood by us only so far as our language is capable of grasping it. But what then happens to those "things" that, by their very nature, must always elude our linguistic articulation? And what do we do with those experiences that, by their very nature, carry us beyond or beneath language, yet still provoke in us the recognition of profound meaning? We may here consider, for example, the mystical experience.

In *The Varieties of Religious Experience*,[9] William James offers an elegant and compelling description of the mystical experience that has long been regarded as definitive. After asking, "What does the expression 'mystical states of consciousness' mean? How do we part off mystical states from other states?", James proceeds to describe "four marks which, when an experience has them, may justify us in calling it mystical . . . ." James lists these marks as ineffability, noetic quality, transiency, and passivity. I shall here quote his description of the first two of these characteristics:

> 1. *Ineffability.*—The handiest of the marks by which I classify a state of mind as mystical is negative. The subject of it immediately says that it defies expression, that no adequate report of its contents can be given in words. It follows from this that its quality must be directly experienced; it cannot be imparted or transferred to others. In this peculiarity mystical states are more like states of feeling than like states of intellect. No one can make clear to another who has never had a certain feeling, in what the quality or worth of it consists. One must have musical ears to know the value of a symphony; one must have been in love one's self to understand a lover's state of mind. Lacking the heart or ear, we cannot interpret the musician or the lover justly, and are even likely to consider him weak-minded or absurd. The mystic finds that most of us accord to his experiences an equally incompetent treatment.
>
> 2. *Noetic quality.*—Although so similar to states of feeling, mystical states seem to those who experience them to be also states of knowledge. They are states of insight into depths of truth unplumbed by the discursive intellect.

They are illuminations, revelations, full of significance and importance, all inarticulate though they remain; and as a rule they carry with them a curious sense of authority for aftertime.

The example of the mystical experience is admittedly extreme, and it may be too much to ask of any philosophy that it provide the means for its investigation. But for a philosophy to restrict the possibility of meaningful experience to the realm of the linguistic, or the realm of the *possibly* linguistic, is to deny us experiential access to the entire range of that which is in principle ineffable and which denies all possibility of discursive articulation. As James notes, there are other sorts of experience—such as falling in love, or appreciating the aesthetic power of music—that are similarly ineffable, but none of us can honestly deny the existence of such experience, or the sense of profound meaning that such experience is able to convey. Any account of human experience that describes it as meaningful only to the extent that it can be understood within the boundaries of the linguistic must prove incapable of being extended to the investigation of such experience, experience that meaningfully addresses a far deeper level of human nature than that which allows for articulation within the cultural and linguistic boundaries of a life-world.

To return now to the topic of meaning-bestowal: Husserl's concept of constitution continues to be misunderstood and misrepresented in the literature, and since it is often resorted to by those who want to accuse him of metaphysical idealism, a central feature of this concept has to be clarified.[10] An extremely simplified account will suffice for our present purpose: When Husserl described the intentionality of consciousness as constituting its object, he was not claiming that consciousness is the ground of the extra-mental existence of its object. He was not here concerned with the object as it might exist outside of the act of consciousness. This is not to say that Husserl denied the extra-mental existence of objects or of the independent existence of the physical world. He did not. Husserl's claim was merely that objects as we are conscious of them are always meaningful, and the meaning that they possess is bestowed upon them by our acts of consciousness. Consciousness, in other words, injects meaning into the sensible material with which it is presented (i.e., the hyletic data), and this meaningless data is thereby transformed into meaningful objects. I shall return to Husserl on constitution in just a moment, but this brief clarification should be sufficient to indicate the similarity between this sort of meaning-bestowal and Gadamer's account of the meaning-achievement of language: Just as, for Husserl, consciousness bestows meaning on its object, so too, for Gadamer, does language bestow meaning on its object. By exchanging language for consciousness, Gadamer has avoided one of the most notorious difficulties faced by Husserlian phenomenology—namely, its reliance on the operation of a transcendental subjectivity. Language, by its very nature as a form of communication, must be an intersubjective achievement. Moreover, as the "location" of this intersubjective activity is our lifeworld, its originary conditions lie not in "the transcendental" but in the historically situated present, the conditions of which themselves belong to an historically evolving tradition.

Yet, as I have already explained, Gadamer's account presents us with a different set of problems, the most serious of which, in my opinion, lies in precisely that meaning-bestowal I have just described. While Gadamer's account avoids the difficulties accompanying the positing of transcendental subjectivity as the ground of meaning, it nevertheless retains the view of meaning as bestowed upon the object of consciousness by linguistic intersubjectivity. For both Husserl and Gadamer (and Heidegger as well), moreover, the meaning that's bestowed is constituted always with regard to the comprehensive context of meanings belonging to the lifeworld of which it is a part. In this sense, Husserl, Heidegger and Gadamer might all be described as "intellectualizing" the nature of meaning, and we might even suggest that they all propose some form of epistemological idealism, for the object fully exists for us, according to these thinkers, only after we, whether as subjectivity or intersubjectivity, have bestowed upon it the meaning that consciousness has constituted.

Perhaps ironically, given that he's the one most often regarded as an idealist, Husserl is the only one of these thinkers to actually investigate the extent to which the independently existing object toward which consciousness comes to be directed might contribute to its cognition. I'm referring here to his investigations of genetic phenomenology that he began to pursue in the early 1920s, particularly those published in *Analyses Concerning Passive and Active Synthesis: Lectures on Transcendental Logic* and several of the early sections of *Experience and Judgment*. The question that motivated these analyses was precisely, "What is the nature of prepredicative experience?" Husserl's lengthy and detailed analyses obviously cannot be described here. I also felt that an adequate summary would have been far too long and technical for presentation in *Aesthetic Genesis*, which I wanted to keep as accessible to non-specialists as possible. But I now recognize that a careful presentation, if even only a brief one, will be absolutely essential for the further elaboration of some of the theses for which I argued in *Aesthetic Genesis*, and I hope to be able to return to this project in the future. Meanwhile, I shall have to rest content with the admittedly bold claims that I have made regarding the contribution of objectivities to our cognition of the objects of consciousness, and I remain confident that something like the account that I have offered will prove to be more or less correct and true.[11]

NOTES

1. In "Disclosedness and Signification: A Study of the Conception of Language Presented in *Being and Time*" (*Eidos*, vol. 1 [1979], 199–210), I demonstrate that there is also a philosophy of language to be found in *Being and Time*. But Heidegger's view of the nature, ubiquity and power of language develops along quite different lines throughout his subsequent writings.

2. From the mid-1970s until around 2000, the identification of Heidegger as a "philosopher of embodiment" was commonplace. He was typically represented as standing side by side with that other "existential philosopher", Merleau-Ponty. Fortunately, this state of affairs has changed. See, for example, D. Cerbone's article, "Heidegger and *Dasein*'s Bodily Nature: What is the Hidden Problematic?," *International Journal of Philosophical Studies*, vol. 8 (2000), 209–230. Cerbone argues, basically (and correctly), that consideration of the body does not belong to Heidegger's project of the explication of *Dasein*. A more indirect response to the earlier, uncritical reading of Heidegger as a philosopher of embodiment has been offered by commentators who attempt to "apply" Heidegger's thought to environmental issues. See, for example, Frank Schalow, *The Incarnality of Being: The Earth, Animals, and the Body in Heidegger's Thought* (Albany: SUNY Press, 2006).

3. Martin Heidegger, *Being and Time*, tr. John Macquarrie & Edward Robinson (New York: Harper & Row, 1962).

4. Hans-Georg Gadamer, *Truth and Method*, Second Revised Edition, translation revised by Joel Weinsheimer and Donald G. Marshall (New York: Crossroad, 1990).

5. Gadamer is probably referring here to Plessner's book *Lachen und Weinen* [*Laughing and Crying*] (1941). While Plessner's project and goals were quite different from my own—he's usually referred to as the founder of philosophical anthropology—it can be noted in passing that his view of intentionality might be located somewhere between the received view in phenomenology and my own. Plessner locates intentionality in a consciousness that originates in and through the behavior of the organism interacting with its environment, and particularly with those elements of the environment that restrict the freedom of its activity and self-expression. Plessner in this way conceives of a consciousness that is independent of a transcendental ego and essentially bound to, and by, the natural world.

6. The passage is from TM's Supplement II, "To What Extent Does Language Preform Thought?" This "supplement" was added to the first (1975) English translation of (the second edition of) TM; it had first appeared two years earlier as a separately published paper, "Jusqu'à quel point la langue préforme-t-elle la pensée," in E. Castelli, ed., *Demitizzazione e Ideologia* (Rome: A. Milani, 1973).

7. *Gesammelte Werke* vol. 8 (1993), 350–362; quotation from 350 [my translation].

8. Robinson quotes from Richard Palmer's translation in the latter's "Gadamer's recent work on language and philosophy", which appeared in *Continental Philosophy Review*, vol. 33 (2000). Gadamer's text of this 1992 paper is published in his *Gesammelte Werke*, vol. 8 (1993), 400–440; the quotation is from page 407 [my translation].

9. William James, *The Varieties of Religious Experience: A Study in Human Nature* [The Gifford Lectures on Natural Religion Delivered at Edinburgh in 1901–1902] (New York: Random House, 1902). The quoted passages are found on 370–371.

10. The claim that Husserl is to some extent committed to metaphysical idealism is not without merit, but that claim cannot be made on the basis of the misunderstanding of his concept of constitution that I here discuss. For more on this, see *Roman Ingarden's Ontology and Aesthetics* (Ottawa: University of Ottawa Press, 1997), especially 41–49: "Chapter Two: Ingarden's Interpretation of Husserl, A. Introduction: Husserl and Metaphysical Idealism."

11. In "Consciousness, Intentionality, and Causality" (in M. Szatkowski and M. Rosiak, eds., *Substantiality and Causality* [Berlin: Walter de Gruyter, 2014; *Philosophische Analyse/ Philosophical Analysis* vol. 60], 129–149), I suggest that "Husserl was incorrect in identifying objectivation as an operation performed by the intentionality of the cognizing subject's consciousness. I maintain, rather, that this objectivation operates as a process of formal causality, and that this operation of objectivation, proceeding in accordance with the (formal) structure of the cognized object, informs the structure of the intentional act of the cognizing subject. This is simply another way of reformulating what I called above the 'new Copernican hypothesis of

phenomenology'" (142). This paper also addresses concerns raised by Joshua Boyce in his contribution to this collection, "A Relational Theory of Truth," regarding my discussion of materialism and modern science.